MW00461824

Submit all requests for reprinting to:
Peak Performance Publishers
28677 San Lucas Lane #201
Bonita Springs, FL 34135
Chris@DrZimmerman.com

Published in the United States by Peak Performance Publishers

Composition by Peak Performance Publishers
Cover Design by McPherson Graphics

First Edition

DEDICATION

I would like to dedicate this book to my children. They truly are in their own right, Women of Worth and a joy to my heart.

To Kathy, my firstborn, who loves and cares for me and is such an encouragement by her own faithfulness to the Lord and to those who know her.

To Vickie, who would bring joy to any Mom's heart as she serves the Lord so faithfully in the role of a Pastor's wife for many years and has so much love for them as well as her family.

To Karen, as she has so many times given me words of wisdom and insight when mine was sadly lacking. I never fail to be grateful for her life and loving concern.

To Terry, I am so thankful for all the years the Lord gave her to raise a family she loved and is now with Jesus in all His glory.

To Chris, who has lovingly supported me in some desperate times of my life and shown me love when I needed it the most. And, has worked tirelessly and endlessly to process this book.

Having children who love and live for Jesus is the second desire of my heart, having a loving and close relationship with Jesus and to grieve not the Holy Spirit, being first. We all send forth this book with the prayer that God will use His Words to encourage hungry hearts!

INTRODUCTION

Spending some time with the Lord, reading the Bible and praying to God about the cares of my life and asking for His help has been a priority for many years. I began journaling in 1987. Most of what you will be reading in this book is a direct quote from one of those journals. The Ladies Class I taught at Coventry Baptist Church, Fort Wayne, IN gave me a small leather bound book which provided writing space for two days on each page. There was only room to write maybe three sentences for each day, but it was a start. In the beginning, I would write a scripture that was meaningful to me as I read the Bible that day. Then gradually, I begin to communicate my thoughts to the Lord and then state a brief prayer. Eventually, I wrote in between the lines, in the margins, above and below the printed scripture; the pages were a mess but I knew the Lord could read it. Let me encourage you, if you've never kept a journal, you need to! It is my prayer that as you read these daily readings that you too, will begin to record your thoughts and prayers each day. It's hard to begin anything new but this is something you need to do! We can drop money in the offering plate, extend a helping hand, say an encouraging word, minister in so many great ways but when you give your first thoughts of the day to the Lord, He can cause the rest of it to be more fruitful. What God speaks to you through His Word is worth recording and can be so meaningful to you when you reread it. Every day, I read what I wrote a year ago on that day and it keeps me sober! Seriously, it lets me focus on where I've been and what I want to be. The desire of my heart is to love and serve and please my Lord. Reading, studying, and meditating in His word every day is the way to know Him. My prayer is that this book will be helpful to you and as you read it each day.

JANUARY 1

FROM THE BEGINNING OF THE YEAR TO THE END

Deuteronomy 11:12 New King James Version (NKJV)

"A land for which the Lord your God cares; the eyes of the Lord your God are always on it, from the beginning of the year to the very end of the year."

Every year is a challenge and is full of uncertainty, but here's the promise: *His eyes are on it, God cares for it from the beginning to the end of it!* He is the source of our mercy and His mercy endures forever. Be enriched in the Word, as it will always be! Heaven and earth as we know it will pass away but God's Word is forever! Romans 16:20 Message Bible (MSG), *"Stay alert like this and before you know it, the God of peace will come down on Satan with both feet, stomping him into the dirt! Enjoy the best of Jesus."* The love of Jesus is the One who lights our soul as well as our path. So many do not live at their best, but flounder in their struggles of living. He enables you to *"enjoy the best of Jesus,"* as, *"The Lord cares where you are and is with you from the beginning of the year to the very end of it."*

In my journal on January 1, 2010, I wrote: "Who knows but Him what the year holds?" Little did I know that this particular year would mean the loss of my husband, Louie, the love of my life, followed shortly thereafter by the death of my youngest daughter, Terry. The scripture says, *"enjoy the best of Jesus"*, and I can now do that as I know that's what they're doing and I will see them again!

JANUARY 2
GOD'S BLESSING ON YOUR LIFE

1 Thessalonians 5:23 (NKJV)

"Now may the God of peace Himself sanctify you completely; and may your whole spirit, soul, and body be preserved blameless at the coming of our Lord Jesus Christ."

As you start a new year, you may be inclined to want to make new vows regarding your diet, behavior, spending habits, etc., and that's good to make improvements. Paul's prayer for the people in Thessalonica was for them to be sanctified in their spirit, soul and body. He wanted every one of them to be set apart for service and to live holy lives before the Lord. The result? "They would be blameless at the coming of their Lord." Listen, you want the Lord to approve of your conduct when He returns. Blameless doesn't mean you are sinless, but free from reproach and being full of regret. Can you do that? Probably not; but look at the verse. "The One who calls you is faithful, He will do it," as you allow Him to settle within your spirit, soul and body, you can be blameless at His return. You serve a loving, faithful Lord; He wants you to be right before Him and He will help you. God knows how you struggle with the body parts, your soul and spirit are more willing than your body, but He's a Big God, let Him do it!

JANUARY 3

EVERYTHING I DO IS KNOWN TO YOU

Romans 12:1 (MSG)

"So here's what I want you to do, God helping you: Take your everyday, ordinary life—sleeping, eating, going-to-work, and walking-around life—and place it before God as an offering. Embracing what God does for you is the best thing you can do for him. Don't become so well-adjusted to your culture that you fit into it without even thinking. Instead, fix your attention on God. You'll be changed from the inside out. Readily recognize what he wants from you, and quickly respond to it ..."

Psalm 119:167-168 Living Bible (LB), *"I have looked for your commandments and I love them very much; yes, I have searched for them. You know this because everything I do is known to you."* VS. 165, *"Those who love your Word have great peace of heart and mind and do not stumble."* VS. 162, *"I rejoice in your laws like one who finds a great treasure."* Romans 5:5 (MSG), *"... we can't round up enough containers to hold everything God generously pours into our lives through the Holy Spirit!"* Shut every other door of your life and be determined to know Him and to recognize what He wants from you. The key is to respond quickly to what you sense God is saying to you in His Word. Do it in your every day, ordinary life your sleeping, eating, going-to-work, walking-around life. The more time you spend in His Word, the more natural it will be to respond to Him; because it is so true, everything we do is known to Him.

3

JANUARY 4

GOD ALLOWS SOME TIMES OF DARKNESS IN OUR LIVES

John 12:24 (NKJV)

"Most assuredly, I say to you, unless a grain of wheat falls into the ground and dies, it remains alone; but if it dies, it produces much grain."

The last thing in the world we want to be is obscure. We struggle for acceptance and fight with all our might for recognition. It is a faith stretching experience when we find ourselves alone and buried, as if six feet of dirt is on top of us. The world's way is choosing the talented, the gifted; God's way is choosing the helpless. That grain of wheat, if given the choice, would remain above ground and forever be a single grain of wheat, but when buried and processed through much darkness and time it becomes many grains. Similarly, God allows some times of darkness and brokenness in our lives that we may become more obedient and fruitful. You will either give up and surrender or be put on a shelf. God empties us so that He might fill us. We want maturity without suffering and pain. We want God to answer our prayers and leave us alone. We want to do God's work our way... Acts 17:28 (NKJV), *"...for in Him we live and move and have our being,"* We have nothing; it is God and God alone. Nothing exists, transpires, happens, or is even thought of, apart from the presence of God. So, if you find yourself "buried" for a time, know that God knows where you are, you are not alone... the best place in all the world is in His Presence.

JANUARY 5

HE GIVES US THE "WILL" AND THE "WON'T" POWER"

Romans 12:1 (NKJV)

"I beseech you therefore, brethren, by the mercies of God that you present your bodies a living sacrifice, holy, acceptable to God which is your reasonable service."

Before we trusted Christ, we used our bodies for sin; now we want them to be used for His glory. The Spirit of God dwells there; it's God's temple. Jesus had to take a body to accomplish God's purpose. So we must yield our body for the Holy Spirit to use us. Each day, surrender your body to Him and then spend time in His Word so He can transform your mind and prepare your thinking for the day. Romans 12:2 (NKJV), *"...be not conformed to this world but be transformed by the renewing of your mind..."* The world wants to change your mind so it exerts pressure from without. The Holy Spirit changes your mind by releasing power from within. If the world controls your thinking, you're a conformer; if God controls your thinking, you're a transformer. Memorizing God's Word will gradually make you spiritually minded. Your mind controls your body and your will controls your mind. Many people think they can control themselves by "will power" and generally fail. He gives us the "will" power and the "won't" power when we surrender to Him. Yield to Him and let Him work what is best for you. Ephesians 1:8 (LB), *"For how well He understands us and knows what's best for us at all times."* If you have a right relationship with God, you will have a right relationship with people. Yield your spirit, mind and body to Him for your *"acceptable service."*

5

JANUARY 6

GOD GIVES EACH ONE A MEASURE OF FAITH

Romans 12:3 (NKJV)

"For I say, through the grace given to me, to everyone who is among you, not to think of himself more highly than he ought to think, but to think soberly, as God has dealt to each one a measure of faith."

Every believer is a living part of Christ's body and has a spiritual function to perform of building up "The Body." We belong to each other and we need each other. Don't be guilty of guarding your own turf ... thinking that no one can do this as well as you can. It is not wrong to recognize your gift but it is wrong to have a false evaluation... both to over-estimate and to under-estimate. We are saved by grace and we are "gifted" by God's grace through faith "according to His measure" as stated in verses 3-6 of this chapter. Some can belittle their gifts and not use them; others can boast about gifts they simply do not possess. Both are guilty of false pride. God places the gifts He wants exercised in the local body of believers so they can grow in a balanced relationship. We may not see results of our ministry but God sees and blesses. Encouragement is as much a blessing as teaching or preaching. Spiritual gifts are tools to build with, not toys to play with or weapons to fight with. Don't think of yourself more highly than you ought to think but do use what you have been given to build up others and to glorify Him.

JANUARY 7

HE SATISFIES EVERY NEED

Acts 17:25-28a (LB)

"And human hands can't minister to His needs--for He has no needs! He himself gives life and breath to everything and satisfies every need there is. He created all the people of the world from one man, Adam, and scattered the nations across the face of the earth. He decided beforehand which should rise and fall and when. He determined their boundaries. His purpose in all of this is that they should seek after God and perhaps feel their way toward him and find him—though He is not far from any one of us. For in Him we live and move and are!"

There is no life outside of Christ, just existence. The people in Corinth were suing one another; Galatians were biting and devouring each other; women in Philippi were at odds with each other and splitting the church. They began to judge and criticize each other, each sure the other was not spiritual at all. When some people come into the church you know they're going to be a problem. What do you do in a marriage when you differ on a matter? You find something you do agree on, a common ground, and build on that. Whether in the home or the church, Jesus gives life and breath to everything and satisfies every need there is. Our purpose in living is to seek after God and find Him...for in Him we live and move and are!

JANUARY 8

THE LORD IS CLOSE TO THOSE WHOSE HEARTS ARE BREAKING

Romans 5:3 (LB)

"We can rejoice too when we run into problems and trials for we know that they are good for us—they help us learn to be patient."

Receive the trouble/pain because when it comes, God is up to something in your life. God gets blamed for a lot of things He didn't do but He still can work your difficulties into blessings, in spite of the Devil's schemes. But, receiving and being accepting of pain and problems is not a natural reaction for anyone. Again, the best response I know is God's Word. Psalms 34:15 (LB), *"For the eyes of the Lord are intently watching all who live good lives, and He gives attention when they cry to him."* VS. 17-19, *"Yes, the Lord hears the good man when he calls to him for help, and saves him out of all his troubles. The Lord is close to those whose hearts are breaking. The good man does not escape all troubles—he has them too. But the Lord helps him in each and every one."* If it concerns you, it concerns Him. We live in a fallen world that loves sin and bad things do happen to God's people, but we have a refuge and a place of safety; also, we have His promise that He will be with us. While we pray, He works, and in the meantime, we learn patience.

JANUARY 9
BEHAVE LIKE A CHRISTIAN

Romans 12:10-13 (NKJV)

"Be kindly affectionate to one another with brotherly love, in honor giving preference to one another, not lagging in diligence, fervent in spirit, serving the Lord; rejoicing in hope, patient in tribulation, continuing steadfastly in prayer; distributing to the needs of the saints, given to hospitality."

Behave like a Christian. Christian fellowship is more than a handshake; it is sharing the burdens and blessings of others. When life becomes difficult, reach out to someone else; don't become cold and uncaring. When life is unfair, rejoice in the hope you have in the promises of Jesus. If is not natural to be kind. But God can give you the power to do it. Offer to push the grocery cart of an older person who is struggling; bring in the mail/newspaper for a disabled person; surprise a friend by picking up the check at lunch. And when feeling really generous, offer to babysit! When you do things for someone else, you are showing brotherly love, you are "giving preference and not lagging in diligence," plus you are serving the Lord. As for being "patient in tribulation," the best help is in reading scripture. Micah 7:8-9 (LB), *"...and when I sit in darkness, the Lord himself will be my Light. God will bring me out of my darkness into the light and I will see His goodness."* It helps to continue steadfastly in your prayer time and to help those in need by being hospitable. In other words, first focus on Jesus and then others; it will help you behave like a Christian!

JANUARY 10
ACCEPT AND RECEIVE ONE ANOTHER

Romans 14:1-4a (NKJV)

"Receive one who is weak in the faith, but not to disputes over doubtful things. For one believes he may eat all things, but he who is weak eats only vegetables. Let not him who eats despise him who does not eat, and let not him who does not eat judge him who eats; for God has received him. Who are you to judge another's servant? Indeed, he will be made to stand, for God is able to make him stand."

The point is to accept and receive because God does that for you. Some people think that believers who follow strict rules are more mature...not necessarily so. VS. 3, *"...sometimes they become judgmental and critical."* Do not allow your knowledge of the Word to cause you to condemn others. Christian fellowship is not based on diet or religious calendars, but is found in accepting and receiving. VS. 4, *"Our Master is the One who is able to make us stand and it is before Him we stand or fall."* No one has the right to "play God" in another's life, but we can advise, pray and admonish. It is encouraging to know that our success in our walk before the Lord does not depend on the attitudes and opinions of others. I found that God blesses those I disagree with and it's okay for *"He is the One who made him to stand."* If we would yield to the Holy Spirit, we'd find that all need to grow. The strong Christian needs to grow in love; the weaker Christian needs to grow in knowledge. The weak must learn from the strong and the strong must love the weak. It is God who makes us all to receive, accept and to stand!

JANUARY 11

DON'T LET YOUR CONCEPT OF GOD BE LIMITED AND DON'T STOP WHERE YOU ARE

Jeremiah 29:11-13 (LB)

"For I know the plans I have for you says the Lord. They are plans for good and not for evil, to give you a future and a hope. In those days when you pray, I will listen. You will find me when you seek me, if you look for me in earnest."

We tend to put God in a box of our own limited understanding. God cannot be confined to our knowledge of Him. He's a God of surprises. If you've ever had surprise lilies, you know how delightful they are ... nothing that night and the next morning, dozens of blooms! God loves to give us delightful blessings and even the desires of our heart. He acts in unexpected ways and people. We shouldn't despair because the present is painful and the future uncertain. He is the Lord of all history and it is as Eugene Peterson says, "Every morning we wake up to something that has been going on for a very long time." Even though He is the creator of everything, He cares for you individually and has a good plan for your life. Don't let your concept of God be limited, and don't stop where you are; resolve each day to seek after Him. *"You will find me when you seek me, if you look for me with all your heart!"*

JANUARY 12

WE NEVER RECEIVE ANYTHING UNTIL THE WORD COMES

1 Kings 17:5-7 (NKJV)

"So he went and did according to the Word of the Lord, for he went and stayed by the Brook of Cherith, which flows into the Jordan. The ravens brought him bread and meat in the morning, and bread and meat in the evening; and he drank from the brook. And it happened that after a while the brook dried up, because there had been no rain in the land."

When God forces us to move or change, He's got something better for us. For Elijah, the brook dried up and the birds didn't show up! VS. 8, *"Then the Word of the Lord came to him..."* We never receive anything until the Word of God comes to us; sometimes from Him and sometimes from someone else. God never dries up a brook unless he's got a widow. Most of us only see the birds are gone and so is the water. God has a geographical place for every one of us! The widow told Elijah, *"I have some for myself and my son."* Come to the place where you say, *"I cast myself upon you Lord Jesus, if I die, I die, but I will make a sacrifice."* God says that if we will trust Him, we will see a miracle. The widow gave up her last hope of life. Determine within yourself that you will give the Lord only that which is of value to you. Obedience is the key that opens the door of life. It's giving of self/substance that produces the supply. VS. 24, *"Then the woman said to Elijah ... the Word of the Lord in your mouth is the truth."* All things happen according to the spoken Word of God; I repeat: we never receive anything until the Word of God comes to us.

JANUARY 13

TO KNOW THE LOVE OF CHRIST

Ephesians 3:17-18 (NKJV)

"...that Christ may dwell in your hearts through faith; that you being rooted and grounded in love may be able to comprehend with all the saints what is the width and length and depth and height—to know the love of Christ..."

Faith is to believe, trust and to commit. We believe in Jesus Christ; we trust in Him for salvation; we commit ourselves to His will and way. Faith is the channel through which God's gracious gift of salvation flows through us and in us. Grace is God's part; that place of free love and special favor. God, in His mercy, does not give us what we deserve; and God in His grace gives us what we do not deserve. God is love and when God relates that love, it becomes grace and mercy. Science with its entire means of measuring cannot "guess" as to the size of the universe. God is greater than the universe He created. He is omnipresent, present in all space and in every moment of time. He is love. Wherever He is, there is His love. How wide is God's love? How long? How deep? How high? Yet, Paul prayed we might grasp the answers in our minds. It is broad enough to include all people. It is long enough to extend from eternity to eternity and to go to any length in expressing itself. It is as deep or profound as the very nature of God and high enough to reach the limitless heights of heaven itself. Thank you, Lord, for letting us know You and Your love.

JANUARY 14
THEN THE WIDOW GAVE

Mark 12:44 (NKJV)

"...for they all put in out of their abundance, but she out of her poverty put in all that she had, her whole livelihood."

Jesus sat opposite the treasury and saw how the people put in money into the treasury. Mark 12:41 *(NKJV), "...and many who were rich put in much and then the widow came..."* Your giving is measured by its cost, not its amount. God is concerned about the Spirit in which we give and by what we keep. The coins made certain sounds as they dropped in and the rich made a display of the amount they gave, enjoying the sound as the large coins rolled around. The widow gave just a few cents and Jesus said it was the largest gift of the day. "This poor widow has put in more than all those who have given" were His exact Words. Your giving is measured by what it cost you, not the amount of the gift. She had nothing left. The widow gave out of deep devotion and worship. Giving is meant to be in grateful response to all God has granted us; it is a privilege to do it.

JANUARY 15
YOUR REASON FOR RIGHT LIVING

Romans 13:11-12 (LB)

"Another reason for right living is this: you know how late it is; time is running out. Wake up for the coming of the Lord is nearer now than we first believed. The night is far gone; the day of his

return will soon be here. So quit the evil deed of darkness and put on the armor of right living."

We are not our own bosses to love or die as we ourselves might choose. <u>Romans 14:8</u> (LB), *"Living or dying, we follow the Lord. Either way we are his."* <u>Romans 14:10b-12</u> (LB), *"Remember, each of us will personally stand before the Judgment Seat of God. For it is written," 'As I live,' says the Lord, 'every knee shall bow to me and every tongue confess to God.' Yes, each of us will give an account of himself to God."* <u>Romans 15-13</u> (LB), *"God who gives you hope will keep you happy and full of peace as you believe in him. I pray that God will help you overflow with hope in him through the Holy Spirit's power within you."* We need to saturate ourselves in the Word of God and in prayer knowing He already given you everything you need. <u>1 Corinthians 3:21b-23</u> (LB): *"He has given you the whole world to use, and life and even death are your servants. He has given you all of the present and all of the future. All are yours, and you belong to Christ and Christ is God's."* He has given you everything you need to live right.

JANUARY 16
THERE ARE NO LIMITS TO WHAT GOD CAN DO

<u>Ephesians 3:20</u> (NKJV)

"Now to Him who is able to do exceedingly abundantly above all that we ask or think, according to the power that works in us..."

God exceeds our greatest expectations. God can do even more than we can think or even imagine. Push your imagination to the limit...God can do more than that. Ask beyond your dreams...God can do more than that! Super Abundantly!! There are no limits to what God can do. Look at what the verse says, it's according to God's power working in us. Too many times we sit on the side lines, as it were, and want God to work. God does work, but only to the extent we are willing for Him to work. We need to ask, "What do you want me to do in this?" People are not led to Jesus by clever arguments or neat soul winning packages, but always by the gracious and powerful influence of God's Holy Spirit. We have everything when we have Christ. Philippians 2:13 (LB), *"For God is at work within you, helping you want to obey him, and then helping you do what he wants."* Thank Him today for His power working in you because there are no limits to what our God can do!

JANUARY 17
GOD ALWAYS DOES JUST WHAT HE SAYS

1 Corinthians.1:9 (LB)

"God will surely do this for you for He always does just what He says and He is the One who invited you into this wonderful friendship with His Son, even Christ our Lord."

We need to believe exactly what the Bible says; if not, you'll believe what you "feel." Which is more trustworthy; your feelings or the Bible? When you received Christ, you were placed by the Holy Spirit in Him. Before you were placed in Christ, you were in Adam, dead in sins. But when you were saved, you were placed in Christ and that was the work of the Holy Spirit. This new position is a work engineered through the cross by the Holy Spirit to a new relationship in Jesus, in whom we now live and abide, according to the Word of God. You now have two addresses: one where you live here and one in Christ. The one in Christ is unchanging, eternal and unalterable. Your level of fellowship may change but your relationship will not ever change. It is a work of grace. God reached down, took you out of a life of sin and placed you in a life of righteousness in Him through an act of grace. You didn't do it; all you did was respond to His love. God seated us with Him (in Christ). Our position in Him is the source of our security both in eternity and in our earthly experience. There is no other source, no other way. "God always does just what He says."

JANUARY 18
THE BRIGHTEST AND THE BEST

1 Corinthians 1:26-31 (MSG)

"Take a good look, friends, at who you were when you got called into this life. I don't see many of the "brightest and the best" among you, not many influential, not many from high-society families."

When you became a Christian, it didn't make you instantly the "brightest and the best," giving you impeccable manners and morals. The early Corinthians brought their hard-drinking, sexual, promiscuous behavior into the church. After Paul had been their Pastor for over a year, he wrote: "Isn't it obvious that God deliberately chose men and women that the culture overlooks, and exploits and abuses, chose these "nobodies" to expose the hollow pretensions of the "somebodies?" That makes it quite clear that none of you can get by with blowing your own horn before God. Everything that we have—right thinking and right living, a clean slate

17

and a fresh start—comes from God by the way of Jesus Christ. That's why we have the saying, "If you're going to blow a horn, blow a trumpet for God." I am weak; Satan is strong; Jesus is stronger. We can have victory no matter what, but God doesn't provide armor for our backsides, so don't turn and run. God rarely speaks to us through visions and dreams but He re-speaks His Word to us in particular situations. Set your sights on becoming one of the "brightest and the best" but also know that God will teach you and use you where you are and who you are.

JANUARY 19
DO YOU KNOW WHERE YOU'RE GOING

Hebrews 11:8 (NKJV)

"Abraham obeyed when he was called to go out to the place which he would receive as an inheritance. And he went out, not knowing where he was going."

By faith, Abraham obeyed God and went out, without knowing where he was going. Oswald Chambers says, "We have to continually revise our attitude towards God to see if we are going out of everything, trusting God entirely. Each morning we wake it is to be a 'going out,' building in confidence on God. Do you believe in a miracle working God and will you go out in surrender to Him until you are not surprised an atom at anything He does?" God knows what He's doing; do you know what you're doing and where you're going? He is the author and finisher of my faith, my life. I cannot control what happens to me but I can control what I say and do about it, i.e. how I respond; and then let God controls the rest. Hardships, trials, and pain are a part of life. Will God tell me what

He's going to do? I don't think so! But He will tell me Who He is and He will direct my steps when I "go out" with Him.

JANUARY 20
SPIRIT CAN ONLY BE KNOWN BY SPIRIT

1 Corinthians 2:15-16 (LB)

"But the spiritual man has insight into everything, and that bothers and baffles the man of the world, who can't understand it at all. How could he? Man certainly has never been one to know the Lord's thoughts or to discuss them with Him or to move the hands of God by prayer. But strange as it seems, we Christians actually do have within us a portion of the very thoughts and mind of Christ."

1 Corinthians 2:9 (NKJV), *"Eye has not seen nor ear heard, nor have entered into the heart of man the things which God has prepared for those who love Him."* VS. 10, *"But God has revealed them to us through His Spirit. For the Spirit searches all things, yes the deep things of God."* VS.12, *"Now we have received not the spirit of the world but the Spirit who is from God, that we might know the things that have been freely given to us by God."* It is the Spirit of God within us that keeps us walking when we don't understand. We have to have His Spirit to trust Him when things don't change rather than when they do; when you can't see, when things make no sense. Mostly, we believe in one outcome…ours…and the way we want it! Trust in God, His Plan, His character, Who He is and what He does. It is not the spirit of the world that helps you do this. Spirit can only be known by Spirit. Have spiritual wisdom and that only comes through His Word.

JANUARY 21

GOD WANTS YOU TO BECOME SOMETHING

Romans 5:2 (LB)

"For because of our faith, He has brought us into this place of highest privilege where we now stand and we confidently and joyfully look forward to actually becoming all that God has in mind for us to be."

God wants you to become something! God has a very special plan for your life. It began a long time ago when He created you. He carefully and lovingly formed you exactly how He wanted you to be - your looks, abilities, birthplace, birthday...nothing was accidental. God has something in mind for you that He wants you to become. In order to do that, we're inclined to think we need to do a righteous program of self-improvement. The harder we try, the more frustrated we become. God has to do the changing; your trials are not accidents. Patience, endurance and steadfastness grow when difficulties and temptations put us under the scrutiny of the Holy Spirit. Our self-centered defensive, selfish behavior has a way of surfacing when problems come. It is "because of our faith, He has brought us into this place of highest privilege." He draws you unto Himself through the circumstances He has arranged just for you and for that purpose. So "stand confidently and look forward to actually becoming all that God has in mind for you to be." Trust Him to help you become all that He wants you to be!

JANUARY 22

SEEK THE WELFARE OF THOSE WHO WOULD DESTROY YOU

Jeremiah 29:7 (NKJV)

"And seek the peace of the city where I have caused you to be carried away captive and pray to the Lord for it, for in its peace you will have peace."

Almost in the same breath God told Jeremiah to tell the Jews to pray for the peace of the city of Babylon in which they were held captive for 70 years, He tells them He has a good plan for them (VS.11), *"Many suffered and died there, but God told them to pray for Babylon and to seek its welfare for in its welfare, they would find their own."* In it, they would discover God's best plan. Why not in the good times? The purifying and testing come from challenging circumstances, not from what our senses, emotions or intellect tell us. So when He tells us He's working all things for our good and we see everything going wrong—we have to continually claim the promise in His Word and believe He's doing exactly that. Then thank Him for whatever happens. God alone can remake and remold from within and He does that as we submit. Our part is to believe He has taken over and then accept joyfully and with thanksgiving and praise every circumstance God uses to bring about the transformation needed in our lives. We want to "see" the good; God wants us to "believe" so we may experience the good.

JANUARY 23

GOD WILL BLESS YOU IN THE PAIN OF UNDESERVED SUFFERING

2 Corinthians 12:9b-12 (LB)

"My power shows up best in weak people. Now I am glad to boast about how weak I am; I am glad to be a living demonstration of Christ's power, instead of showing off my own power and abilities. Since I know it is all for Christ's good, I am happy about "the thorn," and about insults and hardships, persecutions and difficulties; for when I am weak, than I am strong—the less I have, the more I depend on Him."

Circumstances that rip our self-sufficiency are blessings in disguise. Every blow shows we cannot handle our own situation. The more trying the circumstance, the more we realize our need of Him. Each trial gives us opportunity for growth. When we trust our lives to Him, we can be sure that <u>no one</u> can mistreat us unless God allows it. So thank and praise Him in (<u>not for</u>) every evil thing that comes your way. God will bless you if you endure the pain of undeserved suffering. What credit is in enduring the suffering you deserve for having done wrong? But if you endure it having done right, God will bless you, as is explained in <u>1 Peter 2:19-20a</u> (LB*): Praise the Lord if you are punished for doing right! Of course, you get no credit for being patient if you are beaten for doing wrong..."* God carefully designed the universe and just as carefully designed you and your circumstances. *"What I want from you is your true thanks; I want your promises fulfilled. I want you to trust me in your times of trouble, so I can rescue you, and you can give Me glory,"* Psalms 50:14-15 (NLT)

JANUARY 24

NOTHING HAPPENS TO US WITHOUT HIS KNOWLEDGE

Romans 8:3b (LB)

"He destroyed sin's control over us by giving Himself as a sacrifice for our sins."

God may see every sparrow in existence and number the hairs on your head, but the fact remains sparrows do fall and tragedies do happen. Children are objects of abuse; people we love die from horrible diseases despite our prayers. We are prone to wonder why God didn't do something to prevent it; why does He allow sin and evil to prevail. Some come to the conclusion that it's because of our or someone else's sin. The truth is...bad things do happen to good people. God didn't create evil because He is love. He made humans with a free will and the capacity to choose to do evil. Evil remains in the world with God's permission, but is always subject to His will. Nothing evil can touch us without His permission. God sent His Son to break the power of evil in our lives. "He destroyed sin's control over us by giving Himself as a sacrifice for our sins" Romans 8:3b (LB): *"Receive God as the all-powerful God He is and know absolutely nothing, happens to us without His knowledge."* Believing this, we can praise and thank Him in every circumstance evil in our lives. Every difficult situation, even tragedy, will ultimately be changed by Almighty God. God will work in us to transform it to fit into His intended plan for your life. Praise Him, and release His power to work in any situation for your good!

JANUARY 25

PRAISE GOD FOR ALL CIRCUMSTANCES

Ephesians 5:20 (NKJV)

"Giving thanks always for all things to God the Father in the name of our Lord Jesus Christ."

If someone inherits a lot of money, we say: "How wonderful!" If someone dies and goes to heaven, we say, "How sad!" We are to praise and thank God for all things. We mentioned yesterday the fall of the sparrow, the abuse of children and loved ones who die; some will die and some will fall and some will not die...our praise must be for both instances! How do we combat evil face to face? Sometimes Jesus took charge and sometimes He stood quietly by and let it happen. So what are we to do? First, know that we have no power – the overcoming force is God Himself. We have to learn to focus on Him and not the evil that is against us. Do not give the enemy your attention; give it to Jesus. We just want to respond to the wrong being done...get in our licks and put right the wrong. If our action is prompted by the evil circumstance, rather than by faith in the power of God, we allow evil to overcome us. Always keep your eye on God and thank Him for everything. You're not thanking Him for the evil or bad situation; you're thanking Him for Who He is; for His goodness and mercy in all things. Set your mind and will to accept God's Word that He is in charge regardless of what your feelings or apparent circumstances may be. The final outcome is in His capable hands.

JANUARY 26

CALL THINGS THAT DON'T EXIST AS THOUGH THEY DO

Romans 4:17b (NKJV)

"God who gives life to the dead and calls those things which do not exist as though they did."

Abraham and Sarah were past the age of childbearing; yet they called those things which did not exist as though they did. Romans 4:18-24 New International Version (NIV), *"Against all hope, Abraham in hope believed and so became the father of many nations just as it had been said to him...Without weakening in his faith, he faced the fact that his body was as good as dead—since he was about 100 years old—and that Sarah's womb was also dead. Yet he did not waver through unbelief regarding the promise of God, but was strengthened in his faith and gave glory to God, being fully persuaded that God had power to do what He had promised. This is why "it was credited to him as righteousness." The words "it was credited to him" were written not for him alone, but also for us, to whom God will credit righteousness—for us who believe in Him who raised Jesus our Lord from the dead."* It is your Word, Lord God, and is just as true for us when we don't waver in unbelief but believe You. The same power that raised Jesus Christ from the dead works in our dead hearts and bodies to quicken us to believe that those things which do not now exist can become reality. You are the Lord God Almighty. Psalms 18:24b (MSG), *"God rewrote the text of my life when I opened the book of my heart to his eyes."* God does rewrite and reroute our lives when we believe His Word and "call the things the things that do not exist as though they do."

JANUARY 27
STEP INTO THE WATER

Isaiah 43:2 (NKJV)

"When you pass through the waters, I will be with you; and through the rivers, they shall not overflow you."

God doesn't open up a path or give you help before you need it. When you are confronted with obstacles, keep walking. The waters didn't part for the fleeing Israelites until they stepped their feet into the water. We worry about problems we "envision;" all kinds of difficulties, some of which never happen. We want God to clear the way before us for miles but God wants us to "step into the water." His promise is that "they will not overflow (overcome) you;" but you have to be in the floodwaters before you can claim that promise. Faith isn't learned in comfortable surroundings; and how we hate discomfort. The cross wasn't comfortable, for sure, but God the Father was with His Son. Trust Him today as "you pass through the waters, He will be with you."

JANUARY 28
GOD WORKS BEHIND THE SCENES

Isaiah 45:9 (NKJV)

"Woe to him who strives with his Maker!"

God is in charge of every storm, every war, every famine and pestilence, earthquake, tornado, hurricane, every wave of the ocean (saying you will go this far and no farther), every birth and death, every flower that grows in the field, every sparrow...living or dead, for He is Lord. Our part is to choose whether or not to believe Who He is. God has never been late and never will be. His timing is as perfect as He is. We are always fussing because our estimates are usually wrong, or we turn in our bids late! "Woe is the man who fights with his creator." God works behind the scenes and sometimes in the lives of the ungodly to bring good into our lives. Job knew he was innocent; and his conclusion was "Though he slay me, yet I will trust Him." It is interesting that it was when God had Job pray for his abusive friends that He restored his happiness and wealth. God had a perfect plan for his life as He does for yours. Isaiah 45:6b-7a (NIV), "*I am the Lord and there is no other; I form the light and create darkness*" but every single thing He does is with you in mind; so be accepting of the "light and the dark" as He is in charge of both and He is your Maker. He works behind the scenes for you!

JANUARY 29
DON'T MURMUR AND COMPLAIN

1 Corinthians 10:10 (LB)
   "Don't murmur against God and His dealings with you..."

On August 24, 1998, I wrote the following in my journal: "We offer thanks when the sun shines and grumble when it rains! Having lived in Fort Wayne, IN (which I nicknamed Fort Rain) for 39 years makes me really appreciate the last 8 months. When I walk into my kitchen, which has a skylight (now living in Florida), I see solid sunshine; only once has it been cloudy. Many, many mornings I grumbled at the appearance of darkness and gloom. But are we to thank God only for what we want? Doesn't everybody fuss and complain—what's the difference? Everything!! Life depends on little things! Marriages fail over them; a mechanic makes a small mistake and a great airliner crashes; wars break out over small misunderstandings. One angry Word results in a shooting. We get an "attitude" at the breakfast table or in the long line at the grocery store. Grumbling is so easy to do that we all do it and so well! To complain is a natural response—no one had to teach you how to complain. By grumbling/complaining, we actually are accusing God of not knowing how to manage His world or how to schedule our day, even though He has said that He scheduled every day of our lives before we began to breathe in Psalms 139:16 (LB), *"And don't murmur against God and His dealings with you as some of them did, for that is why God sent his Angel to destroy them."* "All these things happened to them as examples—as object lessons to us—to warn us against doing the same things; they were written down so that we could read about them and learn from them in these last days," 1 Corinthians 10:10-11 (LB),*"We need to read, heed and believe His Word. Unbelief is the root of our murmurings and complaints and is also the indication that we have little confidence in the One who does "all things well."* So stop murmuring against God and His dealings with you!

JANUARY 30
THANK HIM FOR WHAT HE IS ABLE AND WANTS TO DO

Psalms 62:9 (LB)
"The greatest of men, or the lowest—both alike are nothing in His sight. They weigh less than air on scales."

Merlin Carothers said that he thought since his grumblings were legitimate, he had the right to do them. For instance, if the bathroom was left messy by another family member and he had to gobble his breakfast so he wouldn't be late; the car wouldn't start; he hit every red light, then these were valid complaints and it was okay. The first step is to admit you're a habitual complainer. Make an agreement with God not to grumble, instead "Thank God for everything!" The Holy Spirit had to show him that this is what he had taught. God will do the changing; it is His power that brings transformation. Keep your eyes on Jesus and thank Him for what He is able and wants to do. In time, you'll see the very things you used to grumble about coming back to vex you again. He'll use those incidents to bring about change in you. Once they made you stumble, but now they become opportunities for God to show up! Some go through their entire lives believing, if I had just had the right breaks, I could have been...you fill in the blanks...if my marriage or my profession had been different...whatever. Can you accept that God has you exactly where He wants you? He hasn't overlooked a single thing. We all make bad choices and then live in the consequences. Right now, praise and thank Him for your situation, as is. Submit every aspect of your mess to Him, at every turn. You may weigh less than air on scales, but He is a Mighty God!

JANUARY 31
BE FILLED WITH MY JOY

John 17:13 (LB)
"I have told them many things while I was with them so that they would be filled with My joy."

Jesus prayed for us that His joy might be perfected in us and that we might experience His delight and that it might be fulfilled in us. Whatever happens, we are to be glad in the Lord ...not necessarily for the happening itself, but Philippians 3:1 (LB), says *"Whatever happens, dear friends, be glad in the Lord. I never get tired of telling you this and it is good for you to hear it again and again"* So you say, "Well, that's hard to do!" Here's what is hard, friend, the cross was hard! Jesus willingly suffered the strain and weight of all our sin to provide for us a way to heaven, plus the coming of the Holy Spirit to help us live our life here *"...for how well He understands us and knows what's best for us at all times,"* Ephesians 1:8 (LB). We can be glad in the Lord, regardless of what is happening in our lives. Paul said that he never got tired of telling you to be glad in the Lord because we needed to hear it again and again. That is so true, we have to turn to the Word and repeat His promises over and over until our mind agrees with our heart and we sense His Presence, love and joy more than our pain. Jesus prays for you that you may experience that.

FEBRUARY 1
INTO EVERY LIFE SOME RAIN MUST FALL

Ezekiel 34:26b (NKJV)
"And I will cause showers to come down in their season; there shall be showers of blessing."

Ask yourself this question today, as I did, "What is my season today, Lord?" If it's a time of dryness and drought, then it's a season for some showers. Is it a time of heaviness and darkness? Then, this too must be a season for showers, and notice Ezekiel

30

makes the word "showers" plural. A season of showers can do a lot for a dry and withered heart. He can send showers of comfort, healing and grace. "Let your heart become a valley low and God will rain on it 'till it will overflow," Streams in the Desert. Job's season of thorns became flowers after You rained on him, Lord. You received your crown of glory after your crown of thorns. The fruitful life seeks rain as well as sunshine; both are required for growth. The promise is the showers will become seasons of blessings. Deuteronomy 33:25 (NIV) tells us that, "...your strength will equal your days," and that's good in all the seasons in which you live. We just need You to permeate our lives with Your Presence, Lord!

FEBRUARY 2
DO YOU LACK WISDOM

James 1:5 (NKJV)

"If any of you lacks wisdom, let him ask of God who gives to all liberally..."

Jesus told His disciples in Luke 21:15 (NKJV), "For I will give you a mouth and wisdom which all your adversaries will not be able to contradict or resist." If you need wisdom, Jesus will be generous in giving it to you as He gave you the mouth in which to speak. He is so pleased when we make the choice to consult and obey Him. With His wisdom comes the absence of fear. On our own, we can go through deep valleys or soar to new heights and neither one changes us. On the other hand, God's wisdom provides balance, insight and stability. None of which is natural and you get it only when you ask for it. God's wisdom is so needed in hard confusing situations; we need His strength to continue in spite of swirling circumstances. His promise is that He will give it to us generously and it will be such that "none can contradict us." When we use His Word in our responses, not only will He be pleased, He is also glorified! Just remember, it is His wisdom, not yours, so give Him the praise and glory!

FEBRUARY 3
MONEY

1 Timothy 6:9-10 Holman Christian Standard Bible (HCSB)

"But those who want to be rich fall into temptation, a trap, and many foolish and harmful desires, which plunge people into ruin and destruction. For the love of money is a root of all kinds of evil, and by craving it, some have wandered away from the faith and pierced themselves with many pains."

Money itself is not your problem... it's how you handle it and your attitude toward it. A poor person or a wealthy person can have a love for money that will ruin their life. It appears the focus of the world in which we live today is all about money as it seems to be the basis of all our decisions. Job tells us, *"We brought nothing into the world and we can take nothing out."* Nothing you accumulate here in these short years on earth will go with you beyond the grave. Our real problem lies in that we want more than we need and "things" always require more things. When you do this, you fall into the temptation of taking shortcuts and before you know it, you're caught in a greed trap. The scripture says that the love of money is a root and those roots spread all over your life and can cause you to "wander away from your faith." The things that you allow to come into your home because of the love of money will not only jeopardize it, but your relationship with God, and will "pierce you through with many pains." God measures what we give, rather than what we have.

FEBRUARY 4
BE COMFORTED

Isaiah 40:1 (NKJV)

"Comfort, yes, comfort My people!" says your God."

This world is full of hurting hearts. Before you can ever be a comfort to others, you must go through what is wringing out the hearts of the hurting. If you, yourself are wounded, you will learn in the process how to help the wounded. If you are experiencing some really great sorrow, it could be that years from now, you'll be able to be of help to someone going through much the same thing. You will actually be able to bless God for the discipline learned in the experience as you help others. James 1:2-3 (Weymouth), *"Reckon it nothing but joy whenever you find yourself hedged in by various trials. Be assured that the testing of your faith leads to power of endurance."* God, often hedges us in for protection but we don't see it that way and struggle to be set free. You are there for the experience so spend the time listening and learning. God doesn't comfort us so we will feel comfortable, but to enable us to comfort others.

FEBRUARY 5
I'M YOURS

<u>Ephesians 1: 4</u> (NIV)

"For He chose us in Him before the creation of the world to be holy and blameless in His sight."

"Long ago, even before He made the world, God chose us to be His very own through what Christ would do for us; He decided then to make us holy in His eyes without a single fault—we who stand before Him covered with His love," <u>Ephesians 1:4</u> (LB). That is true whether I ever live it out or not. My body, soul, and spirit are Yours, Lord, made by You, kept by You and redeemed one day by You. You have sealed me until the day of redemption and You've committed Yourself for my growth in truth and holiness. Your promise is to cover me with Your love so that I stand without a single fault on that day when salvation from sin is complete. I truly *"do not count my life dear to myself, so that I may finish my race with joy, and the ministry which I received from the Lord Jesus."* <u>Acts 20:24</u> (NKJV). So be it, Jesus. Be it praise, thanksgiving, despair or destruction, I am Yours. Your love is perfect, whatever state or form, and I receive it! I belong to You!

FEBRUARY 6
WE HAVE THIS MOMENT

<u>Ephesians 2:19</u> (LB)

"<u>Now</u> you are no longer strangers to God and foreigners to heaven, but you are members of God's very own family..."

Ephesians 3:20 (NIV), *"Now to Him who is able to do immeasurably more than all we ask or imagine..."* Recently I read that most people spend 58 minutes out of every 60 thinking about: 1) the past; 2) regretting lost joys or pleasures; 3) feeling shame for things done badly; and 4) or, living in the future, either longing for or dreading it. Only one person in a thousand knows how to live in the present, which is really all we have. Each moment is rarely repeatable...seldom ever happens again. To relive the past and worry about bad decisions and mistakes is futile and weakening. To consider the future is important, true, but we have no guarantee we will have it. What we have is this moment. We have now. I've tried, since reading this to check my thoughts to see if what I'm thinking is in the past, present or things yet to be and I have to constantly bring myself in line to keep centered on "now." Scripture tells us that, *"Now we have every grace and blessing. Every spiritual gift and power are ours now during this time of waiting for the return of our Lord Jesus Christ,"* 1 Corinthians 1:7 (LB). Put your hopes and prayers into today and live expecting the Lord to be gracious unto you.

FEBRUARY 7

LISTEN

1 Kings 19:11-12 (NKJV)

"Then He said, 'Go out, and stand on the mountain before the Lord.' And behold the Lord passed by, and a great and strong wind tore into the mountains and broke the rocks in pieces before the Lord, but the Lord was not in the wind; and after the wind an earthquake, but the Lord was not in the earthquake, and after the

earthquake a fire, but the Lord was not in the fire; and after the fire a still small voice."

The Lord speaks clearly in His Word, and sometimes He only whispers. (Satan whispers too, but it's all lies; just look at your past). Notice, God wasn't in the wind, the earthquake or the fire, but "in a still small voice." God was in all of them but not for Elijah. That's why we need to be listening so we can discern what He is saying to us. God speaks all the time but only ears that are listening will hear. In Revelation 2 and 3 we read seven times, *"He who has ears to hear, let him hear."* Jeremiah 7:13 (NKJV), *"... I spoke to you, rising up early and speaking, but you did not hear...,"* God is telling Jeremiah that He has spoken to His people but because of their wickedness, they are not listening. Romans 10:17 (NKJV), *"So then faith comes by hearing and hearing by the Word of God."* Be a person who seeks what to know, as is stated in Luke 8:18 (NKJV), *"Therefore take heed how you hear ..."* The Mountain-Maker and Earth- Shaper owns it all. Humble yourself before the Lord God Almighty. Open His Word and let your heart and ear hear what He speaks into your spirit. Today, listen!

FEBRUARY 8
JESUS LOVES ME

John 17:23 (NKJV)
"I in them, and You in Me; that they may be made perfect in one, and that the world may know that You have sent Me, and have loved them as You have loved Me."

You need to realize that God loves you as much as He loves Jesus; put that with 1 John 4:18a (LB), *"We need have no fear of someone who loves us perfectly; his perfect love for us eliminates all dread of what he might do to us."* You get a major hook up when you believe that! Not only does He love us but He helps us be perfected, i.e., being made or in the process of being made perfect. Perfect love casts out fear. Outer circumstances that loom out at us have to fall in place to fit perfectly into the Plan that God is working out for our lives. We may not see that Plan but we can and do see Jesus; and we know that God sees and knows His Plan and that it is good. The established and accomplished facts of Ephesians 1:3 (LB), tells us that He, *"...has blessed us with every blessing in heaven"* and that in Vs. 18, *"the eyes of our heart are flooded with light so that we can see something of the future he has called us to share."* When that kicks in, we can truly entrust our circumstances to Him. Reading the scriptures every day really aids the mindset. Feelings fight like crazy for control—never doubt what you believe and stop believing your doubts. Doubts have a hard way to go if you feed them enough scripture! The truth is Jesus Loves you!!

FEBRUARY 9
GOD IS KIND, BUT NOT SOFT

Romans 2:1-10 (MSG)

"Those people are on a dark spiral downward. But if you think that leaves you on the high ground where you can point your finger at others, think again. Every time you criticize someone, you condemn yourself. It takes one to know one. Judgmental criticism of others is a well-known way of escaping detection in your own crimes and misdemeanors. But God isn't so easily diverted. He

sees right through all such smoke screens and holds you to what you've done. You didn't think, did you, that just by pointing your finger at others you would distract God from seeing all your misdoings and from coming down on you hard? Or did you think that because he's such a nice God, he'd let you off the hook? Better think this one through from the beginning. God is kind, but He's not soft. In kindness He takes us firmly by the hand and leads us into a radical life-change. You're not getting by with anything. Every refusal and avoidance of God adds fuel to the fire. The day is coming when it's going to blaze hot and high, God's fiery and righteous judgment. Make no mistake: In the end, you get what's coming to you—Real Life for those who work on God's side, but to those who insist on getting their own way and take the path of least resistance, Fire! If you go against the grain, you get splinters, regardless of which neighborhood you're from, what your parents taught you, what schools you attended. But if you embrace the way God does things, there are wonderful payoffs..."

Finding fault is not worth the find!

FEBRUARY 10
LIVING WORDS

John 6:63b (NKJV)

"The Words that I speak to you are spirit, and they are life."

John 6:63b (MSG), *"Every Word I've spoken to you is a Spirit-Word, and so it is life-making."* Spend time studying, reading and meditating in God's Word each day and if you really want an eye-opener and desire to improve your quality of life, memorize some of it. Memorizing scripture is the most important habit you'll ever have to improve your life. It's like a planted seed; it will produce life in you. Write scripture down on a card and place it where you'll see it often during the day. It takes a while before you really learn it but reflecting often and referring to it will help you gain insight into your problems and enable you to help others with theirs. It's the best habit out there, go for it! Every "you" and "your" you read can become "me" and "mine;" just know that it was written for you. When you read something that sounds too good to be true, know that He had you in mind and that it was written for you! James 1:25 (NKJV) reminds us, *"... to not be a forgetful hearer but a doer of the Word."* It isn't enough to hear and know, as the last part of the verse says, *"... this is the one who will be blessed in what he does."* You aren't blessed until you do something with the insight you've been shown. Make a life with His Words...every Word is a Spirit-Word, and so it is life-making.

FEBRUARY 11
EXPERIENCE GOD'S LOVING KINDNESS

Psalms 125:1-2, 4 (LB)

"Those who trust in the Lord are steady as Mount Zion, unmoved by any circumstance. Just as the mountains surround and protect Jerusalem, so the Lord surrounds and protects his people. O Lord, do good to those who are good, whose hearts are right with the Lord."

Psalm 51:1 (NKJV), *"Have mercy upon me, O God, according to Your loving kindness; according to the multitude of Your tender mercies, blot out my transgressions. Wash me thoroughly from my iniquity and cleanse me from my sin."* Regardless of our circumstances, we are as steady as the mountains surrounding Jerusalem because the Lord protects those who trust in Him. The promise is He will give good to those whose hearts are right with the Lord. When you err, acknowledge and confess your sin, as David did. Then ask for His tender mercy according to His measure of loving kindness. David loved the Lord but one of the hardest experiences of his life was facing the sin of his affair with Bathsheba. David's response when rebuked was, *"I have sinned against the Lord."* David had sinned against Bathsheba, Uriah, as well as the nation he ruled, but none of it was as offensive as His sin against the Lord. Thank you, God for your loving kindness that covers our sin when we confess and respond rightly to You.

FEBRUARY 12
SUBMISSION BRINGS STRENGTH

James 4:7 (NKJV)

"Therefore submit to God. Resist the devil and he will flee from you."

Eugene Peterson wrote in his introduction to the Book of Judges: "God it turns out does not require good people in order to do good work. He can and does work with us in whatever moral and spiritual condition he finds us. God, we are learning, does some of his best work using the most unlikely people. It's almost as if God is saying, 'Well, if that's all you're going to give me to work with, I'll use these men and women just as they are,' and get on with working out the story of salvation." Twice in the Book of Judges, we read there was no king in Israel and the people did whatever they

40

felt like doing, which accounts for their moral and political anarchy. Whatever you are when God calls you to a higher level of responsibility, know that He's also calling you to a lower level of humility. Peter Marshall, Chaplin of U.S. Senate, prayed, "Lord, when we are wrong make us willing to change and when we are right, make us easy to live with." Each time God blesses us with good things, He runs the risk that it will take our focus off of Him. The more He blesses us, the more self-absorbed we tend to become. Submission to God actually brings us strength; we find that a submitted life has the power to overcome. When our enemy meets that kind of resistance, he runs!

FEBRUARY 13
COMPLETE YOUR TASK

Acts 20:24 (LB)

"I consider my life nothing to me, if only I may finish the race and complete the task the Lord Jesus has given me."

"When God is preparing us for a great work, the enemy always comes to confront us. We should accept it as evidence of God being in it and claim double the blessing, victory and power. Power has always been developed through resistance. The force and damage of an artillery shell is determined by the amount of resistance at the point of impact. Electricity is produced by the friction of rotating turbines. We can gain power from Satan as God uses him as an instrument for our blessing and ultimate good. Tribulation is a door to triumph. No one wins until he has walked the winepresses of woe. In anguish, Jesus said, *"In this world you will have trouble"* John 16:33 (LB). But, also, *"Take heart, I have overcome the world."* Someday we will understand. We wrestle our crowns from the giants we conquer. Tribulation was in the lives of all the greats such as Paul, Martin Luther, John Wesley," Streams in the Desert. Our goal is to finish and complete whatever Jesus has assigned for us today. Friction and Resistance are often much of the assignment but also serve as a door opener to complete the task.

FEBRUARY 14
GOD'S LOVE IS ETERNAL

Psalms 103:17 (MSG)
"God's love though, is ever and always, eternally present to all who fear Him."

When Louie and I went for pre-marital counseling (we were young whippersnappers, ages 66-67), our Pastor asked us if we would like to say anything to one another as we exchanged our vows. I thought about it for a moment and we both agreed to do so. At the given point in our ceremony, the Pastor indicated I would be first. I took both of Louie's hands, looked into his eyes and began: "Louie, how we praise God the Father of our Lord Jesus Christ who has blessed us with every spiritual in heaven because we belong to Christ..." and continued on for most of the next 12 verses of Ephesians 1. When I finally shut up, Louie had nothing to say ... his comments were in his pocket on a 3x5 card and remained there. Later this card was included in the pages of our Wedding Book. In reality, I may have spoken good words but he lived them out every day of our lives. He never missed a Valentine's Day, Proposal Day or Anniversary to take me to the beach, kneel in the sand, and again ask me to marry him. "God's love though, is ever and always, eternally present to all who fear Him." Today, Louie is in heaven praising God for the gift of His love in bringing him there. Maybe there is someone you need to remember on this Valentine's Day in love. Even though you can never match the love of Jesus, He is pleased when you try!

FEBRUARY 15
SOME THINGS ARE GOOD TO HEAR AGAIN AND AGAIN

Philippians 3:1 (LB)

"Whatever happens to you dear friends, be glad in the Lord. I never get tired of telling you this and it is good for you to hear it again and again."

You can learn to thank God and be grateful for every inconsequential, little thing that happens in your life. God will use your praise to draw weary and unhappy people to you and then to Himself. Try using small upsets as a point to praise and watch Him turn things around. Are you glad for the upset? Not really, but if you've determined beforehand (mind set, will set) that you will use these events as a reason to voice your praise, then you might recognize this is God's way of getting your attention so you will pause and acknowledge Him. (This gives me some insight as to why I am such a Master-Messer!) As you begin to do this privately, it will eventually carry over into your public life as well. In time, you will be able to thank Him for an upset that caused you to turn your thoughts toward Him...start doing this today and before you know it, you'll do it automatically. God has this incredible way of matching your praise to equal your problems! You've heard all this before but the scripture says, *"it is good that you hear it again and again."*

FEBRUARY 16
COMPLETE THE TASK GOD HAS GIVEN YOU

Acts 20:24 (MSG)

"What matters most to me is to finish what God started: the job the Master Jesus gave me of letting everyone I meet know all about this incredibly extravagant generosity of God."

Paul said, *"I consider my life worth nothing to me, if only I may finish the race and complete the task the Lord Jesus has given me,"* Acts 20:24 (NIV). God gives you work to do and when He is preparing you for something great, the Enemy always comes to confront you, causing you to doubt and question. You need to accept this as evidence that God is in it, He is at hand to help you through His blessing and power. Power has always been developed through resistance. It's just as true in the spiritual world as in the physical. God can turn Satan's power and use it as an instrument of blessing to you. He is God! Tribulation is a door to triumph. Jesus said, *"In this world you will have trouble, but take heart, I have overcome the world,"* John 16:33 (NIV). What has God given you to do that you haven't yet finished? He finished His work and wants you to finish yours!

FEBRUARY 17

SPEAK GOD'S WORD INTO YOUR LIFE

Hosea 10:12 (LB)

"Plant the good seeds of righteousness and you will reap a crop of my love; plow the hard ground of your hearts for now is the time to seek the Lord ..."

Hosea 12:6 (LB), *"Oh, come back to God. Live by the principles of love and justice, and always be expecting much from him, your God."* Hosea 14:8-9 (LB), *"... I am living and strong! I look after you and care for you. I am like an evergreen tree, yielding my fruit to you throughout the year. My mercies never fail. Whoever is wise, let him understand these things. Whoever is intelligent, let him listen. For the paths of the Lord are true and right, and good men walk along them."* Jude 20-21; 24-25 (LB), *"You must build up your lives ever more strongly upon the foundation of our holy faith, learning to pray in the power and strength of the Holy Spirit. Stay always within the boundaries where God's love can reach and bless you. Wait patiently for the eternal life that our Lord Jesus Christ in his mercy is going to give. And now—all glory to him who alone is God, who saves us through Jesus Christ our Lord; yes, splendor and majesty , all power and authority are his from the beginning; his they are and his they evermore shall be. And he is able to keep you from slipping and falling away and to bring you sinless and perfect into his glorious presence with mighty shouts of everlasting joy!"* Nothing is more powerful than God's Word. Speak these scriptures into your life and live in them today!

FEBRUARY 18
STOP COMPLAINING

Philippians 2:13-14 (LB)

"For God is at work within you, helping you want to obey him, and then helping you do what he wants. In everything you do, stay away from complaining and arguing."

I had no idea of how much I complain until I started trying to quit! (Much like trying to quit smoking, I suspect). It's so automatic! If I ever shut up complaining, I find it is so much easier to be glad! Quit grumbling and start praising God in (not for) every dark and crooked thing you see and watch God's light penetrate the darkness. Do I really believe that? Yeah, Lord, Your Word says so. Beware, though of the dangerous dogs all around you, as they don't believe a word of it. We have no idea of what this day will hold, but we do know who holds the day and it is He that works within you, helping you want to obey Him and then helping you do what He wants. It is the "old man" in us that looks for what's wrong in our lives instead of what's right. Wise up and learn the benefits of praise to the One who has already ordered up what's on your plate for today. Praise Him before He fixes you and be amazed at how quickly you are made right. Above all, and in everything you do, stop complaining and grumbling. *"Whatever happens, dear friends, be glad in the Lord. I never get tired of telling you this and it is good for you to hear it again and again,"* Philippians 3:1 (LB).

FEBRUARY 19

THE POWER OF THE LIFE-GIVING SPIRIT IS MINE

Romans 8:1-3 (LB)

"So there is now no condemnation awaiting those who belong to Christ Jesus. For the power of the life-giving Spirit—and this power is mine through Christ Jesus—has freed me from the vicious circle of sin and death. We aren't saved from sin's grasp by knowing the commandments of God, because we can't and don't keep them, but God put into effect a different plan to save us. He sent His own Son in a human body like ours—except ours are sinful—and destroyed sin's control over us by giving himself as a sacrifice for our sins."

The power of the life-giving Spirit is mine and that power gets me through life's low–lying humiliations. I recognize that before You, I am wretched, miserable, blind, and naked, but I am covered with the love of Jesus and the power of the Holy Spirit. When Jesus died on the cross, You have truly saved me from sin and death. Nothing passes through my life until it first passes You. You have poured Your favor out on me and I give You praise. You destroyed sin's control over me by the sacrifice of Your Life that You gave for my sins when You went to the cross. Thank You Jesus! I could never do this on my own...never be saved from sin's death grip and grasp, even in knowing Your commandments, could never keep them; so thank You for providing a way for me to come to You. I know you live in me and I hope You are happy here.

FEBRUARY 20
TRUST IS THE LANGUAGE OF THE HEART

Psalms 37:3 (LB)

"Commit everything you do to the Lord. Trust Him to help you do it and He will."

Trust is the language of our heart. Faith is an act of our will and belief comes from the mind; but trust comes from the heart. Faith and belief refer to something about to happen or is taking place. Trust is to see, feel and lean on His great heart of love through delays, reversals, difficulties, rejection and all evidence to the contrary. Trust in Him. We are to always praise and reverence Your Name. Your business on earth is the supreme concern of life and all of our personal "stuff" no matter how we view it, is secondary. No prayer of any human on earth has any power until that lesson is learned. God, have Your way in this world and in my heart. Your will be done today in all I do. "Commit everything you do to the Lord; trust Him to help you to do it and He will."

FEBRUARY 21
THE LORD IS GOOD

Nahum 1:7 (LB)

"The Lord is good. When trouble comes, He is the place to go! And He knows everyone who trusts in Him!"

The Lord is good and He is the One we run to in times of trouble. All the forces that come against us can be used to bring us straight to Jesus. " An eagle will wait perfectly still on a mountain cliff, watching the sky fill with lightening and darkness until he feels the burst of the storm screaming around him, then he dives straight into the winds, using the power of the storm to carry him above it. This is how God wants us to use the storms that threaten to destroy us... use the power of the thing that comes against you to rise above what is threatening you," Streams in the Desert.   Satan attacks our bodies and plans our defeat. God heals us and we come out better for it. Psalms 138:2b-3 (LB) *"... for your promises are backed by all the honor of your Name. When I pray, You answer me and give me the strength I need."* Help us not to just read, but believe and heed Your Words, as Your Word is the way that it is!

FEBRUARY 22

GOD DETERMINES THE TIME OF YOUR DELIVERANCE

Ecclesiastes 11:5a (MSG)

"So you'll never understand the mystery at work in all that God does."

"We would love it if God would visibly show us and encourage us and sometimes He does. But how wonderful it is when we just trust Him either way. He really wants us to remember that His promises and His Word are more dependable than anything we can 'sense or feel.' We receive more when we trust Him without the visible evidence. Strangely, it's those who trust Him without any evidence except His Word that always receives the greater amount of visible evidence of His love. Many unanswered prayers come with 'my time has not yet come' recorded underneath," George G. Trumbull. "God has a fixed time and an ordained purpose and He who controls the limits of our life also determines the time of our deliverance," Selected. God is ever working in our lives and sometimes we see it; sometimes we can only see where He's been; and sometimes we just need to blindly follow knowing that He who controls the limits of our life also determines the time of our deliverance. When the shadows deepen and you do not know the way, keep walking, He will always lead you into the Light.

FEBRUARY 23
I WANT TO WALK STEADILY WITH YOU

1 Peter 5:10 (NKJV)

"But may the God of all grace, who called us to His eternal glory by Christ Jesus, after you have suffered a while, perfect, establish, strengthen and settle you;"

Exodus 33:21 King James Version (KJV), *"And the Lord said, "Here is a place by Me, and you shall stand on the rock."* Put a spiritual splint on me and hold me quiet until I believe I can walk steadily with You all the time. I want to stand still until Your insight is so ingrained in me that it becomes a permanent habit to choose You in everything. Lead me forward, plan my days that I may do well what you have left me here to do for Your glory, remembering if I receive glory, You get none. My spirit is justified before God at salvation, but the "sinful nature" still resides in my body. If I allow it to control me, I will sink under the power of my Enemy. If I understand the love God has for me, I will make a practice of placing my faith in Him. If my cell phone loses its power, I plug it into an electrical outlet to recharge it. The power source is always available but I have to plug it in to receive it. God is our source of power and I must stay plugged into Him. The spiritual law of abiding, making the right choice, being steadfast (not wavering) and believing is the thing that keeps me connected. The natural law of sin and sickness loses its grip over me when I'm connected to You. Pluck my heart strings over and over until I am humbled and blended in harmony with Your Spirit.

FEBRUARY 24
GOD DELIGHTS IN EVERY DETAIL OF YOUR LIFE

Psalms 37:23 (LB)

"The Lord directs the steps of the godly. He delights in every detail of their lives."

You read your Bible, pray, go to church, help others, witness—do you think that's all that God's interested in? He takes pleasure in His children just as you do...every detail we enjoy in our life...eating, working, resting, playing; every human activity except sin can be done for God's pleasure if we do it in faith and with an attitude of gratitude. You can wash dishes, clean house (even iron, uggh), dispense pills, raise a family, set up a computer program, sell cars, push grocery carts, all for the glory of God. Like a proud parent, God watches and is pleased when you use the abilities He's given you for His glory. Be thankful you can do them! There are no unspiritual abilities, just misused ones! Do the things you were designed to do. "God delights in every detail of your life."

FEBRUARY 25
HE OWNS IT ALL

Psalms 104:32 (MSG)

"He takes one look at earth and triggers an earthquake; points a finger at the mountains and volcanoes erupt!"

Holy, Holy, Holy is my God! Years ago and perhaps today in countries where there is a king, the king owns the land, all of it! People could build houses and live in them; they owned the house but the King owned all the land and the people were grateful for the privilege of living there. Our King owns it all. He lets me live in His house, sleep in His bed, breathe His air, eat His food, drive His car, see with eyes He has made; write checks on His bank account. It's all His! I own nothing but my relationship with Him and He's the One that made that possible. He alone can say, "It's Mine, Mine, it's all Mine!" One look from Him can trigger an earthquake; point a finger and volcanoes erupt. Every day You give us new opportunities to trust You, Almighty God, help us to recognize and respond to them.

FEBRUARY 26
YOU ARE THE APPLE OF HIS EYE

Isaiah 43:4b (LB)

"You are precious to me and honored, and I love you."

We need to let those Words soak in when we go through heartache, financial stress, body pain, and also when the enemy comes in like a flood. My weakness needs Your strength; whatever concerns me, concerns You. *"Whoever touches you, touches the apple of My eye,"* Zechariah 2:8 (NKJV). God says in 1 Kings 12:24b (MSG), *"I'm in charge here!"* He is the God who owns it all and He owns my circumstances. I didn't come to where I am by accident; I am where He wants me to be. He is the Keeper of my finances; I am to depend on Him because we read in Philippians 4:19 (LB) *"And it is He who will supply all your needs from His riches in glory ..."* It is as though He who whispers, "I am aware of every interruption, every weakness you have." The problems will leave as we learn to see Him in everything. He owns your every experience and He owns you. Even though you are insufficient, the Word of God says, "I am precious and honored in His sight and yeah, the apple of His eye."

FEBRUARY 27
YOUR SITUATION IS AN OPPORTUNITY FOR SOMETHING ABOUT TO HAPPEN

1 Kings 12:24b (MSG)
"This is God's Word ... I'm in charge here."

We seem to always be looking around for someone to blame for what we're experiencing instead of looking to see what God can do. Our situation is an opportunity for something about to happen. That's why some promises seem unfulfilled, prayers unanswered and circumstances unfair. Your discontent in some of this is so you won't feel so comfortable here; you need to realize you're not home yet! This isn't the end of you or your story. Everything that breaks your heart is temporary. Use the things you experience to accomplish God's purposes. You can use the very things that come against you to "walk over the backs of your enemies," with God helping you. God said, "I'm in charge here." Or, "This thing is from Me," (NKJV). This was spoken by the Lord to tell a rebellious king to return home and stop fighting; but it is just as true for you today. If you're having financial problems, going through difficult circumstances, or times of sorrow, God could be saying, "This is from Me." Rejection and disappointment go with the territory but this territory isn't your home. God sees the completion; we see in part. Let that part be enlightened with the knowledge that "He is in charge!"

FEBRUARY 28
GOD WILL SETTLE AND ESTABLISH YOU

1 Peter 5:10 (LB)

"After you have suffered a little while, our God, who is full of kindness through Christ, will give you His eternal glory. He will personally come and pick you up and set you firmly in place, and make you stronger than ever."

We all experience times of highs and they are usually followed by almost depression! In the morning, you're singing and in a good mood; by evening, almost silent. God shines His light on your life all the time, in the good times and the bad. He lifts you up to strengthen you so you may go deeper still. He lights your way so He can send you out into the night. This is not for you, but for you to help someone else. If you haven't been in the night, you don't know how to help someone that is there. Satan loves a good fight and we feel like we're trapped. Actually we have the Word working for us, He doesn't. It is time for you to realize God keeps your soul in His hand and His promise is "after you've suffered a little while, He will personally come and pick you up and set you firmly in place and make you stronger than ever." You need to realize that part of His makeover includes perfecting, establishing and settling you.

FEBRUARY 29
YOU CAN TRUST GOD IN ALL YOUR EXPERIENCES

Isaiah 60:1 (LB)

"Arise; my people let your light shine for all the nations to see. For the glory of the Lord is streaming from you."

Are you letting your past bother you? Too many people keep going over and over what happened years ago... your past can be an albatross around your neck or it can become the wind beneath your wings. A missionary was brutally raped and asked this question, "Can I thank God for trusting me with this experience even if He never tells me why?" Some things are never explained to us but the secret of trust is never found in answers; it's in acceptance. Whatever happens, has happened, or will happen, know that God is in charge. You can either believe that or you will go through life thinking God is unfair. You need to bury the past; if not, you'll live with its ghosts. Rehashing old hurts is like watching a sad movie over and over, hoping for a different ending. It ain't gonna happen! Learn from your mistakes, get over them, and move on. "Arise and shine and let the glory of the Lord stream from you!" You can learn to trust God in all your experiences!

MARCH 1
HIS HAND AND HIS HEART ARE ALWAYS OPEN TO YOU

Matthew 17:20b (NKJV)

"Nothing is impossible with God."

Actually, nothing is impossible for you as your cast all your anxiety on Him and experience His peace. It is possible to have all your thoughts and desires of the heart purified in the deepest sense of the Word. It is possible to see all your circumstances as God's will and be accepting rather than complaining. It is possible to become strong by taking refuge in God. Everything that works in your life is subject to Him and His will and every bit of it gives you a more blessed sense of His Presence and power. All divine possibilities cause you to bow before Him and teach you to hunger and thirst more for Him. You are able to have as much of God as you want. He always has His hand and heart open to you. Whose fault is it if you come away lacking or empty-handed? He gave His life that you may KNOW Him and the power of the resurrection and because of that, nothing is impossible with God Almighty!

MARCH 2
WAIT PATIENTLY

Psalms 37:7 (NKJV)

"Be still before the Lord and wait patiently for Him."

Oswald Chambers said: "One of the greatest strains of life is waiting for God." Jesus said that He would take care of us and He knows our needs better than we do. Never let your desires to receive what you want become stronger than your desire for the will of God to be done. His patience eliminates your wavering and wobbling before Him. Waiting is more than just hanging on. The Lord was accused of being demon possessed, ridiculed, beaten and crucified and He endured it all because He knew heaven was just ahead. The Lord said that He would come and His Word is just as good as His Presence. He is your Rock and steady foundation. Trust Him completely and wait patiently for Him to act. James 1:4 (LB), "...so let your patience grow and don't try to squire out of your problems." For when your patience is finally in full bloom, then you will be ready for anything, strong in character, full and complete." Wait patiently on the Lord!

MARCH 3

WE KNOW THE LOVE OF CHRIST BY EXPERIENCE

Ephesians 3:16-19a Revised Standard Version (RSV)

"That according to the riches of his glory he may grant you to be strengthened with might through his Spirit in the inner man, and that Christ may dwell in your hearts through faith; that you being rooted and grounded in love, may have power to comprehend with all the saints what is the breadth and length and height and depth, and to know the love of Christ ..."

VS. 16, *"that you be strengthened with might through His Spirit"* means to be infused with power and as a result, be fortified or invigorated through His Spirit, as that is the agent that activates the power. *"In the inner man"* is your spiritual being. The Holy Spirit is the One who causes the power to be active and effective in your life. God has a limitless reservoir of strength and power... tapping into

57

this source is up to you. VS. 18, *"Only God can help us comprehend that the power is fully able to accomplish its goal."* It is broad enough to include all men; long enough to extend from eternity to eternity. It is as deep as the very nature of God and as high so as to reach the limitless heights of heaven itself. And, it is as deep as the profound nature of God Himself. VS. 19, We *"know the love of Christ"* by experience!

MARCH 4
ALWAYS BE THANKFUL

1 Thessalonians 5:18 (LB)

"No matter what happens, always be thankful, for this is God's will for you who belong to Christ Jesus."

The natural thing to do is to be ungrateful and think on what is not right in your life. The natural thing is to be thankful only for the things that seem good at the time! But when the Holy Spirit has control, we are able to give thanks all the time in (not for) everything. That includes adversity, hard licks, unfairness, and lumps right along with the blessings. I have to ask, do I really believe 1 Thessalonians 5:18 and give God thanks in everything? Yea, Lord, my intellect knows; now help my emotions to agree that no matter what happens, to always be thankful. I know that You hold the keys to this life and the next. It is your Holy Spirit who reveals Jesus to me...Your beauty, holiness, glory...I bow before the King of Heaven and magnify Your great Name. There is none like you! I will praise you and give thanks, no matter what!

MARCH 5

FOLLOW THE HOLY SPIRIT'S LEADING

Ephesians 5:25-26 (LB)

"If we are living now by the Holy Spirit's power, let us follow the Holy Spirit's leading in every part of our lives. Then we won't need to look for honors and popularity which lead to jealousy and hard feelings."

This scripture is such good advice for our day to day living; because if we are living by the power of the Holy Spirit, we won't need to look for honor and popularity among people. These things only lead to jealousy and hard feelings. It is the Holy Spirit that produces love, joy, peace (which is our relationship to God); longsuffering, kindness, goodness (our relationship to others); faithfulness, gentleness, self-control (our inner-self relationship). The best response we can give to the Giver of gifts is to put them in action. He has given you exactly what He wants you to use; and as you use what He has given you, He gives you more. Focus all your attention on Him. When we do this, we're not prone to go out and tell others all about ourselves...what we are like ... but we'll be talking about our Mighty God and Savior and Who He is. Let the Holy Spirit lead your life.

MARCH 6
DON'T PICK ON PEOPLE OR JUMP ON THEIR FAILURES

<u>1 Corinthians 10:12</u> (LB)

"So be careful. If you are thinking, "Oh, I would never behave like that"—let this be a warning to you. For you too may fall into sin."

When we look at another's sin, we might be prone to say, "I'm bad, but certainly not that bad." If I do this, I become a Pharisee and violate something very important about my own relationship with Jesus. God graciously reminds me that there is NO SIN OF WHICH I'M NOT CAPABLE! And it is only His restraining hand that keeps me from being as bad as I could be! It is almost dangerous for a Christian to be right most of the time; as the spirit of pride creeps in. Rejoicing in the failure of another can be spiritually devastating. To say, "I told you so" is not an attractive trait as it reveals pride, self-wisdom and shows there is something very sinful going on in your own heart. "Let him who thinks he stands, take heed lest he fall" <u>Luke 6:37</u> (MSG). Don't pick on people, jump on their failures, and criticize their faults— unless, of course, you want the same treatment. Don't condemn those who are down; that hardness can boomerang. Lord, help us to learn and live by Your commands, not just read them, but know what You say and then do them!

MARCH 7

IT'S OKAY TO BE ALONE

Genesis 32:24 (NKJV)

"Then Jacob was left alone; and a Man wrestled with him until the breaking of day."

I've certainly cringed from the reality of being alone and to grieve and cry is hard, but that's not what the Lord had in mind. When left alone with You, Lord, what better state of mind and well-being could I possibly have? Jacob, when left alone, became a prince; Peter was left alone on the rooftop to have a vision; Moses was alone when he received his assignment as the bush burned; many old-timers such as John the Baptist, John on the Isle of Patmos, Gideon, Joshua, all received their commission of the Lord while alone. Think of what it would be like to be alone without You! If we fail to be alone with You, we have little blessing to pass on to anyone else. True, we may have less time to work but what we do will have more meaning and power. Jacob may have wrestled all night but he did receive his blessing. There is no way of measuring the value of our time alone with You, dear Lord.

MARCH 8

LAUNCH OUT INTO THE DEEP

Luke 5:4 (MSG)

"When he finished teaching, he said to Simon, "Push out into deep water..."

How deep, Lord? It all depends on how completely we are willing to cut off our ties to what is on shore; and how great our need really is, plus how anxiously we regard what's next! It also depends on how much we trust His Word and that which He is speaking into our lives. As we are "put out into the deep," we embrace in detail His goodness, mercy, grace and finite loving care. We go "out into the deep" to gain the work of the Holy Spirit in us. It is there we lose our sorrows and concerns and take on His calmness and peace and experience His abiding Presence. "Putting out into the deep" is to be immersed in His purposes, not our own. In Simon's case, it was for a better catch; whatever He has in mind for you, will always be for your good. He is the One who invites you to do it. He created us for going into the deep places and He is the One who makes those places fit in harmony with His own purpose and plan. Deep waters always flow and never become stagnant. God will always want you to share whatever you learn in your deeps.

MARCH 9
SUBMIT TO THE LORD'S PROCESSING

Hebrews 6:12 (RSV)

"...so that you may not be sluggish, but imitators of those who through faith and patience inherit the promises."

Those who have gone before us call from their lofty heights saying: "We did it; you can too!" We need faith and patience so teach me Lord, don't let me squirm out of one lesson of Your loving discipline because I'm discouraged, doubting or lonely. Don't throw me in the scrap heap because I've not passed the test; give me another chance! The old blacksmith, in order to test a piece of metal, heats, hammers, and then throws it into cold water to see if it stands the test. After doing this a few times, he then knows if it will be tempered or fall to pieces. The Lord does the same thing ... puts me in the fire, water and heavy blows ... help me, Lord, to stand and not be unwilling to submit to Your processing. It takes 11 tons of pressure on a piano string for it to be tuned ... just tune me, Lord, to be in harmony with You. It was Job who said, *"And when He has tried me, I will come forth as gold."* When the fire is the hottest, stand still, for later on will come the harvest. Hebrews 12:11 (RSV), *"For the moment all discipline seems painful rather than pleasant; later it yields the peaceful fruit of righteousness to those who have been trained by it."*

MARCH 10
GOD CAN RESTORE, USE AND BLESS OUR BROKENNESS

Isaiah 41:15 (LB)
"You shall be a new and sharp-toothed threshing instrument..."

You said, *"I will make you a sharp-toothed threshing instrument to tear your enemies apart,"* and you can do it Lord, even to a wimp and a worm, when I look to You. What greater contrast is there from a worm to a sharp-toothed threshing instrument? A worm is so easily squashed; a threshing tool with sharp teeth can cut through a mighty rock! You, Almighty God, can turn one into the other. You can take an individual or a nation and turn their weakness into great strength. So I need to take heart, You can make me stronger than my circumstances or situations. You can make me into a threshing tool that can plow through the hardest situations, just like a plow share cuts through hard dirt. The verse says, *"I will make you..."*

On earth, we look for the Big, Brave and the Beautiful—the strong victorious people; God looks for the broken, the failed, and the weak to build His kingdom. Isaiah 42:3 (LB), *"...He will not break the bruised reed nor quench the dimly burning flame."* He will encourage the fainthearted, those tempted to despair. He will see full justice given to all who have been wronged." In Him, there is no bruised reed that God cannot restore, use and bless.

MARCH 11
THERE'S A SMALL CLOUD RISING

1 Kings 18:44 (NLT)
" ... I saw a little cloud about the size of a man's hand rising from the sea. "

Mostly we miss the "small cloud risings" all around us because we have such a fixation on what is "big." Every big thing though starts with something small...like a small step or a small seed, and usually it is all we have at the time. If you're not willing to start with something small, you'll probably never start at all. In this particular instance, the small cloud had great potential and so does your small beginnings. Your problems are opportunities for God to show He strong; His strength is made perfect in your weakness. The "small cloud rising" came about as Elijah bowed himself upon the earth and put his face between his knees. As a result, the small cloud brought an abundance of rain. We're prone to view health and prosperity as an indication of God being with us. But it is in the mundane, the small experiences that we learn to live in total dependence on the One who brings about our deliverance. He helps us switch from anxiety to total trust. We need to spend some time bowing upon the earth with our face between our knees and then to step out believing His Word. That small cloud rising over you could result in an abundance of blessings.

MARCH 12
THERE IS NONE LIKE YOU!

Isaiah 45:5 (KJV)

"I am the Lord and there is none else, there is no God beside me! I girded thee though thou hast not known me."

Isaiah 45:5 (LB), *"I am Jehovah; there is no other God. I will strengthen you and send you out to victory even though you don't know me."* What an awesome Mighty God You Are; You rule, you reign victoriously! You know my desire is to be obedient; God help me to be willing to follow you; not me providing and doing, but you…all the way! It takes gumption, grits, guts and grace to continue where there is nothing being revealed to follow. The only way to live is to keep looking to You. Keep the eyes of my soul open and responsive to you. Don't let me be involved in pettiness and paltriness, but fix my gaze on You, not the drudgery of things here. A surf rider is not distressed by the overtaking waves but dives clean through to the other side. Distress, persecution and tribulation are nothing but "set-ups" to prove You to be more than a conqueror. Praise God, not in spite of, and in the middle of all your struggles and watch Him work! It is the constant love of Jesus and knowing that I am held completely by Your hand that lets me rely solely on Your care alone. Truly, there is none like You!

MARCH 13
PRAY ABOUT EVERYTHING

Matthew 6:33 (RSV)

"0 "But seek you first His kingdom and His righteousness all these things shall be yours as well."

For most people, when prayer fails, so does their spiritual life. Pray privately and to the point. You can't pray wrong, it's a matter of centering on Jesus. If you want to know how to pray ... pray! Pray to a personal God. One man said that in his entire life, he had only conversed five times with his father, so when he said, "Our Father," it made him wonder if He was going to abandon him too. God's promise is that He will never leave us or forsake us, He is personally our God. Ask God where to go, what to do, things to buy...God wants you to pray about everything; ask Him to provide for your family. Sometimes there are long spans of time in between your requests and His answers. Sometimes you may hear "It's not good for you now," or "Wait," even "No!" Development needs to take place first within you ... God moving in your life is more important than what you're asking for. Always include praising God when you pray. Psalms 22:22b (RSV), *"In the midst of the congregation, I will praise thee."* (LB), *"I will stand up before the congregation and testify of the wonderful things you have done."* This encourages you to stand up before others to praise, worship, adore, honor and glorify Him. Pray persistently. It isn't that God didn't hear you the first time; you are just reminding Him that you're waiting but be sure, though, to thank Him for answering you. And remember, He wants you to want Him more than any other thing He could ever give you.

MARCH 14

SEE THAT YOU EXCEL IN GIVING

1 Corinthians 8:7-8 (LB)

"You people there are leaders in so many ways---you have so much faith, so many good preachers, so much learning, so much enthusiasm, and so much love for us. Now I want you to be leaders also in the spirit of cheerful giving."

Giving makes you more like God. *"God gives to all generously and ungrudgingly,"* James 1:5 New Revised Standard Version (NRSV). Giving draws me closer to God. *"Your heart will be wherever your treasure is,"* Matthew 6:21 (NIV). Giving breaks the grip of materialism as described in Matthew 6:24. Giving is a test of maturity. If you are untrustworthy with worldly wealth, who do you think will trust you with true riches of heaven? Giving is an investment for eternity. You will store up real treasure for yourself in heaven; it is a safe investment for eternity, plus you will live a fruitful Christian life down here as well. Giving blesses you. 1 Timothy 6:18-19 (RSV), *"They are to do good, to be rich in good deeds, liberal and generous, thus laying up for themselves a good foundation for the future, so that they may take hold of the life which is life indeed."* Proverbs 22:9 (LB), *"Happy is the generous man, the one who feeds the poor."* Deuteronomy 15:10b (RSV), *"Give generously and God will bless you in all your work and in all that you undertake."* Remember the generosity of Jesus as He willingly gave His life for us." There is more happiness in giving than in getting.

MARCH 15

THE BORROWER IS A SLAVE TO THE LENDER

Proverbs 22:7 (LB)

"Just as the rich rule the poor, so the borrower is servant to the lender." VS. 7 Modern Language, *"... the borrower is the slave to the lender."*

Being on the wrong side of interest can ruin your life. You need to earn interest, rather than pay interest. Debt enslaves, obligates, undermines joy, erodes giving opportunities and unravels character flaws. It will cause lack of contentment, patience, trust, self-discipline and affect your Christian witness. Why would you want to do something that would cause you to do evil in His sight? If you're already in debt, how do you free yourself from it? Make the decision to have a plan, stick with it and give yourself time; find a partner that will help you be accountable. Start a small savings account; if you're determined, God will help you. Savings makes a person free and wise, as well as enhances your joy. It lets you respond to giving opportunities. It strengthens your character and provides a powerful witness. Ecclesiastics 3:17 (LB), *"In due season, God will judge everything man does, both good and bad."* Living within your means is a good way to live. Proverbs 23:12 (LB), *"Don't refuse to accept criticism, get all the help you can."* Listen to Proverbs 23: 12 (RSV), *"Apply your mind to instruction and your ear to Words of knowledge."* VS. 18, *"Surely there is a future, and your hope will not be cut off."* Go to God's Word every day for encouragement and instruction, you will find that He will direct you to live a debt-free life.

MARCH 16

THE WORD OF GOD IS MY DELIGHT

Psalms 119:77 (LB)

"Now let your loving-kindness comfort me, just as you promised. Surround me with your tender mercies that I may live. For your law is my delight."

The Word of God reveals the mind and will of God. Ephesians 5:18 (RSV), *"... to be filled with the Holy Spirit ..."* and Colossians 3:16 (RSV), *"Let the Word of Christ dwell in you richly ..."* Psalms 119:96-98 (LB). *"Nothing is perfect except your Words. Oh how I love them. I think about them all day long. They make me wiser than my enemies because they are my constant guide."* VS. 102-103 (LB), *"No, I haven't turned away from what you taught me; your Words are sweeter than honey."* VS. 105 (RSV), *"Thy Word is a lamp to my feet and a light to my path."* We should never neglect God's instructions. Scripture isn't mere musings; it is God directing us as surely as He led the Israelites with a cloud by day and fire by night. In Psalms 119, we find the meaning of being obedient and faithful to His Word. Develop an appetite for the Word, it is delightful. A little dab will not do you! Learn how to discern good from evil. We live in a permissive society with suggestive lifestyles and it is impossible sometimes to tell the Christian from the unbelievers. Let the Word of God be a lamp to your feet to light and illumine your path. When you read it, obey it. God will equip you with the strength to keep His Word.

MARCH 17

THE THINGS OF HEAVEN ARE JUST BEYOND WHAT WE'RE LOOKING AT

2 Corinthians 4:16-18 (MSG)

"So we're not giving up. How could we! Even though on the outside it often looks like things are falling apart on us, on the inside where God is making new life, not a day goes by without his unfolding grace. These hard times are small potatoes compared to the coming good times, the lavish celebration prepared for us. There's far more here than meets the eye. The things we see now are here today, gone tomorrow. But the things we can't see now will last forever."

The things of heaven are just beyond what we're looking at, at earth's level. We should never give up or lose hope. We stare at what we see ... disappointment, failure, pain and sorrow and on the outside it often looks like things are falling apart on us but on the inside God is making new life within us. Not one day goes by without His unfolding grace. Truly, every evil intent Satan hurls against us is small potatoes compared to the lavish celebration being prepared for us this minute. Just beyond what you're looking at is a whole host of *"His salvation wonders on display in His trophy room. Earth-Tamer, Ocean-Pourer, Mountain-Maker, Hill-Dresser, Muzzler of sea storms,"* Psalms 65:6 (MSG). What we see today is so brief but all our salvation wonders will be forever. While our worldly life is wasting away as it is controlled by the laws of nature; our inward nature (born at our second birth) has eternal value. Life is like grass, very short lived; but life with Jesus is both now and forever.

MARCH 18
FIND OUT WHAT GOD IS UP TO AND GET IN ON IT!

1 Corinthians 15:58 (RSV)

"Therefore, my beloved brethren, be steadfast, immovable, always abounding in the work of the Lord, immovable, always abounding in the work of the Lord, knowing that in the Lord your labor is not in vain."

I need to get off of what I'm down to and get on to what God is up to! Here's what you're down to: you think you won't get what you need or you might lose what you've got. You struggle with material wants, unmindful that God knows what you need and He has a bountiful supply. You need to be more concerned with your relationship with Him more than what you want. God has work for each one of you to do and sometimes your wants hinder the effectiveness of your work. Or, Satan can discourage you in your work by getting your eyes off the ministry and onto yourself. God is more concerned about your attitude than He is your actions. You need to "be steadfast, immovable and always abounding in the work of the Lord;" and when you do this, you will find out what God is up to; so get with it and get on it! God wants to be involved in your life and please believe this; you want to be involved in what God wants!

MARCH 19
HE IS IN CHARGE

2 Peter 5:10 (LB)

"After you've suffered a little while, our God, who is full of kindness through Christ, will give you his eternal glory. He

71

personally will come and pick you up and set you firmly in place, and make you stronger than ever."

The most difficult ingredient in suffering is time. A sharp pain is easily endured but body or heart pain over a period of years needs God's grace to not despair. Prolonged pain burns like fire. God knows how much pain we need to be purified. *"He sits as a refiner and will closely watch as the dross is burned away"* Malachi 3:3 (RSV). He stops the fire the moment He sees His image in the suffering. His plan may be hidden for a very long time but we have to believe He is in charge. Focus on the lesson to be learned more than on the deliverance. The reasons behind it all will more than justify the One who brought you to it. Don't try to steal tomorrow out of His hand. Wait for Him to personally come and pick you up and set you firmly in place, just as He promised. You will become stronger than ever before.

MARCH 20
THE LORD IS MY STRENGTH AND SONG

Isaiah 12:2b (LB)
"I will trust and not be afraid for the Lord is my strength and song; he is my salvation."

The One, who merely spoke and the world began, opened His mouth and the universe came into existence has become my salvation and He is <u>my</u> strength and song. That is true because You said so. Your promises are backed by all the honor of Your Name. Fear can block that flow of strength, so instead of trying to fight my fear, I trust in You. There is no limit, NONE, to how much

You can strengthen me. You are my song; You rejoice over me in singing and I want to join You in singing Your song! Zephaniah 3:17 Modern Language (ML), "*The Lord your God is in your midst, a mighty God who will save. He will rejoice over you with delight, He will rest you (quiet you) in His love. He will be joyful over you with singing.*" (LB) puts it this way, "*Is that a joyous choir I hear? No, it is the Lord himself exulting over you in happy song!*" The Mighty Voice that spoke the universe into existence rejoices over you in song!

MARCH 21
GOD WILL DEAL WITH YOUR TOMORROWS

Matthew 6:34 (MSG)

"*Give your entire attention to what God is doing right now and don't get worked up about what may or may not happen tomorrow. God will help you deal with whatever hard things come up when the time comes.*"

You are not to worry about tomorrow...housing closures, bankruptcy, unemployment, and business failures all create fear and depression. No one knows where to go for answers, as we all are so inadequate. God has predicted a time of shaking of kingdoms and materials, as stated in Hebrews 12:26-27 (RSV), "*... but now he has promised, yet once more, I will shake not only the earth but the heaven. This phrase, yet once more, indicates the removal of what is shaken, as of what has been made, in order that what cannot be shaken may remain.*" Today's society and the business world has been shaken to the very core, yet God and His kingdom remain rock solid. God is more than able to make all grace abound to you, so that in all things at all times, having all that you need, you will abound in every good work as described in 2 Corinthians 9:8. Your family, your health, your spiritual and material security is secure; your present and your future is guaranteed in His promise of His unshakeable kingdom. Man's resources are not your source. It is merely one conduit He may or may not choose to use to meet your needs. Philippians4:19 (KJ), *"My God shall supply all your need according to his riches in glory by Christ Jesus."* You are not to worry about tomorrow!

MARCH 22
JESUS IS CONTINUALLY WITH YOU

Psalms 73:23-24 (NKJV)

"You hold me by Your right hand. Nevertheless, I am continually with You. You will guide me with your counsel and afterwards receive me to glory."

It is in the knowing that Jesus is continually with you that gets us through the dull, dreary, days and commonplace duties of living. Learn the secret of abiding in Jesus. It's a test you can give to every high emotion to see what the outcome of it will be. If it is an emotion kindled by the Spirit of God and you do not let it have its way, it will react on a low level--the higher the emotion, the deeper you'll sink. But if the Spirit of God has stirred the emotion, let the consequences be what He wills. You can't stay on the heights of emotion, but you must walk in the light of what you received there, when God through His Spirit, has stirred you. When God uses the thing that should have destroyed you to develop you, say: Psalms 119:71 (RSV), *"It is good for me that I have been afflicted that I may learn your statues."* It is during hard times of stress and adversity that you learn truly that He is holding you and is continually with you.

MARCH 23
HIS WORD IS BETTER THAN GOLD

Psalms 119:59 (RSV)

"When I think of thy ways, I turn my feet to thy testimonies." *VS. 72,* *"The law of thy mouth is better to me than thousands of gold and silver pieces."*

When you think of God's way and your turn your feet to obey Him, turn quickly because any delay whatsoever will cause you to waver. Once you're distracted, more than likely, you will not do it at all. Job 23:11 (RSV), *"My foot has held fast to His steps, I have kept His way and have not turned aside."* Job started out in VS. 8 by saying, *"But He knows the way that I take and when He has tried me, I shall come forth as gold."* VS. 12, *"I have not departed from the commandment of his lips,"* as the Word of God was better to him "than thousands of gold and silver pieces." It is so important to believe and cling to His Word. There are times when we go forward, He is not there; and backward, we do not perceive Him; turn to the left and seek Him, but do not behold Him; to the right and cannot see Him. It happens. None of which changes the fact that He knows the way that you take and when He has tried you, you shall come forth as gold. It is one of His promises and every one of them are backed by all the honor of His Name. Trust His Word.

MARCH 24

HAVE FAITH TO BELIEVE GREAT THINGS AND STRENGTH TO ACCOMPLISH THEM

Joshua 3:15-16 (RSV)

"And when those who bore the ark had come to the Jordan, and the feet of the priests bearing the ark were dipped in the brink of the water...the waters coming down from above stood and rose up in a heap far off."

It is incredible that in David's day when one reached out to just "steady" the ark he was struck dead. Yet the priests carrying the ark dared to approach the raging water of the Jordan where the sacred ark could have been swept away but when their feet merely touched the water, they found themselves standing on dry ground. We never test the power of God in our lives until we attempt the impossible. "When we move forward in faith, it helps God carry out His good plan. Faith always honors God and God honors faith. Attempt great things for God and expect great things from God. When taking things from God in the supernatural that are normally impossible, it is easier to take a lot than to take a little. It is when we launch out into the deep, that we find *"all things are possible with God,"* Luke 18:27 (NIV). Draw from the Source—take His faith to believe great things and His strength to accomplish them," Days of Heaven upon Earth.

MARCH 25
LEARN TO LIVE IN CHAOS

Proverbs 13:33 (LB)

"Humility and reverence for the Lord will make you both wise and honored."

I would love for the unsettled and restless thoughts to go away but I know that I need to learn to live in the chaos, accept each day as it comes, as You are in the middle of it. A thing doesn't have to be "right" for it to be going on—life happens; pain hurts; people experience sorrow; my goal is in communication with You. When I get distracted and focus on lesser things, You are with me, just waiting and watching in the background. A successful day is one in which I stay in connection with You all day long. God will never open a door for me that He has closed; He opens other doors. And, He holds me responsible for what I do not see. I lose when I think of "what might have been." He reminds me that I have shut doors that never should have been closed. I am not to fear when He brings back the past ... let memory have its way—God ministers to me in memory. Only He can turn what "might have been" into something good in the future. Humility and reverence for the Lord will show how to live in a way that will honor Him.

MARCH 26
GOD WILL MEET MY EVERY NEED

Psalms 34:19 (KJV)

"Many are the afflictions of the righteous; but the Lord delivereth him out of them all."

In You, I am complete; in You, I have everything. Open my capacity to experience You. Remove the clutter from my heart. As my yearning for You increases, I will lose the desire for other things. I desire You and Your favor. It is impossible for me to have a need You cannot meet. Never be fooled by appearances; things that are visible are fleeting, but things that invisible are everlasting. I can never fix the problem if I am obsessed with fixing the blame. How I say something is as important as what I say. I can never be persuasive when I'm abrasive. Faith in God is never an exemption from trials but it will sustain me during them. I Peter 4:12-13 (MSG), *"Friends, when life gets really difficult, don't jump to the conclusion that God isn't on the job. Instead, be glad that you are in the very thick of what Christ experienced. This is a spiritual refining process, with glory just around the corner."* Real maturity takes place in pain—I'll never know how strong I am until I have a need. 2 Corinthians 4:12 (MSG), *"Our lives are at constant risk for Jesus' sake, which makes Jesus' life all the more evident in us. While we're going through the worst, we're getting in on the best!"* Through the good and the bad, He meets our every need.

MARCH 27

HOW TO LIVE A CREATIVE LIFE

Galatians 6:1-5, 7-8, 14-17 (MSG)

"Live creatively, friends. If someone falls into sin, forgivingly restore him, saving your critical comments for yourself. You might be needing forgiveness before the days out. Stoop down and reach out to those who are oppressed. Share their burdens and so complete Christ's law. If you think you are too good for that, you are badly deceived...Don't compare yourself to others. Each of you

must take responsibility for doing the creative best you can with your own life. Don't be misled: No one makes a fool of God. What a person plants, he will harvest. The person who plants selfishness, ignoring the needs of others—ignoring God!—harvests a crop of weeds. But the one who plants in response to God, letting God's Spirit do the growth work in him, harvests a crop of real life, eternal life. For my part, I am going to boast about nothing but the Cross of our Master, Jesus Christ. Because of that Cross, I have been crucified in relation to the world, set free from the stifling atmosphere of pleasing others and fitting into the little patterns they dictate...It's not what you and I do...It is what God is doing, and He is creating something totally new, a free life! I have far more important things to do—the serious living of this faith!"

What a mouthful of great advice from Paul. How much time do you spend on you and how much do you spend in ministry? Galatians 6:10b (MSG) *"Every time you get the chance, let us work for the benefit of all, starting with the people closest to us in the community of faith."*

MARCH 28
WHAT ARE YOU DOING HERE

1 Kings 19:1 (KJV)

"And Ahab told Zezebel all that Elijah had done and withal how he had slain all the prophets with the sword."

Ahab was not only a wimp but a blabbermouth. When he couldn't have the plot of ground he wanted, he got into bed, covered up his head and whimpered until Jezebel did his dirty work for him. Now he can't wait to tell Jezebel that Elijah has just killed 850 of her private stock. It was true, he had killed 450 prophets of Baal and 400 prophets of Asherah, and now running for his life and prays to die. This is a man who had received a special power from the Lord. Having the power of God in your life is never an easy thing. Elijah is about to receive a visit from the Lord. VS. 9, "What are you doing here Elijah?" If God should suddenly appear in this room and ask you that question, could you say, "I'm about doing what you planned and sent me to do?" Look at Elijah's response, "I, even I only am left." He wasn't giving a thought to what God might have had in mind in his predicament; he's having a pity party. The Lord passes by and there is a great wind across the mountains, followed by an earthquake, then a fire and after that, a still small voice. Elijah heard it (give him credit for hearing it!) Again he's asked, "What are you doing here Elijah?" His reply, "All your covenant people have left and I, only I am left alone." The Lord ignores his pitiful plea and promptly gives him another assignment! If God has given you a special assignment, He has also given you what you need to see it to completion. You need to be listening in case the next voice you hear should be, "What are you doing here?!"

MARCH 29
HE WILL NOT DISREGARD THE SMALL AND INSIGNIFICANT

Isaiah 42:3 (LB)

"He will not break a bruised reed, nor quench the dimly burning flame. He will encourage the downhearted, those tempted to despair."

"He won't brush aside the bruised and the hurt and He won't disregard the small and insignificant," is another translation. In our world, we look for the big, brave, and the beautiful ... the strong, victorious people; God looks for the broken, the failed, and the weak in which to build His kingdom. In Him, there is no "bruised reed" that God cannot restore, use and bless. He can take a life crushed by pain and sorrow and turn it into an instrument of total praise. Our saddest failure can become heaven's glory. Our life becomes what we focus on the most. If we dwell on our disappointments and sorrows, they will become our life. If we focus on the goodness, greatness and love of Jesus, that's what we'll have. You are the only one who can let the Lord turn your sorrow into joy. When my Louie died, it was the greatest pain I have ever known, but knowing and realizing what his life is now, has become my greatest joy. I am so blessed in knowing the love he is experiencing this moment! You can become bruised but not broken. Why? Because His Word states, *"He will encourage you and will not quench a dimly burning flame."*

MARCH 30
USE WEALTH WISELY

1 Timothy 6:17 (HCSB)

"Instruct those who are rich in the present age not to be arrogant or to set their hope on the uncertainty of wealth, but on God, who richly provides us with all things to enjoy."

Jesus Calling: "It's impossible for you to have a need God cannot meet." Yet we constantly flit here and there to find fulfillment. Material achievement is temporary. Buy the latest smart phone and see how long before it is outdated! If God has blessed you with money, He probably meant for you to use a good portion of it to help those who do not have enough. Always be humble and grateful and never become arrogant. Those who regard money as a status symbol need to see what the verse says about the "uncertainty of wealth." Do not run after money, run after "God, who richly provides us all things to enjoy." Money has a way of strangely disappearing. Paul says to use your wealth to do what is good and to be rich in good works. It is one thing to be known as affluent; it is so much better to be known as being rich in good deeds. Use what God has allowed you to have wisely.

MARCH 31
YOU ARE WITH ME

On March 31, 2010, I called on Dr. Jesus, (Dr. Love) for release of pain for my husband, Louie. It looked like you had forsaken him but You came and gloriously redeemed him. Thank you, Lord! I have to "rouse myself up and get the mind of Christ" about Louie's death for he is not dead, but risen! I am keenly aware of the enemy's attack on my body and emotions—you lose devil; Jesus is calling me to trust Him. He is the One who drives away my sorrow and heals my brokenness. Help me to find you at every turn today, when I seek you with all my heart. Clear my mind and calm my fears; draw near so I may receive Your peace; tune out other voices so I can hear Yours. At this very hour (6:55a.m.) four years ago today, Louie came to live with You and left such a hole in my heart. Fill it with your loving, living Presence. He said, "Good morning, Jesus" to you for the first time and now he can join in praise with millions who never stop lifting their voices together in adoration and thanksgiving. What a joy! He has total deliverance, forever and ever. The storms of bereavement still roll over me but only drive me to my knees, actually on my face, in total dependence and trust in You. You don't keep me from the storms, but You are my protection and safekeeping in them.

APRIL 1

JEHOVAH HIMSELF IS CARING FOR YOU

Isaiah 54:2, 4-7 (RSV)

"Enlarge the place of your tent and let the curtains of your habitation be stretched out; hold not back, lengthen your cords and strengthen your stakes. Fear not, for you will not be ashamed; be not confounded, for you will not be put to shame; for you will forget the shame of your youth and the reproach of your widowhood you'll remember no more. For your Maker is your husband, the Lord of Hosts is His Name and the Holy One of Israel is your Redeemer, the God of the whole earth He is called. For the Lord has called you, like a wife forsaken and grieved in spirit, like a wife of youth when she is cast off says your God. For a brief moment I forsook you, but with great compassion I will gather you."

If you have ever experienced the grief of being a widow, you will find much comfort in these verses. If you have been the "wife of youth that has been cast off" you will really cling to the promise of "your Maker being your husband." I have served both roles and it is truly a time when you believe these particular scriptures. Should you find yourself with children, no home in which to live, no job or money. It seems as if the Lord has cast you off; but look at the promise: "For a brief moment I forsook you, but with great compassion, I will gather you." He does I; so if that is your life today, be encouraged. You are hob-knobbing with the Elite...*the*

Lord of Hosts is His Name; the Holy One of Israel is your Redeemer. It is but a brief moment, until He will gather you with great compassion; you have His Word. It may well be April Fool's Day but he is no fool whose God is the Lord!

APRIL 2
THE HOLY ONE OF ISRAEL IS YOUR REDEEMER

Psalms 121:5-7 (LB)

"Jehovah Himself is caring for you. God is your defender. He protects you day and night. He keeps you from all evil and preserves your life. His eye is on you as you come and go and always guards you."

When my husband was in the hospital before he died, this scripture was a poster by his bedside. And yet, he died. Nonetheless, he surely lives in God's Presence today and I am convinced that His eye never left him as he left me to go and live with Jesus and He is continually caring for him today. God's hand is ever at work in his life and God's unseen power controls everything for His purpose. Afflictions cannot injure us when blended with submission. Hard situations, circumstances, and troubles come when we're on Christ's "other side." God may never reveal to us what we so yearn to know but He owes us no explanations. We need to believe He will keep every promise He makes. His Word working His will is the way it is. We just need to believe that regardless of what is going in our life, He is caring for us; He is our defender; He protects us day and night and preserves our life; and His eye is on us as we come and go. The more we trust God, the more He meets our needs. The more He meets our needs, the more we are encouraged to trust Him. God is always at work within us. With problems comes the keen anticipation to see how He will either use them or rescue us from them.

APRIL 3
TODAY, PLEASE LISTEN

Hebrews 4:7b (RSV)

"Today when you hear His voice, do not harden your hearts." *(MSG) "Today, please listen, don't turn a deaf ear."*

God said the Words, "Today, please listen, and don't turn a deaf ear" three times in this chapter; it wasn't just spoken to people living in the days of Moses but for our entire lifetime, as well. God means what He says and "today" is now. His powerful Word is as sharp as a surgeon's scalpel cutting through everything in our lives, whether doubt or defense; laying us open to listen and to obey. Nothing and no one is impervious to God's Word—we can't get away from it, no matter what! Hebrews 4:16 (MSG): *"Jesus has been through weakness and testing, He has experienced it all and not once did He sin. So let's walk right up to Him and get what He's so ready to give us, take His mercy and accept His help."* KJV states, *"Let us therefore come boldly unto the throne of grace that we may obtain mercy and find grace to help in time of need."* We're so ready to listen to ill advice from well-meaning friends; to bad reports from the doctor; to political schemes that threaten our very existence. We need to be listening, not harden our hearts, but be receptive to what He is speaking into our lives when He says, "Today, please listen."

APRIL 4

MY PRAYER

Philippians 4:13 (MSG)

"Whatever I have, wherever I am, I can make it through anything in the One who makes me who I am."

Truly, you know me better than I know me. Nothing in me is unknown to You. Since You look at me through Your eyes of grace, I need not fear You or what You're seeing. You are healing me in body and spirit; probe further in my mind, refresh me and renew me. You are my resident tutor; teach me Lord. I just need to listen for You, knowing You not only care, but You are love. Something of real worth is in "listening" for You; and to seek, actively seek, Your deepest blessings. My heart is open to receive more of what you desire to disclose. Work God, in my behalf that I will bring honor and praise to Your Holy Name and Word. We think of the abundant life as health and wealth; You say it is in learning to live in total dependence on You. Every moment switch me from anxiety to speaking Your Name and to know what You're up to. You are here, You care, You love, and You can help me do this, in Jesus Name I pray.

APRIL 5

HIS PEACE IS AVAILABLE TO US

John 16:33 (RSV)

"I have said this to you that in me you may have peace. In the world you have tribulation ..."

Jesus spoke these Words to His disciples to encourage and also to warn them. "You may have peace in me" was telling them it is available for the taking. But "... in the world you will have tribulation." It is for certain that if we share in His suffering, we will be more conformed to His likeness. We are enlarged spiritually in understanding as we endure hardships, as it softens our heart and makes us more sensitive and tender toward others and more receptive to the Holy Spirit. Every stinging sorrow we are spared results in either an unclaimed or missed blessing. (With that thought in mind, don't dread the stinging blows but rather look for the blessing sure to follow...bring 'em on!) 2 Corinthians 4:16-18 (MSG), "So we're not giving up .... Even though on the outside it often looks like things are falling apart on us, on the inside, where God is making new life, not a day goes by without his unfolding grace. These hard times are small potatoes compared to the coming good times, the lavish celebration prepared for us. There's far more here than meets the eye. The things we see now are here today, gone tomorrow. But the things we can't see now will last forever." He says that in the world we will have tribulation but to be of good cheer as He has overcome the world and His peace is available for every stinging blow!

APRIL 6
JEHOVAH THE LORD IS MY STRENGTH AND SONG

Isaiah 12:2 (ML)

"Behold, God is my salvation; I will trust and not be afraid, for JEHOVAH, the Lord, is my strength and song; yes, He has become my salvation."

The One who spoke the universe into existence is my strength and song; yes, He has become my salvation. He is my absolute unlimited power. The human weakness in me, when consecrated to You, is like a magnet drawing your power into my own neediness. Fear can block that flow of strength so I depend on the truth of Your Word, "I will trust and not be afraid." Instead of trying to fight my fear, I will trust You. Confidently trusting You, there is no limit, NONE, to how much you can strengthen me. You are my song. You want to share Your joy, making me constantly aware of Your Presence in me. You want me to join You in singing Your song!

APRIL 7
HE HAS MADE WIDE STEPS FOR MY FEET TO KEEP ME FROM SLIPPING

Psalms 73: 1-2 (ML)

"Surely God is good to Israel, to those whose hearts are pure; but as for me, my feet had almost stumbled, my steps had nearly slipped."

How good God is to those whose hearts are clean and pure but in this Psalm, Asaph is saying, "but my feet had almost stumbled, my steps had nearly slipped." Ever been there? 2 Samuel 22:27 (LB), *"You have made wide steps for my feet to keep them from slipping."* (ML), *"Thou stretchest my stride on the ground on ankles that never grow weak."* (KJV), *"Thou hast enlarged my steps under me; so that my feet did not slip."* How good God is even when we almost slip! One of the things that cause us to slip is to doubt. Doubt is not a sin but to retain it until it masters you is. The serpent in the garden said, "but God won't let you eat of that tree, will He?"

Causing Eve to think God was holding out and this led to spiritual decay and the beginning of doubt and sin for the rest of us. You can starve your doubts by feeding them a steady diet of faith and by believing God wants you to have a good, clean heart. He does this by going before you to make wide steps for your feet to keep them from slipping!

APRIL 8
THE PROSPERITY OF THE WICKED IS A SLIPPERY PATH

Psalms 73:3 (ML)

"For I was envious of the arrogant, when I saw the prosperity of the wicked."

How many times have we looked at the prosperity of the wicked and been envious? People, who seemingly have everything, often have nothing. They are often like shells...outwardly beautiful but nothing inside and are constantly seeking pleasure but finding only emptiness. There is a vast difference between pleasure and happiness and an even greater distance between pleasure and peace. Peace with God and peace within are life's greatest treasures. True values in life are spiritual, not material. Psalms 73: 11-12 (RSV), *"And they say, 'How can God know? Is there knowledge in the Most High? Behold these are the wicked: always at ease, they increase in riches."* Psalms 73:18-20 (LB), *"What a slippery path they are on—suddenly God will send them sliding over the edge of the cliff and down to their destruction: an instant end to all their happiness, an eternity of terror. Their present life is only a dream! They will awaken to the truth as one awakes from a dream of things that never really were!"* It is like someone walking on ice, one minute they are on their feet and the next, they are on their back! We are never to envy the prosperity of the wicked.

APRIL 9

GOD'S PRESENCE MAKES THE DIFFERENCE

Psalms 73:21-24 (RSV)

"When my soul was embittered, when I was pricked in heart, I was stupid and ignorant; I was like a beast toward thee. Nevertheless I am continually with thee; thou dost hold my right hand. Thou dost guide me with thy counsel and afterward thou wilt receive me to glory."

Asaph got a good look at himself; his soul was embittered, life wasn't fair and what's worse, God wasn't fair either! His feelings were hurt; pouting; his values were out of focus. He behaved and reacted in animal fashion. He came to worship with questions and went away with answers when God whispered in his soul. You can't get right with yourself until you get right with God. He realized the Presence of God and the fact that he was continually with Him; He was holding his right hand and guiding him with His counsel…glory here, glory there! God's Presence makes all the difference.

APRIL 10

THESE THINGS WILL SURELY COME TO PASS. JUST BE PATIENT

Habakkuk 2:1-3 (LB)

"I will climb my watchtower now and wait to see what answer God will give to my complaint. And the Lord said to me, Write my answer on a billboard, large and clear, so that anyone can read it at a glance and rush to tell others. But these things I plan won't happen right away. Slowly, steadily, surely, the time approaches when the vision will be fulfilled. If it seems slow, do not despair, for these things will surely come to pass. Just be patient! They will not be overdue a single day!"

I can remember posting this entire scripture on poster board and hanging it on the inside door of my basement. My washer and dryer were in the basement, as well as a TV room, so I went up and down those basement steps many times each day and always read this scripture. I noted the challenge was not to write my complaints, but my <u>answer</u>. I was experiencing a very painful time of divorce, a marriage of 25 years was falling apart and I needed to know that *"these things I plan won't happen right away. Slowly, steadily, surely, the time approaches when the vision will be fulfilled... for these things will surely come to pass."* I needed to know the truth of these scriptures. God had not moved out of my house, my husband had   Reading these verses many times a day gave me courage and hope. And I found the rest of the verse to hold true as well, as repairmen for the washing machine and air-conditioner read and commented on it, as well. God knows your complaints, but He also knows when you believe His Word and focus on His answers.

APRIL 11

FOCUS ON YOUR PURPOSE, NOT YOUR PROBLEM

Habakkuk 1:5 (LB)

"The Lord replied: "Look and be amazed! You will be astounded at what I am about to do. For I am going to do something in your own lifetime that you will have to see to believe."

Prophets generally spoke to people on God's behalf, but Habakkuk spoke to God about people. Habakkuk's name means "strong embrace;" and he was a prophet with deep emotions. Years ago, statistics reported there are 54 million disabled people in our society with special needs and problems and the rate only increases. We may not have a physical handicap but we all seem to capitalize on what's wrong in our lives. You need to focus on your purpose and not your problem. Never stop looking at your purpose and ask yourself, "What purpose can I fulfill in this problem?" The Lord says, "Look and be amazed! You will be astounded at what I am about to do...you will have to see it to believe it." Instead of throwing up your hands and looking at the impossible, turn to the Lord. Don't let your troubles make you selfish and self-centered. Focus on the needs around you. Look beyond what is temporary to the eternal. Jesus focused on His passion, not His pain. His passion is you. Focus on triumph, not your trial. If you will let go of what you hold in your hand, He will let go of what is in His!

APRIL 12

STRIP DOWN, START RUNNING AND NEVER QUIT

Hebrews 12:1-10 (MSG)

"Do you see what this means...it means we'd better get on with it. Strip down, start running—and never quit! No extra spiritual fat, no parasitic sins. Keep your eyes on Jesus, who both began and finished this race we're in. Study how he did it. Because he never lost sight of where he was headed, he could put up with anything along the way: the Cross, shame, whatever. And now he's there, in the place of honor, right alongside God. When you find yourselves flagging in your faith, go over that story again, item by item, that long litany of hostility he plowed through. That will shoot adrenaline into your souls!"

We all have a race to run and we need to have a goal in mind. When an athlete runs, he isn't dressed in a suit, vest and tie, but he's stripped down to aid in his sprint. We need to strip down (get rid of those parasitic sins hanging all over us); start running (get up and get going); never quit (and never give up); with our eyes on Jesus...not on those around us or the obstacles looming ahead. Jesus never lost sight of His finish line. And He knew that the cross was ahead of Him. When you're prone to be flagging in your faith, go over His race, and consider His treatment and how He finished! Now, He's in His place of honor, right alongside God Almighty. Your challenge is to keep your eyes on Jesus! Your problems aren't for your punishment; they are for your training.

APRIL 13

GOD WILL DO IT

<u>2 Samuel 10:12b</u> (MSG)

"And God will do whatever He sees Needs Doing."

What is your greatest need today? Do you believe God will do whatever He sees needs doing? God must have wanted us to believe it because it's stated again in 1 Chronicles 19:13b (MSG), *"And God will do whatever He sees needs doing."* Both instances were in reference to God defending His people in battle; but it is just as true in our lives, as well. God sees our inward parts and knows our needs. Our bodies get sullied by the things and people with which we associate. Our innards (spirit) get blurred when the outer comes in contact with what's ungodly. But you will never have a desire (that has been placed in you by the Holy Spirit) in which He doesn't intend to fulfill. Everything you can comprehend through faith belongs to you. You draw close to God by opening the Bible and your spirit to receive from Him in how to do this. God will do whatever He sees needs doing in you when you are open to receive it. God puts a natural instinct into your heart to enable you to receive what He has spoken. He who breathes heavenly hope into you will not deceive or fail you. God will do it because He has said that "He will do what He sees needs doing!"

APRIL 14

DESPERATION IS BETTER THAN DESPAIR

Lamentations 3:16-24 (MSG)

"He ground my face into the gravel. He pounded me into the mud. I gave up on life altogether. I've forgotten what the good life is like. I said to myself, 'This is it, I'm finished. God is a lost cause.' I'll never forget the trouble, the utter sense of lost, the taste of ashes, or the poison I've swallowed. I remember it all—oh how well I remember--the feeling of hitting the bottom. But there's one thing I remember and remembering, I keep a grip on hope. God's royal love couldn't have run out, his merciful love couldn't have dried up. They're created new every morning. How great your faithfulness. I'm sticking with God. (I say it over and over), He's all I've got left."

You didn't "ground my face into the gravel," it was of my own doing but I do recall the *"utter sense of being lost;"* the taste of *ashes and I remember hitting the bottom."* You've brought me through a lot of dirt but "I'm sticking with You." Faith doesn't create desperate days but sustains you in them. The alternative to desperation is despair. Shadrach, Meshach and Abednego faced a desperate situation but they didn't despair but said, *"Our God is able to save us but even if He does not, we will not serve or worship any other."* God is walking in the depths of your blazing fire and His *"royal love does not run out; keep a grip on hope, His merciful love hasn't dried up, it is new every morning!"* You will survive desperation; just don't despair.

APRIL 15

YOU ARE A GOD WHO GIVES AND GIVES AND GIVES

Hebrews 6:13 (MSG)

"When God made his promise to Abraham, he backed it to the hilt, putting his own reputation on the line. He said, 'I promise that I'll bless you with everything I have—bless and bless and bless!'"

You are a God who gives and gives and gives. You poured out Your life like a drink offering for my sins. Thank You, Jesus. Help me to receive from You the full measure of whatever You see that needs doing within me. Let me be receptive and attentive and open me up to receive Your abundance. Direct my attention to You, searching for You every moment, not just while I'm sitting here. Stay close and help me keep my mind focused. One person has said that he sets the timer on his watch every hour to remind him of his need to turn his thoughts to You either in Your Word or in prayer. Grant peace to my hurting heart. I know you are Lord, You are God Almighty. Isaiah 26:3 (NLT), *"You will keep him in perfect peace whose mind is stayed on you, because he trusts in You."* Joni E. Tada said that when she gets to heaven, she'll be glad to get out of that wheelchair and to be able to walk and run but the thing she will be most thankful for is a new heart that is perfect toward You. Your best blessing is Yourself, dear Lord!

APRIL 16
GO UP HIGHER

Revelation 4:1b (MSG)

"Ascend and enter. I'll show you what happens next." (KJV) "Come up hither, and I will show thee things."

We are constantly being challenged to "go up higher." New heights bring new temptations and Satan uses that state of elevation to bring us to a precarious pinnacle beyond our ability, where we dare not move, and then pulls the rug out from under us. God will lead you "to go higher" but when He elevates you, instead of clinging to a pinnacle, you find yourself walking on a great tableland, a Rock. When God gives me a truth, sometimes it lasts for that day. God wants, once He has shown me a truth, to work my way through it and walk in the light of it ... not for the moment for but for my entire life. "I want to scale the utmost height and catch a gleam of glory bright" ... to walk on that tableland that is stable and secure. John was invited to *"Ascend and enter. I'll show you what happens next"* and he was caught up in deep worship! Any height you can attain in your spiritual life is for the purpose of deeper relationship with your Lord and to enhance your time of worship.

APRIL 17
HE BUT SPOKE AND THE WORLD BEGAN

Psalms 33:4-11 (LB)

"For all God's Words are right, and everything he does is worthy of our trust. He loves whatever is just and good: the earth is filled with his tender love. He merely spoke and the heavens were formed

and all the galaxies of stars. He made the oceans, pouring them into his vast reservoirs. Let everyone in the entire world—men, women and children—fear the Lord and stand in awe of him. For when he but spoke the world began! It appeared at his command. And with a breath he can scatter the plans of all the nations who oppose him, but his own plan stands forever."

Our God is in the Psalms. When my hungry heart finds the living truth, I gain new strength for daily living. Pain, sorrow and grief lose their grip of terror as fear flies away. I'm encouraged as I see how others long ago won victories in the same arenas, as I read in the Psalms. It makes my heart *"well up in praise"* (VS.1) when I read this entire chapter. It is so true, everything God says and does is worthy of our trust and praise. He but spoke and when He opened His mouth, the world began! And as He spoke the entire world into existence, He can just as easily scatter the plans of any nation who oppose Him. VS. 7 Emphasized Bible says, *"Who gathered as into a skin-bottle, the water of the sea, delivering into treasuries the roaring deeps!"* All that, plus He saves our souls ... there is none like the God of the Psalms!

APRIL 18
PURSUE A LOVE RELATIONSHIP

Hebrews 12:1 (ML)
"So then, encircled as we are with such a great cloud of witnesses all about us, let us get rid of every impediment and the sin that ensnares us so easily and let us run steadily the course mapped out for us."

God pursues a love relationship with you and encourages you to seek one with Him Jeremiah 29:13 (NKJV, *"And you will seek me and find me when you search for me with all your heart."* You are His workmanship and there is no one else in all the world exactly like you! *"For we are God's handiwork created in Christ to devote ourselves to the good deeds for which God has designed us."* Ephesians 2:10 says that God's plan for your life is personal ... no dream, no esteem. Do you want to go out for the rat race or for God's race? Dedicate your whole life to the Lord. People get hung up just trying to fit in. Learn to say, "Yes, Lord." And then, "Now what was the question?" Offer yourself, i.e., your time, treasures, as a living sacrifice, dedicated wholly to Him. Do not conform to the standards of this world but let God transform you. Then you will know the will of God...what is good, and perfect. Perfect means it fits you perfectly. Strip off everything that slows you down or holds you back. Run with patience the race God has set before you. Don't let your possessions possess you. Don't live as close to sin as you can because you will become ensnared. That's a lot of "don'ts", so DO pursue that love relationship, as there are a great cloud of witnesses all around you.

APRIL 19
GOD IS THE GOD OF WHATEVER YOU NEED

Psalms 146:5-8 (LB)

"But happy is the man who has the God of Jacob as his helper, whose hope is in the Lord his God. It is God who made the earth, the heavens, and the seas and everything in them. He is the God who keeps every promise and gives justice to the poor and oppressed and food to the hungry. He frees the prisoners and

opens the eyes of the bind; he lifts the burdens from those bent down beneath their loads. For the Lord loves good men."

Maybe you resent that things aren't better for you right now and you hold God responsible. Look at the needy people listed in these verses ... poor, oppressed, hungry, prisoners, and blind, heavily burdened. God is the God of whatever you need. Psalms 147:11 (LB), *"His joy is in those who reverence him, those who expect him to be loving and kind."* Are you looking at another person for companionship, intimacy, friendship, or understanding? That person may leave you, either by choice or by death. One of life's most frightening experiences is to be orphaned or widowed. God watches over you not just to observe, but to help. *"Happy is the man who has God as his helper ... He is the God who keeps every promise."* He is the God of all whatever's.

APRIL 20
TO GOD, THE NIGHT SHINES AS BRIGHT AS DAY

Psalms 139:12 (LB)

"For even darkness cannot hide from God; for you the night shines as bright as day. Darkness and light are both alike to you."

"It is better to walk in the dark with God than to walk alone in the light." The day before my husband died, I had copied that quote in my journal from Streams in the Desert that morning as well as: "Trouble and darkness are meant to teach you ... never try to get out of a dark place except in God's timing. Premature deliverance can circumvent God's work of grace. Commit it to Him and be willing to abide in the darkness, knowing He is there. Touching anything of His mars His work. Moving the hands of the clock to suit you can never change the time." Your situation may be very difficult and filled with uncertainty, very serious, but perfectly right. The reason behind it all will more than justify the One who brought you to it, for it is the platform from which God will display his Almighty grace and power. He will not only deliver you but in doing so, impart a lesson you will never forget. You will be unable to thank Him enough for doing exactly what He has done. I spoke these words at my husband's funeral and they are just as true for me today as they were then. I am unable to thank God enough for doing exactly what He has done! Thank you God for deliverance from darkness into Your marvelous light!

APRIL 21
IT'S UP TO US TO GATHER IN GOD'S PROVISION

Psalms 104:27-28 (LB)

"Every one of these depends on you to give them daily food. You supply it and they gather it. You open wide your hand to feed them and they are satisfied with all your bountiful provision."

The Psalmist was addressing "the whale that plays in the sea" in the above scripture. As humans, we do not live in a spoon-fed world. God gives richness to the soil, fertility to the seed, provides sun and rain. But we must plant, work the soil and harvest. Even birds must scratch and wild animals hunt. He may supply it, but it is up to us to gather it. Work is a blessing. The world's oldest profession is not prostitution ... horticulture is and it started in the Garden of Eden. VS. 30 (RSV), "*Then You send your Spirit and renew the face of the ground.*" (If you cut down a tree, plant another for those who come after you). God provides a bountiful provision for all His creation. He opens wide His hand to provide us a bountiful provision of whatever we need; but it is up to us to gather it in.

APRIL 22
EXPERIENCE THE KNOWLEDGE OF GOD

2 Peter 1:2 (NKJV)

"Grace and peace be multiplied to you in the knowledge of God and of Jesus our Lord as His divine power has given to us all things that pertain to life and godliness through the knowledge of Him ..."

This scripture contains every source of help I need to walk before You and I can never exhaust all Your resources. No more than I could ever breathe all the oxygen in the air or a fish could drink a river dry. But I can increase my knowledge of You. In knowing You and what your Word says will give me the knowledge to cope with life at its worst. A discouraged person is in a helpless state and is not able to stand against the devil's schemes, nor is he able to prevail in prayer for others. Flee from every symptom of the deadly foe of discouragement as you would run from a snake. Never be slow to turn your back on it unless you desire to know the taste of bitter defeat. Having "the knowledge of God and knowing He has given me His divine power to deal with all things that pertain to my life" means He, through His Word and His Presence has granted me not only the wisdom I need but blessed me with HIS grace and peace as He does it!   I will say His Word out loud and know this promise is for me.

APRIL 23
GOD WILL SUPPLY ALL YOUR NEEDS

Philippians 4:19 (NKJV)

"My God shall supply all your needs according to His riches in glory."

I may not always understand You but trusting You anyway will keep me close. I would love for the unsettled restless thoughts to go away but You say to learn to live in the chaos as You are here in the middle of it. Accept each day as it comes. It doesn't have to be "right" to be going on—life happens; pain hurts; people are great and people are awful; but my mindset is communication with You. A successful day is one in which I have stayed in communication with you all day. 1,000 things may be on my plate but what I need is You. My deepest and most constant need is Your peace and when I do sit quietly with You, You shine a light in my heart and its total belief in You that calms all my concerns. Weeds of pride, selfishness, and worry are more than met...killed...or at best, made sick enough to leave! It is in moving through the day that I constantly need to maintain openness before You. You will supply all my needs; and my greatest need is fulfilled in being with You.

APRIL 24
LOOK AT JESUS

Hebrews 3:1b (MSG),

"Take a good hard look at Jesus. He's the centerpiece of everything we believe, faithful in everything God gave him to do."

When Paul received his sight, You also gave him spiritual insight into Yourself. His whole preaching centered on that insight; he was "determined to know nothing but You and You crucified." We all need to: *"Take a good hard look at Jesus; He's the centerpiece of everything we believe in."* In You, I am complete; in You, I have everything. Open my capacity to experience You. Remove the clutter from my heart. As my yearning for You increases, I will lose the desire for other things. I desire You and Your favor. It is important for me to have a need I cannot meet. Never be fooled by appearances ... for the things that are visible are fleeting, but the things that are invisible, are everlasting. That's why *"taking a good hard look at Jesus and keeping Him as the centerpiece of everything I believe in"* will keep me focused on what is important. Heaven's things are just beyond what I'm looking at, at earth's level. God will hold me responsible for the things I do not see. If the centerpiece of my life is Jesus, I will be seeing things a-right.

APRIL 25
HE GETS THE LAST WORD, YES HE DOES

1 Peter 5:9 (MSG)

"The suffering won't last forever. It won't be long before this generous God who has great plans for us in Christ—eternal and glorious plans they are!—will have you put together and on your feet for good. He gets the last Word: yes, He does!"

Worrying over what's been lost or taken from you will never make things better but will only prevent you from making and improving on what remains. No calamity in life will bring only evil if you will immediately take it to God in fervent prayer. It is through pain and sorrow and afflictions that God gives you fresh and new revelations of Himself. God selects only the best for His most noble afflictions as those who have received the most grace from Him can endure. No trial ever hits you by chance but by God's divine direction. No arrow is haphazard but is aimed as a special message to touch only the heart and home of the one intended. It will reveal God's grace and glory if you are accepting. A hostile resentful bitter heart will destroy you and your health. Spiritually deep people are those who come through the deep anguishing fires of the soul. If you pray to know Jesus, you might find Him in a furnace of pain. Be encouraged as it doesn't last forever and before you know it, He *"will have you put together and on your feet for good! He gets the last Word, yes He does!"*

APRIL 26
WE HAVE A FUTURE IN HEAVEN AND THE FUTURE STARTS NOW

1 Peter 1:3-5 (MSG)

"What a God we have! And how fortunate we are to have him, this Father of our Master Jesus! Because Jesus was raised from the dead, we've been given a brand-new life and have everything to live for, including a future in heaven—and the future starts now! God is keeping careful watch over us and the future. The Day is coming when you'll have it all—life healed and whole."

Holy, Righteous and True are You, O Lord, and we commend this day unto You. Because of Your death, we have been given a brand-new life with everything to live for ... a future in heaven...and the future starts now! We may not "feel" like we're enjoying the journey because of situations and circumstances, but the truth is, you never die and your ordained future began the day you accepted Jesus as Savior. Our capacity for knowing Jesus is enlarged when we are brought to Him by difficulties and situations that try to tear down and break our faith. It is then that we get to know *"what a God we have!"* We realize He is taking time to deliver us and also it gives us time to lean on Him and trust Him. *"God is keeping careful watch over us and our future"* and He is the Holy One, the only One who can walk us safely into the day when *"life will be healed and whole."*

APRIL 27
LOVE MAKES UP FOR PRACTICALLY ANYTHING

1 Peter 4:7 (MSG)

"Everything in the world is about to be wrapped up, so take nothing for granted. Stay wide-awake in prayer. Most of all, love each other as if your life depended on it. Love makes up for practically anything."

In human relationships, we mostly love and respect those who do the same for us. We tend to love those who love us and hurt those who hurt us. As we learn to honor and love the Lord, we find that we can love Him even in our trials, in the very things that hurt us so much. Even though there are times when God doesn't allow his saints to feel the fire, there are other times when He does. Fire causes pain and when it does, we place faith in His goodness and love that permitted it. Out of it will come something worthy of praise to Him that otherwise would not have happened. In the book of

Daniel, the three in the fiery furnace came out of it with everything they went in with, except the ropes that bound them. Sometimes God removes the shackles in or during the affliction. Whatever is happening in our life, we know He is wrapping His arms of love around us. And since *"the world is about to be wrapped up, we need to stay wide-awake in prayer and truly love each other as if our life depended on it, as love makes up for practically anything!"*

APRIL 28
QUIETNESS AND CONFIDENCE SHALL BE YOUR STRENGTH

Isaiah 30:15 (NKJV)

"For thus says the Lord God, the Holy One of Israel: 'In returning and rest you will be saved; in quietness and confidence shall be your strength."

Quietness and confidence could be better phrased "utter and complete trust." Trusting in God's strength instead of our own is the only way to find true rest. In this particular instance, the Israelites chose to depend on the strength of Egypt's horses and chariots for their defense and then found to their dismay that VS. 17 was so true: *"One thousand shall flee at the threat of one and were left like a lone pole on top of a mountain."* We need to totally trust in our God and not waste our time wondering if we are adequate…we are more than adequate with the power of the Holy Spirit within, to handle anything the day brings. Our strength comes as we wait on the Lord as VS. 18 tells us, *"Therefore the Lord will wait that He may be gracious to you and therefore He will be exalted. Blessed are all those who wait on him."* The Lord waits in order that He may be exalted; and that He may bless you. Where is your confidence and strength; is it in utter trust in God and His Word, or are you looking for an alternative power source? Thousands of Israelites trusted in Egypt's horses and found themselves running scared from one soldier and abandoned like a lone pole on top of a mountain. Trust God in quietness and confidence; He is able to meets the needs of your day.

APRIL 29
I WILL BUILD YOU AND YOU SHALL BE REBUILT

Jeremiah 21:3-5 (NKJV)

"The Lord has appeared of old to me saying: Yes, I have loved you with an everlasting love; therefore with loving kindness I have drawn you, again I will build you and you shall be rebuilt."

Keep that promise within me, Lord, and rebuild me. The last few years have seemed like You were tearing the old apart, but I'm the one who hasn't done it right. Reshape me. I cling to You for *"good character, spiritual understanding, alert discipline, passionate patience, reverent wonder, warm friendliness, generous love—each dimension fitting into and developing the others"* as I read in 2 Peter 1:5-7 (MSG). You are to be praised. You are Holy God. I love you and thank you for loving me with an everlasting love. You are able to do immeasurably more than I can ask or imagine according to Your power that is at work within me. You will only do as much as I allow You to do so wash me in Your blood, fill me with the power of the Holy Spirit and protect me from each temptation, from every emergency and crisis...every circumstance and all adversity. Whether it is referencing a city or a person, your love covers all, and

I stand in need of your rebuilding grace and power. I cling to your promise of being rebuilt.

APRIL 30
LOVE OF THE WORLD SQUEEZES OUT LOVE FOR THE FATHER

1 John 2:15-17 (MSG)

"Don't love the world's ways. Don't love the world's goods. Love of the world squeezes out love for the Father. Practically everything that goes on in the world—wanting your own way, wanting everything for yourself, wanting to appear important—has nothing to do with the Father. It just isolates you from him. The world and all it's wanting, wanting, wanting is on the way out—but whoever does what God wants is set for eternity."

Isaiah 64:8 (NKJV), *"We are the clay, You are the Potter; we are the work of your hand."* There are days when I flow in harmony and then there are times I seem to be swimming against the current. Help me to realize it and stop struggling and take the hand of One who made me. You may be the one opposing me, the One who caused the current. Help me to not love the world's ways or goods or to be caught up in the snare of wanting, wanting, wanting, but to be resolved to do what You want. Thank You for Your power to overcome the desire to have everything I see. It only isolates me from You and keeps me from focusing on what You're looking at ... what You've already set for me in eternity. Great is my God and greatly to be praised!

MAY 1

WHAT JESUS DID AMONG THEM, HE DOES IN US—HE LIVES

2 Corinthians 4:8-14 (MSG)

"We've been surrounded and battered by troubles but we're not demoralized; we're not sure what to do, but we know that God knows what to do; we've been spiritually terrorized, but God hasn't left our side; we've been thrown down, but we haven't broken. What they did to Jesus, they do to us—trial and torture, mockery and murder; what Jesus did among them, he does in us—he lives! Our lives are at a constant risk for Jesus' sake, which makes Jesus' life all the more evident in us. While we're going through the worst, you're getting in on the best!"

There are times when problems and troubles throw us down but we're not broken; we may become spiritually terrorized (been there, done that) but God doesn't leave our side. We really don't know what to do but we know that God does! What God has done for generations past, He does for us...He lives! We have no way in the world of knowing when we get up in the morning what that day will hold; we can be healthy and well one moment and our life in peril the next...our lives are at a constant risk...but that being true, it makes Jesus' life all the more precious and evident in us. To know His sufficiency is coming to the end of everything in ourselves and circumstances, every trial and problem, and to know that it is there that He makes His life all the more evident in us. While we're going through the worst, we are getting in on the best because it is all necessary for us to be blessed.

MAY 2

EVERYTHING'S GOING TO BE ALL RIGHT

Jude VS. 2 (MSG)

"Everything's going to be all right; rest, everything's coming together; open your hearts, love is on it the way!"

I have love, hope, faith and they all work! Faith is power; power to change the wrong to right and darkness to light when I truly believe "everything's going to be all right." Here's the truth: I rarely will leave worldly things and seek God until I discover the beauty, glory and greatness of God. When I see and want that, then I am willing to forsake the cheap trinkets of the world that I once thought brought satisfaction. God satisfies the hunger of my soul. I have messed up my life so many times, God; save me from killing off the rest of what's left. Help me to open up my heart and help me to be a person of faith. Take the me and get it to what is You. It is through the worst that God reveals His best because *"everything's going to be all right, as love is on the way."*

MAY 3

THERE IS A FORCE THAT HOLDS YOU UP; THE SAME ONE HOLDS YOU DOWN

Philippians 4:13 (NKJV)

"I can do all things through Christ who strengthens me."

There is a force that holds you up. It's the same one that holds you down, speeds you on your way or stops you, but always guides you. It's the Father's hand. God will always use a force to come against you to strengthen you. When He wants to produce more power in your life, He creates more friction. He uses pressure to generate spiritual power and some people can't handle it and often run from it instead of using and receiving it. It is not enough to be propelled, we all need an equally repelling force and that's why God lets pressures and oppositions come against us to further our progress and to strengthen our souls and bodies. We need to thank him for "holding us down" as well as "speeding us on our way." We can do it all through the One who strengthens us.

MAY 4
THE LORD WAITS

Isaiah 30:18 (NKJV)

"Therefore the Lord will wait that He may gracious to you; and therefore He will be exalted, that He may have mercy on you ... Blessed are those who wait for Him."

Many times we read, *"... wait upon the Lord"* as we are so prone to be impatient in wanting the Lord to attend to our affairs and our requests. This verse says that the Lord waits. Sometimes His delays are because He's waiting on us to be ready to receive. We ask for things and we have a preconceived idea of how He's going to do this and that might not be how it's going to come about at all. Our hearts have to change in order to be prepared for the answer, and so the Lord waits. *"Therefore, the Lord waits that He may be gracious to you"* is the first part; and then *"He waits that He may be exalted."* We don't want to miss His mercy and we don't want to miss His glory. Truly, *"blessed are those who wait for Him."*

MAY 5
THE KNOWLEDGE OF GOD

2 Peter 1:2 (NKJV)

"Grace and peace be multiplied to you in the knowledge of God and of Jesus our Lord, as His divine power has given to us all things that pertain to life and godliness ..."

Grace and peace are blessings that spring from the knowledge of God, just in knowing Him. 2 Peter 1:2-3 (LB), *"Do you want to know more and more of God's kindness and peace? Then learn to know him better and better. For as you know him better, he will give you through his great power, everything you need for living a truly good life."* The knowledge of God is a special kind of knowledge; it's a kind that is totally complete. As our knowledge of Jesus grows and we mature, He gives us through His divine power, i.e., resurrection power, knowledge of all things that pertain to our life. Many questions and problems are thus answered when we know what His Word says because then we grow in our knowledge of Him.

MAY 6
JESUS WILL MEET YOUR NEEDS

Luke 9:42 (HCSB)

"As the boy was still approaching, the demon knocked him down and threw him into severe convulsions."

Was the demon afraid of Jesus? Apparently not, as it knocked the boy down right in front of Jesus and sent him into severe convulsions. Satan will stand his ground; you have to get on God's ground. Don't miss this: It was the destructive intent of the demon that brought about the end of the matter! So don't shrink in terror of his evil intentions toward you, as it gets God's attention to defend you! Jesus gave the boy back to his father, healed and whole. He will do the same for you. You don't have to be shrieking and foaming at the mouth to warrant His help; God can do what is impossible for humans to accomplish. Refuse to be stopped by whatever the need is and do something to solidify your faith in the One who can meet every need.

MAY 7
RENEW YOUR MIND EVERY DAY

Romans 12:12 (NKJV)
"Be transformed by the renewing of your mind ..."

You've just overcome a problem? Great! But one is just around the corner waiting to take its place. You're always going to be a "work in progress." That's how spiritual growth happens. And, it doesn't come about by us ... by human effort ... work of self, but by spending time in prayer and having your mind cleaned up in the Word every day. Reading the Word will wash away the debris in your mind you collected the day before. Agree with God, believe what He says is the way that it is. Just as you don't give up on a child when they try, God is pleased when He sees you trying. It's His job to *"...cause you to be governed by the Holy Spirit."* 2 Corinthians 3:8 Amplified Bible (AMP) If you could do it, you wouldn't need Jesus. You need to be transformed by renewing your mind in His Word every day!

114

MAY 8
GIVE YOURSELF TIME TO MOURN

Ecclesiastics 3:4b (NKJV)

"A time to weep, and a time to laugh; a time to mourn, and a time to dance ..."

Grief has to be processed as it is a natural reaction to loss. If you bury your grief, it will cause you to be depressed and anxious. You will become stressed as you search for resolution, as we all need a time to mourn. The Bible says "time" so that tells you there is a beginning and end to it. How much time? The time it takes depends on how great the loss, as well as the spiritual health of the one doing the mourning. God processes our grief so we will again laugh and dance. You need to complete grief or you will repeat it. You will know when it is complete when the time comes that you can remember it without being terrorized by it. You will weep, you will laugh, you will mourn; but you also will dance! Be encouraged!

MAY 9
WHEN YOU PRAY, GET READY

Hebrews 12:12 (LB)

"So take a new grip with your tired hands, stand firm on your shaky legs, mark out a straight smooth path for your feet so that those who follow after you, though weak and lame, will not fall and hurt themselves but become strong."

When you pray, "Lord, give me faith"—get ready! What you're doing is asking for trials—for how else can you know you have faith except as it is exercised? God refines the gifts He gives us through them. He never trains us in tents of ease or luxury but in hard, lengthy and difficult service, which is why there are so many drop outs. We mostly live in the glare of the things of the world so we need a time when He pulls us aside to give us a glimpse of what's next. So know when the hands are tired and the legs shaky, you can keep on that straight smooth path because others are depending on you to do it as they need your strength. The Lord gives you faith; He is with you; He is at hand!

MAY 10
GIVE GOD TIME TO POSSESS YOUR SOUL

Matthew 10:27 (NKJV)
"What I tell you in the dark, speak in the daylight."

All of God's greats spent hours, months, even years alone...Moses in the desert; Elijah on Mt. Horeb; Paul in Arabia. If you are to be used of Him, you too will need to spend great quantities of time of rest in the shadow of El Shaddai. You need a time for God to possess and process your soul and to whisper to you. It is as necessary as your food. There is nothing random in God's kingdom! Everything that happens fits into a pattern for good to those who love Him. Instead of trying to make sense of it—trust, praise and thank Him for it. Even your mistakes and sins can be reprocessed into something good. What He whispers to you in the night, speak that to someone in the daylight.

MAY 11
THE DEVIL'S AIM IS HIGH

Luke 4:1-2 (NKJV)

"Jesus, full of the Holy Spirit, was led by the Spirit into the desert where for 40 days He was tempted by the devil."

There is nothing backward or bashful about the devil; if he didn't hesitate to try to tempt Jesus, he certainly won't back away from you. Anyone full of the Spirit of God will experience times of great conflict. God allows it for the lessons we will learn and for the growth that will come as a result. What does heat do for paint but to give it endurance and a luster it would otherwise not have? He polishes us with afflictions and trials for future service. Charles H. Spurgeon: "I owe more to my Lord's fire, hammer and file than to anything else in His workshop. Sometimes I wonder if I ever learn anything except at the end of God's rod. When my classroom is darkest, I see my best." The Devil loves to attack God's best servants, he aims high; but our God is higher and greater!

MAY 12
GRANT US ALL A TRANSITION OF COMING TO YOU

Psalms 119:168 (LB)

"You know this because everything I do is known to You."

I know that I will reach home in Your perfect timing because everything I do is already known to you. It will not be one moment too soon or too late. I watched my husband, Louie, do that and it wasn't something I understood but I know he is with You and I praise You for that. I pray that You will redeem that horrible processing as You see fit. The days of darkness and bungling of doctors did bring him into your glorious Presence. You are Holy Lord God Almighty; grant us all a transition of coming to You. You've filled the earth with Your tender love. *"Those who rejoice in Your Word have great peace of heart and do not stumble. I long for Your salvation ... "* Psalms 119:165-166a (LB) Thank you for Your love that covers us like a soft cloud that wraps totally around us as you so graciously usher us into Your wonderful kingdom.

MAY 13
GOD DOESN'T CHECK OUT ON US

PSALMS 138:7 (KJV)
"Though I walk in the midst of trouble, You preserve my life."

Mostly, when problems and troubles overwhelm us and continue unchecked, we tend to think You've checked out. Not so ... any more than You left Daniel in the lion's den or the three men in the fiery furnace. It is in the center, the very deepest midst of the trouble that You are there, Your Presence protecting and preserving the life You breathed into us. Oswald Chambers: "We have no right to judge where we should be put, or to have preconceived notions as to what God is fitting us for. God engineers everything." He is in the center of whatever and wherever you are. He never has, nor will He ever, check out on you. But He certainly will be the One who "checks you in."

118

MAY 14

CULTIVATE GOD CONFIDENCE

1 Corinthians 10:12b (MSG)

"You could fall flat on your face as easily as anyone else. Forget about self-confidence, it's useless! Cultivate God confidence."

Bible characters always fell on their strong points, never on their weak ones. Don't rely on your strengths, rely on God. You will never know where temptation will come from. The least likely thing can wind up being your downfall. If you have just come through looking good in a great crisis, beware of the aftermath. Be constantly aware of your great need of God...be dead to doubts and blind to impossibilities! What you consider your strength, could be a double weakness. *"Cultivate God confidence; forget about self-confidence, it's useless!"*

MAY 15

WHAT IS FAITH

Hebrews 11:1 (LB)

"What is faith? It is the confident assurance that something we want is going to happen."

"Faith puts a letter in the mailbox and lets go. Distrust, however, holds onto the corner of the envelope and then wonders why an answer never arrives! Hand your circumstances over to God, allow Him to work," Streams in the Desert. Faith is more than a receiving. You have faith but it only benefits you as you appropriate and use it. Don't worry over it or be anxious; and don't doubt or waiver in unbelief. Faith is believing and being certain of what you do not see. It is the confident assurance that something you want is going to happen and having confidence in the One who can make it happen. Faith doesn't reason or contemplate, only believes in the ability of the Lord God Almighty!

MAY 16
TRUST HIM TO DO WHAT YOU'VE COMMITTED TO HIM

Psalms 37:5 (NKJV)

"Commit your way to the Lord, trust also in him and he will bring it to pass."

One translation says, "Commit your way to the Lord, trust in Him and He will do this." The first issue is "you." Commit your way—that means be willing for Him to answer in whatever way He chooses. He will do this for you...maybe not as you expect, but commit it to Him. Trust Him to do what you've committed to Him. You activate your faith muscles by believing. Keep believing God even though nothing changes. Trust God to do it. *"God will do whatever He sees needs doing ..."* 2 Samuel 10:12 (MSG)

MAY 17
EXTEND YOURSELF

Isaiah 58:10 (MSG)

"If you are generous with the hungry and start giving yourselves to the down and out, your lives will begin to glow in the darkness..."

The (NKJV) says, *"If you extend your soul to the hungry and satisfy the afflicted soul"* ... that's more than giving them a little money or bread, that's giving of yourself, getting involved in their life, letting the down and out know that you don't live an entirely selfish life but you have a concern for them as well. To "satisfy the desire of the afflicted" means to help them find some answers. Isaiah 58 10-11 (LB), *"Then shall your light shine out of the darkness and the darkness around you shall be as bright as day. And the Lord will guide you continually and satisfy you with all good things and keep you healthy too; and you will be like a well-watered garden, like an overflowing spring."* For years, I loved the promise of "the darkness being as bright as the day; of being satisfied with all good things/being kept healthy; flowing like an overflowing spring" never realizing all that was prefaced with *"IF I extend my soul to the hungry and give myself to the down and out, then my life would begin to glow in the darkness."* To realize fulfillment of His Word, we need to comprehend the conditions stated. What a great promise in extending yourself!

MAY 18
HE WAS DESPISED AND REJECTED

Isaiah 53:3 (NKJV)

"He was despised and rejected by men; a man of sorrows and acquainted with grief."

People are prone to believe that suffering is associated with sin. Jesus' suffering was for our sin, not His. He was despised and no one cared. He carried our sin on His shoulders and instead of being grateful, people shunned Him as if He had leprosy. He was "wounded, pierced through; crushed to death for our sins." He took on Himself the punishment for all our wrongdoings. He accepted the entire affliction without response as stated in VS. 7, *"He was oppressed and he was afflicted, yet he opened not his mouth."* Because of His own suffering, He knows how to help you in yours. He endured the shame and pain of the cross, *"He was smitten by God and afflicted,"* VS. 4, but now He ever lives to make intercession for you. Because He was rejected, we are accepted. Thank Him today for being willing to hang there in shame on the cross until all of our sins were forgiven.

MAY 19
ARE YOU UNEMPLOYED

2 Timothy 4:2 (NKJV)
" ... *Be ready in season and out of season."*

When Timothy said, "Be ready in season and out of season," he wasn't taking about time, but about you; whether you feel like it or not. If you do only what you feel like doing mostly that would be nothing. The "unemployed line" in the spiritual realm is endless. Spiritually depraved people refuse to do anything whatsoever unless there's a miracle in sight or some supernatural phenomenon. If you have experienced a new birth and taken your rightful position of being in Him, you will do your best at whatever the Wind Words whisper to you, whether you feel inspired or equipped. You will never hear God say, "If you can't get it right, do nothing at all." If you've done your best, it's a "Well done, good and faithful servant," even if it's mostly a mess. Don't join the ranks of the unemployed where God's works are concerned; be ready in season and out of season. You need not be unemployed spiritually; 'tis the season to serve.

MAY 20
GOD AFFIRMS US, MAKING US A SURE THING IN CHRIST

2 Corinthians 1:20-22 (MSG)

"Whatever God has promised gets stamped with the Yes of Jesus...God's Yes and our Yes together, gloriously evident. God affirms us, making us a sure thing in Christ, putting his Yes within us. By His Spirit He has stamped us with His eternal pledge—a sure beginning of what He is destined to complete."

Oswald Chambers: "We must not measure our spiritual capacity by education or by intellect; our capacity in spiritual things is measured by the promises of God."   And whatever God has promised gets stamped with the, *"Yes of Jesus!"* When the promise states, *"God affirms us, making us a sure thing in Christ;"* what does that do for all your feelings of inadequacy and inferiority? Genesis 1:27 says that we are made in His image, reflecting His nature. What else do you need? We have His stamp of approval for not only a sure beginning; we also have His promise that our destination is complete!

MAY 21

COMPLETE WHAT GOD GAVE YOU TO DO

John 17:4 (NLT)

"I brought you glory on earth by completing what You gave Me to do."

Don't try to do what someone else is doing. A spiritually mature Christian enjoys the accomplishments and gifts others have because they enjoy what God has gifted them to do. *"Let us not become ... competitive ... envying ... and jealous of one another ..." "Galatians* 5:28 (AMP) Time spent in trying to be like someone else is a total waste. God made you unique; there's not another human being in the world exactly like you...there may be some look-alikes, but that's where it stops. He not only has a plan but a divine purpose for you. Jesus told God, *"I brought You glory by completing what You gave Me to do"* ... you need to live for that!

MAY 22

YOUR LIFE IS A PRIZE

Jeremiah 45:6 (NKJV)

"I will give you your life as a prize ..."

Whether I live or whether I die, I have life; I will come out of it living because of You, Jesus! You will have you life, no matter what! Even if you go to hell, you will still have life. When God breathed into you life, it was forever. Possessions, property, blessing all go, but life remains. Strip everything else away, life is left. A life hidden in Christ is all that counts. *"I will give you your life as a prize;"* is that how you view it? It is a prize when you abandon your plan to follow His. God doesn't respond to what you do, you respond to what God is doing, let Him set the pace. He knows a thousand ways to make a way for you. God specializes in impossibilities. <u>Psalms 32:10</u> (MSG), *"God-defiers are always in trouble. God-affirmers find themselves loved every time they turn around."* Your life is a prize when you say, *"I don't want to live my way, I want to live Your way, Your Word's way ..."* <u>Psalms 17:4</u> Paraphrase (MSG)

MAY 23
HE IS AT OUR SIDE IN BAD TIMES

<u>Psalms 91:15</u> (MSG)

    "Call Me and I'll answer, be at your side in bad times..."

One morning last year, I was standing at my kitchen sink getting ready to put a large chicken pot pie in the oven, having just made cookies to take to church for a dinner with missionaries. I looked at the clock and saw that I had about 15 minutes before time to put the casserole in the oven and thought I had time to shower. At that moment, my heart totally stopped and I woke up 15 min. later and took a cookie sheet off my face wondering what happened. The broken dish of pot pie was nearby but I never saw it. I had fallen from a standing position to flat of my back on tile flooring and had vertigo so bad I couldn't lift my head. "Lord, you said *to call on You, that You'd be at my side in bad times* (one of the scriptures I had read that morning) this is a bad time, please help me." He did. It took me 25 min. to scoot on my backside to a purse on the floor in the next room so I could use my cell phone to call 911. God is faithful always and He does respond to His Word when we call on Him!

MAY 24
I NEED TO BE REFUELED DAILY

Psalms 17:4-5 (MSG)

"I'm not trying to get my way in the world's way; I'm trying to get your way, Your Word's way."

Your Spirit is here within, it shouldn't be hard to stay connected and in tune with you and it wouldn't be if we kept our mind and will focused on Your Presence, power and desire for us. There's no lack on Your part! A beautiful float in the Rose Bowl suddenly ran out of gas. The whole parade was held up until gas could be found. Ironically, the float belonged to the Standard Oil Company! The float couldn't run without fuel and neither can I. My gas pump is Your Word and I don't operate well on the "Economy Version;" I require a higher octane. The "Regular" doesn't work for me as my tank requires a more powerful fuel to live rightfully and pleasing to You. *"I'm not trying to get my way in the world's way; I'm trying to get your way, Your Word's way."* I need to be refueled daily with the best You have to offer!

MAY 25

THE FIRST RECORDED PRAYER

Genesis 3:9 (NKJV)

"Then the Lord God called to Adam and said to him, "Where are you?"

When Adam and Eve heard God walking in the garden, they hid themselves among the trees and when God questioned them, Adam admitted that he had done something wrong but it really wasn't his fault. *"It's that woman you gave me, it's all her fault"* and Eve said, *"Don't look at me, the Devil made me do it!"* Some things haven't changed too much in all these years, have they? At least they were talking to God and that is what prayer is all about. They didn't need to tell God they were hiding; He already knew that...He asks them why they were hiding. He knew that too. He asked to give Adam a chance to confess his sin. This first recorded prayer has so many applications that we can make in our own times of confrontation and repentance before the Lord. If you hear God asking you today, *"Where are you?"* If it's in sin, learn from Adam and don't blame anyone else. Be glad He is seeking you out and giving you a chance to make things right with Him.

MAY 26

WE ARE CHANGED INTO HIS IMAGE AS WE BEHOLD HIM

2 Corinthians 3:18 (KJV)

"But we all with open face beholding as in a glass the glory of the Lord."

We want the Lord to manifest Himself <u>to</u> us; God only manifests Himself <u>in</u> us. His promise is: "I will be with you." I continually mess up; He remains faithful. It is so easy to become agitated and frustrated when I'm trying to do the right thing and it all goes south. I falter, fail and repeat mistakes, and God still helps me! People who used to be lights do, at times, flicker out (how true). <u>2 Timothy 4:16-17</u> (KJV), *"All men forsook me... notwithstanding the Lord stood with me."* I have to build my faith on not the fading light but on the Light that never fails. The ones who flicker and fail were meant to go. So, I will turn my gaze on You. The whole verse reads: *"We all with open face beholding as in a glass the glory of the Lord are changed into that same image from glory to glory even as by the Spirit of the Lord."* We gain His light and glory as we behold and gaze upon Him.

MAY 27

TRUST THE ONE WHO PROCESSES YOUR LIFE

<u>Job 23:10</u> (RSV)

"But He knows the way that I take and when He has tried Me I shall come forth as gold."

Truly there wasn't a man like Job on the face of the earth. <u>Job 1:21</u> (RSV), *"The Lord gave and the Lord has taken away, may the Name of the Lord be praised."* He saw nothing but the hand of the Lord as swords attacked his servants and cattle; the fierce lightening and winds that swept away all his sons and daughters; and as he experienced the deadening silence of his home. Yet his response was, *"Though He slay me, yet I trust in Him,"* <u>Job 13:15</u> (RSV) Job trusted God when severely afflicted and all things dear to him were gone. The furnace may be hot but not only can I trust the hand that lights the fire but I have the assurance the fire will not consume, but only refine me and in the processing, "*I really will come forth as gold!*"

MAY 28
IN YOUR FAVOR, OUR HORN IS EXALTED

Psalms 89:17 (NKJV)

"*For you are the glory of their strength and in Your favor, our horn is exalted.*"

I was intrigued when I first read this verse and didn't have a clue about what the Psalmist meant. Then I read further in VS.24 when God said of David: "*For in My name, his horn shall be exalted.*" It means that in God's Name, David would be given power and eventual triumph. David had been chosen and singled out to be holy; yet his beginnings were not spectacular as he was an ordinary shepherd. David's strength (his horn) would be exalted in the God's Name and would bring about his eventual success through God's favor. Later, in Psalms 92:10 (NKJV), David declares, "*But my horn You have exalted like a wild ox.*" What does your horn represent? It should represent power and eventful triumph! In ancient times, the horn always was a symbol of strength.

MAY 29

REACH OUT FOR CHRIST

Philippians 3:12 (MSG)

"I'm not saying that I have this all together, that I have it made. But I am well on my way; reaching out for Christ, who has so wondrously reached out for me."

To embrace Christ and be embraced by Him, to know Him personally, experience His resurrection power, requires embracing and being a partner in His suffering, as well. Most of us shy away from pain like the plague. We want the Light without paying for what produces light. The Light of the world is Jesus but He had to suffer death for our Light to come. A candle burns before light appears; an unlit candle has no light. We can be of little use to others without experiencing some burnings that will ultimately produce the "Light" of our life, and to do that, we have to be submissive. Jesus suffered what was necessary to reach out for you and now it's your turn to partner with Him in order to help someone else. As you reach out for someone, He reaches out for you.

MAY 30

THE THIRD TIME IS NOT ALWAYS A CHARM

Proverbs 29:1 (NKJV)

"He who is often rebuked and hardens his neck will suddenly be destroyed and that without remedy."

A poet wrote: "My old companions fare thee well, I will not go with thee to hell!" Samson lost everything because of wrong relationships. The Bible says that "three times Samson went down" and the third time it was to Delilah. Ungodly relationships can destroy your life. Samson thought because he was special, God would excuse him. He was special and he was specially gifted, but "he went down" the wrong road. It's better to want what you don't have than to end up with what you can't handle. If you find yourself developing an unhealthy relationship, don't go that third time; you could end up destroyed and that without remedy.

MAY 31
USE WHAT GOD HAS GIFTED IN YOU FOR HIS GLORY

James 1:15 (MSG)

"Lust gets pregnant and has a baby: sin! Sin grows up to adulthood and becomes a real killer."

In Judges Chapters 14-16, you can read of Samson's feats of strength: He could tear young lions apart with his bare hands; lift bolted gates and gate posts of the city and carry them away on his shoulders; kill a whole company of men with the jawbone of a donkey because of God's gift of strength. Samson never knew when the Spirit left him until he tried to use it and found he had none. An angel of the Lord appeared to his mother before he was ever born and told her that *"… he would begin to deliver Israel out of the hand of the Philistines …"* Judges 13:5b (NKJV) God gifted him with strength for a purpose. What are you doing with the gifts that God has especially gifted in you? Luke 12:48 (MSG) *"Great gifts mean great responsibilities; greater gifts, greater responsibilities."* Never let lust be conceived within you so that sin grows and becomes a real killer. Use what God has gifted in you for His glory.

JUNE 1

ARE YOU WILLING TO BE NOTHING SO THAT HE CAN BE EVERYTHING

2 Chronicles 16:9 (NKJV)

"The eyes of the Lord run to and fro throughout the whole earth, to show Himself strong on behalf of those whose heart is loyal to Him."

Samson's gift of strength departed from him as did his eyesight and fame. He was imprisoned, jeered, shackled in irons and defeated. Thousands of Philistines shamed him as they celebrated their great victory to their god Dagon for the capture of Samson. Samson was granted his last prayer, "Master God, grant me strength one more time. Let me die with the Philistines." He pushed hard on the two central pillars of the building and so it was he killed more in his death than he had killed in his life." Don't ever discount God's plan. Before he was born, God had told Samson's mother that he would begin to deliver Israel out of the hands of the Philistines. Ultimately, that happened. What about you? God has a plan in place for your life as surely as He did for Samson. 2 Chronicles 16:9 (NIV) *"The eyes of the Lord range throughout the earth to strengthen those whose hearts are fully committed to Him."* God watches to see who will be willing to be nothing, so that He can be everything.

JUNE 2
HE WILL DELIVER YOU...GIVE HIM TIME

Jeremiah 1:19 (NKJV)

"They will fight against you, but they shall not prevail against you. For I am with you says the lord, to deliver you."

God had already told Jeremiah in VS. 18, *"I have made you like a fortified city and an iron pillar."* (MSG) Bible states it this way: *"... immoveable as a steel post; solid as a concrete block wall, you're a one-man defense system."* Jeremiah 1:5b *"... before you were born I sanctified you; I ordained you a prophet to the nations."* VS. 9b-10 *"Behold I have put My Words in your mouth. See I have this day set you over the nations and over the kingdoms."* Later, He told him, *"You are to preach to the people of Judah. They won't listen to a Word you say; you will not have one convert. They'll try to kill you but I will be with you."* How would you like to get that kind of an assignment? If God has given you a difficult assignment, think of Jeremiah; he faithfully preached for 40 years without compromise or even one convert. Yet, God was always with him and He did deliver him. We have to trust and believe in the infallible Word of Almighty God Jehovah!

JUNE 3
HE CAN DELIVER YOU INSTANTLY

Judges 3:9-10 (NKJV)

"The children of Israel cried into the Lord and He raised up a deliverer for the children of Israel who delivered them."

The Prophet Jeremiah may have waited 40 years to be delivered, but God can put someone in position instantly (as He did in the above reference). It might take us years in schooling but God can download a lifetime of living in us in an instant. It is God who works in us and if we're receptive, God can do it all—He can do anything! Mostly, we aren't "instantly" made heroes or judges; we go through valleys, tribulations and tunnels of darkness before He brings us into greatness in anything. A year ago today, I wrote: "Whether I live or whether I die, I live; I come out of it living because of You, Jesus! Strip it all away, life is left. You don't respond to what we do, we respond to what You do. You set the pace. You know a thousand ways to make a way for me." Psalms 32:10 (MSG), *"God-defiers are always in trouble, God-affirmers find themselves loved every time they turn around. Celebrate God!"* He can deliver you instantly; it's His choice.

JUNE 4
HAVE YOUR OWN PERSONAL REVIVAL

Psalms 80:3, 7, and 19 (NKJV)

"Restore us, O God, cause Your face to shine and we shall be saved."

In these three verses, the psalmist says basically the same thing. Because we are restored and His face does shine on us when we with pad, pencil and Bible come to Him to find out what is wrong with us on the inside. Sometimes He does the restoring very quickly. You really can afford to see fewer TV shows. If not, spiritual impressions will soon be lost to your heart. Years ago, people went to the movies to escape God, now the movies come to them in their own homes. The Devil's ideals and standards are accepted without us even realizing it. When you spend time in His Word and look up to His throne, all of heaven comes to you. When The Psalmist said, "*restore us and we will be saved,*" you are saved from evil influences here and now; saved to fulfill God plan and purpose for your life each and every day; and saved for all eternity. You can have your own personal revival every day.

JUNE 5
THE VICTORIES OF YESTERDAY HAVE LITTLE LINGERING VALUE

Genesis 41:1b (NKJV)
" ... *Pharaoh had a dream; and behold, he stood by the river.*"

Pharaoh had a dream as he stood by the Nile River, the life-stream of Egypt. (Please realize that your source of destruction can come from what you consider your greatest asset). In His dream, out of the river came seven fine-looking, fat cows and began to feed in the meadow. Out of the same river, came seven gaunt, ugly cows and ate up the fine-looking healthy cows. Pharaoh awoke and went back to sleep and dreamed seven heads of grain came up on one stalk, plump and good. Then seven thin heads, blighted by the east wind, came and devoured the seven plump, full heads. This troubling dream was the Plan God had for using one Hebrew to save the entire land of Egypt and to reunite one broken family. The best years of your life, the victories can all be swallowed up just as surely as the fat cows and the plump heads of grain...all gone without a trace, leaving you with nothing but defeat and failure. The victories of yesterday can be today's reversals. It happens, it's called life. Listen to me, God saved Egypt through one person and He can do the same thing for you. Defeat and failure is not the end of life. God can use any and all of it, as a means of spurring you onto something richer and better.

JUNE 6
YOUR WORDS ARE HEARD

Luke 1:37 (LB)

"For every promise from God shall surely come true."

If God has made the promise, we can believe it. Daniel 10:12-13 (NKJV), *"Then he said to me, "Do not fear, Daniel, for from the first day that you set your heart to understand, and to humble yourself before your God, your Words were heard; and I have come because of your Words. But the prince of the kingdom of Persia withstood me twenty-one days ... "* Daniel had fasted and prayed for 21 days and the angel is telling him that from the first day he prayed, his prayer was answered but an Evil Spirit (LB) had blocked his path and prevented him from coming to him. But now he would tell him what was about to happen. There may not be anything wrong with you or your prayer but an Evil Spirit can block your answer. How many of us would continue to fast and pray for 21 days about anything? Consider Daniel's reward: VS. 10-11, *"Suddenly a hand touched me ... and he said to me, O Daniel, man greatly beloved, understand the words that I speak to you ... "* Trembling greatly, Daniel received not only strength and peace but the message God sent to him.   Every promise from God shall surely come true.

JUNE 7
TRUST AND OBEY

Mark 9:23 (LB)
"Everything is possible for him who believes."

Oswald Chambers: "He will tax the last grain of sand and the remotest star to bless us if we will obey Him. What does it matter if external circumstances are hard? Why should they not be! If we give way to self-pity and indulge in the luxury of misery, we banish God's riches from our own lives and hinder others from entering into His provision. No sin is worse than the sin of self-pity, because it obliterates God and puts self-interest upon the throne." Make yourself a checklist: Being obedient involves your tongue (what you say); your mind (what you think); and your emotions (how you behave). Do you want to remain the same miserable, complaining, crosspatch or are you absorbing and doing life His way? Be encouraged to obey as you get a fresh touch from Him in His Word. God can encourage and inspire you, but it's up to you to practice obedience. *"Everything is possible for him who believes."*

JUNE 8
BE READY

Psalms 1:3 (NKJV)
"He shall be like a tree planted by the rivers of water that brings forth its fruit in its season, whose leaf also shall not wither..."

Be ready in season and out of season, we're told. We just need to recognize what season we're in. It may be a season of comfort; it may be a season to give comfort; or it may be a time to receive correction. Time is so important. We need to be wise enough to know a blessed life is like a tree that gives fruit in season. God is more interested in your roots than He is in how high your branches. He's more interested in quality than He is in quantity. He is very interested in what comes out of you. That's why He uses your struggles to cultivate the kind of person necessary to produce good fruit. Storms are used sometimes to blow away things or people that hinder what He's working on in you. Be ready for your season, whatever it is!

JUNE 9
HOLD ONTO GOD

Romans 8:35 (NKJV)
"Who shall separate us from the love of Christ?"

Paul lists a number of things: tribulation, distress, persecution, famine, nakedness, peril and sword, indicating some of the troubles that can come in our lifetime. But he hastens to say that we are more than conquerors in all these things. We may be a victim for a while, but we can become super victorious in spite of it all. Not by our own ingenuity or courage, but by holding onto God and His promises. It happens when we don't let any of them affect our relationship with Jesus. Never let any of the things that come against you separate you from the knowledge of His Presence being right there with you. No matter what comes in your life experience, hold onto the love of God and believe that He has not left you for one second. Psalms 73:23 (NKJV), *"Nevertheless I am continually with You; You hold me by my right hand."*

JUNE 10

MY STRENGTH SHALL EQUAL MY DAYS

Deuteronomy 33:25 (RSV)

"As your days, so shall your strength be."

You saved me from the penalty of sin in salvation. Today, I'm being saved from the power of sin. When You come back, I'll be saved from all presence of sin. My strength will equal my days! *"Because God's my refuge, the High God my very own home, evil can't get close to me, harm can't get through the door"* Psalms 91:11 (MSG) (personalized). I really never know anything until I recognize that God knows it all. My humble heart can help me more than my proud mind. God's Word will only bear fruit when sown in peace and that's why the Devil plays so much havoc in my life. If the Devil can't get me upset, he loses control. Oswald Chambers: "We have to take ourselves by the scruff of the neck and shake ourselves and we will find that we can do what we said we could not." God redeemed my life to live it out for Him, and with Him helping me, my strength will equal my days!

JUNE 11

OUR STRENGTH COMES FROM THE LORD

Philippians 4:13 (KJV)

"I can do all things through Christ which strengthens me."

Where we consider ourselves the strongest is where we're least likely to prepare for attack. Satan loves to attack our strongholds. What seems so innocent can be totally destructive.

Flirting with temptation is a guarantee you will at some point actually do it. You need to recognize, avoid and eliminate it, now! Failure to do so won't cut you off from God but it will totally destroy your potential and certainly affect your fellowship with your Savior. And play havoc with your testimony! If you are feeling inadequate today, it's probably because you are. God didn't call us to work for Him but with Him. You don't have ability? No problem; your sufficiency is from God. No money? God is able to make all grace abound to you so that in all things, at all times, you have all you need. No strength? *"I can do all things through Him who gives me strength."*

JUNE 12
OPEN YOUR MIND TO TRUTH

Luke 24:45 (NKJV)

"And He opened their understanding that they might comprehend the scriptures."

Before Jesus ascended to heaven, He was trying to tell the disciples of things to come and they didn't understand a word of it. The Bible says that then He opened their minds to truth. That's exactly what we need to do is to be open to receive from the Holy Spirit the truth of His Word. Hebrews 2:1 (LB), *"We must listen very carefully to the truths we have heard or we may drift away from them."* Veering even slightly off course can put you miles away from where God showed you truth and you can end up in a place you never thought possible. Many times we blame the Devil, when actually it's our own careless drifting and being involved in the cares of this world. When you read, ask the Holy Spirit to bring each thought captive so He can open your understanding, in order for you to comprehend the great truth of the scriptures.

JUNE 13
HE CAN MEET YOUR NEED

<u>John 17:19</u> (LB)

"I consecrate Myself to meet their need for growth in truth and holiness."

God doesn't ask us if we can go through or if we want to go through losses, disasters or death. He allows us to experience these things so that He can meet our need for growth in truth and holiness. In the midst of these things, we can either decide to become sweeter in Spirit or we can become bitter ... more stubborn and critical and fault finding. It all happens, depending on your relationship with God. <u>John 17:21</u> (LB), *"My prayer for all of them is that they will be of one heart and mind just as You and I are Father, that just as You are in Me and I in You, so they will be in us and the world will believe You sent Me."* When we respond rightly to life's surprises, the world does see exactly what our relationship with the Father really is. Jesus has already dedicated Himself to meet our need for growth in truth and holiness, so learn as you groan and know that you are in Him and He is in You!

JUNE 14

THE PLANS OF THE LORD STAND FIRM

Psalms 33:11 (NKJV)

"The counsel of the Lord stands forever, the plans of His heart to all generations."

The plans of the Lord stand firm but we must be prepared to wait on His timing. God's timing is precious and He does things in the very time He has set. It is not for us to know His timing; in fact, we cannot know it—we have to wait for it. If God had told Abraham before he left Haram that he would have to wait 30 years before he could hold his promised son in his arms, his heart would have failed within him. Instead, God graciously withheld that painful information. But the sound of laughter did fill their home in their old age and they soon forgot the long years of waiting. So take heart when God requires you to wait—the One you wait for will not disappoint you. Habakkuk 2:3b (LB), *"If it seems slow, do not despair, for these things will surely come to pass. Just be patient! They will not be overdue a single day!"* The plan of God's heart extends to all generations.

JUNE 15

TAKE A LOOK AT GOD

Psalms 46:10 (MSG)

"Take a long, loving look at me, your High God, above politics, above everything."

<u>Psalms 73:25, 28</u> (MSG), *""You're all I want in heaven! You're all I want on earth! When my skin sags and my bones get brittle, God is rock-firm and faithful. I've made Lord God my home. God, I'm telling the world what you do!"* Focus on God, Who He is and What He is. Stop focusing on your problems. He doesn't need a thing to start with in order to solve what's wrong with you or in you. He flung the stars in place and they still shine every night; He emptied the oceans from His vast reservoirs; He but spoke and the world began, it appeared at His command, and it hasn't stopped yet. There isn't a thing He can't do and He will help you. When He's getting you ready to do something, He often allows you to get into situations in which there are no human solutions. Focus on Jesus more than your problem. He will make you into the kind of person you've always wanted to be. Trust Him regardless of what comes against you. Take a long, loving look at Him; He is rock-firm and faithful!

JUNE 16
JOB KNEW SORROW

<u>Job 2:7-8</u> (LB)

"So Satan went out from the presence of the Lord and struck Job with a terrible case of boils from head to foot. Then Job took a broken piece of pottery to scrape him, and sat among the ashes."

When Job sat alone on his ash heap all troubled over the providence of God (i.e., God working in his life controlling everything for His divine purpose), he might have been encouraged if he had known that literally millions of people would for generations read of his afflictions and find comfort. It is because of his afflictions that he is remembered--without them, we probably would never have known him. Which one of us has not learned that it is through our sorrows that we most clearly experience God's presence in our life? The person who goes through life without them is very shallow indeed. We all need to know heights and depths or we would be dwarfed and undeveloped. Job lost everything in his life that was dear to him but his response was, "Though He slay me, yet will I trust Him." God restored and blessed him, giving him twice as much as he lost. Job may have known deep sorrow but he also personally knew the "Man of Sorrows."

JUNE 17
WE SEEK YOU

Psalms 27:8 (NKJV)

"When you said, "Seek My face," my heart said to You, "Your face, Lord, I will seek."

We seek You, Your Presence; we are so needy. We find ourselves overwhelmed with difficulties, trials and emergencies almost daily. This can be God's way of providing vessels in us that the Holy Spirit needs to fill. Some of these things are nothing but opportunities and God's means of deliverance that we could receive no other way. This is when we "Seek Your face!" We stand still before You and stop our own struggle to be delivered. The very things that threaten to destroy us can be used by God to show us His Almighty power and grace, as we continue to seek and trust You. We spend far too much time seeking what comes from Your hand, asking for blessings. We need to be doing what You said, *"Seek My face"* and be strengthened in our relationship with You.

JUNE 18
WE ALL GET IN A FIX WE CAN'T FIX

Psalms 46:1 (NKJV)

"God is our refuge and strength, a very present help in trouble."

David went from being an exalted and honored King to being hounded and hiding in a cave. His life looked as if it fell apart. We all do some time in that state of existence ... it is called "learning time." It is a time to learn from where your help comes and learn about yourself. This is where God can do some of His best work. It is where your worst failures are confirmed, both to yourself and unfortunately to the whole world about you. It is also the time God bails you out. For all David knew, he was going to die in his cave. We get in a fix we can't fix and this is as good as it gets. Because it is there that we learn to trust God. Never let your sense of security be based on you. God will help you and be with you, no matter what. Trust Him. He will bring you out of the cave. Our only hope is in You, Lord! We really can't fix us; only You can do that!

JUNE 19
PACE YOURSELF

Psalms 80:3 (NKJV)

"Restore us, O God; cause Your face to shine, and we shall be saved!"

Every day you are saved from evil influences and you are saved to fulfill God's plan and purpose for your life. Here's how you do it: Start each day by pacing yourself:

- **P** – Praise God Almighty for Who He is.
- **A** – Accept, be accepting of the plan He has for you today because His Plan is good.
- **C** – Commit your life to the Lord, let Him have His way. *"In all your ways acknowledge Him and He will direct your path,"* Proverbs 3:6 (NKJV).
- **E** – Embrace God's plan for it is perfectly right whether or not you understand it at the time. (MSG) *"Embracing what God does for you is the best thing you can do for God."*

Three times we are told in Psalms 80, *"Restore us and we will be saved"* (VS. 3, 7, and 19). A person with pad, pencil and Bible is sure to find out what is wrong with their life very quickly. Look up to the throne, your advocate sits at God's right hand, heaven is just ahead. PACE yourself today, all of heaven awaits you!

JUNE 20
HE COMES TO FIGHT BY YOUR SIDE

Mark 5:36b (NIV)
"Don't be afraid, just believe."

You walk with God, but sometimes God walks slowly. You become impatient as you wait for God to answer your prayers. Once prayed, you expect God to "hop to" when in reality, it may take years for "what you've prayed for to be prepared." Do you ever consider that God waits for you? Many times He's ready but you aren't! Nor, are you moving with Him, so it's missed. You also over-wait because you lack the confidence to move forward. Psalms 73:24a (NKJV), *You will guide me with Your counsel,"* but you lag behind or run ahead. Your goal is to walk with Him, so as to

146

be available when the timing is right. Blessings happen when you do what is right and what is required...that involves obedience and faith. Stop believing your doubts. You believe every doubt Satan throws at you, so why can't you believe what the Lord says? You have to enter a conflict in order to win and as you enter, He comes to fight by your side. God will deliver you in His determined time. He has a fixed time and an ordained purpose for everything. He who controls the limits of our life also determines the time of our deliverance. Don't be afraid, just believe.

JUNE 21
THE WORD OF THE LORD WORKS

1 Thessalonians 2:12 (LB)

"... that your daily lives should not embarrass God, but bring joy to him who invited you into his kingdom to share his glory."

1 Thessalonians 2:13 (NKJV), *"When you received the Word of God which you heard from us, you welcomed it not as the Word of men, but as it is in truth, the Word of God, which also effectively works in you who believe."* (LB) *"... and it changed your lives when you believed it."* The Word of God works in you. Do not follow the crowd; do not follow the multitude to do evil. Mark 7:8 (LB), *"You ignore God's specific orders and substitute your own traditions."* Proverbs 16:25 (NKJV), *"There's a way that seems right to a man, but its end is the way of death."* Judges 21:25 (NKJV), *"Every man did what was right in his own eyes."* 1 Peter 1:17 (LB), *"Your heavenly Father has no favorites when He judges. He will judge you with perfect justice for everything you do; so act in reverent fear of Him from now on until you get to heaven."* You need to accept

the Word which is at work within you. You must receive the Word and carefully consider how you listen. Revelation 1:3 (NKJV), *"Blessed is he who reads and those who hear the Words of this prophecy, and keep those things which are written in it, for the time is near."* (MSG) says it this way: *"Happy is the one who reads the Book and those who listen to it being read and do what it says."* The Word of God effectively works in you who believe!

JUNE 22
MOVE FORWARD WITH THE KNOWN WILL OF GOD IN YOUR LIFE

Exodus 14:21b (NIV)
"... all that night the Lord drove the sea back with a strong east wind."

We read that *"all that night, the Lord drove back the sea,"* and we know that He merely spoke and the world began, it appeared at His command (Psalms 33 (LB). He can merely "speak" or He can cause an all-night, all-month, all-year happening in order to bring your deliverance, as He is Almighty God! The people whined, *"Have you brought us out here to die in the desert because there were not enough graves for us in Egypt? Why did you make us leave Egypt? Isn't this what we told you, while we were slaves, to leave us alone? We said it would be better to be slaves to the Egyptians than dead in the wilderness ..."* Exodus 14:11-12 (LB). In VS. 15, *"Then the Lord said to Moses, "Quit praying and get the people moving!"* (There's a time to pray and a time to move forward). Result in VS. 18, *"And all Egypt shall know that I am Jehovah."* You may think they were foolish but respond in like manner when you face difficulties. Moses told them, *"Don't be afraid. Just stand where you are and watch, and you will see the wonderful way the Lord will rescue you today ... the Lord will fight for you and you won't need to lift a finger!"* VS. 13-14. You may need to stand still so that you see the solution to your situation. You never know when God will "blow" all night to change things just for you!

JUNE 23
THE LORD IS MY HELPER

Hebrews 13:5-6 (NKJV)

"For He Himself has said, 'I will never leave you nor forsake you.' So we may boldly say: "The Lord is my helper; I will not fear, what man can do to me?"'

I need to get the dread of "what's next" out of me and listen to what You say...to Your say-so. You have said, *"I will never leave you nor forsake you,"* so that I can say, *"The Lord is my helper, I will not fear."* It is through You that I can boldly claim Your promises. I just *" ... need to watch what You do and then do it...mostly what you You do is love us; keep company with you and learn a life of love, learn to love like that ... "* Ephesians 5:1-2 (MSG). In the meantime, I need to do what is within my power to do. It isn't within my power to create the wind or change its direction but I can lift my sail to catch it when it comes. I can't control the Holy Spirit but I can connect with Him and be obedient in doing what He's called me to do as I come under His influence and power. You are my helper. I am not to fear, no matter what. Whether I face giants or grasshoppers, You say, "*I will never forsake you.*" I just need the courage to be bold and believe, "*You are my helper.*"

JUNE 24
DESIRE THE WORD

Ezra 7:10 (ML)

"*For Ezra had disciplined himself to study the Law of the Lord, to practice it and to teach its statutes and ordinances in Israel.*" *(RSV) "For Ezra had set his heart to study the law of the Lord and to do it!*"

Ezra didn't wake up and say, "Behold, I am a spirit-filled teacher!" It took years of disciplined study. Study is more than reading it is delving into the scriptures, running references and finding the treasures that lie within. Learning and knowing means little unless used rightly. Notice he didn't just study, but he put it into practice what he had learned! It has been said, "I am a changed person when I sharpen my focus to believe the Bible was written for me. What do I want from it? I want it to revive my soul, instruct, counsel, comfort, convict, and encourage me. Psalms 19:7 (RSV), "*The law of the lord is perfect, reviving the soul.*" The Law is His instructions and guidelines which are flawless. VS. 8, "*The testimony (statutes) of the Lord are sure (trustworthy and complete in every way), making wise the simple.*" VS. 8, "*The precepts (requirements) of the Lord are right, rejoicing the heart (giving joy to the heart). The commandment of the Lord is pure (radiant), enlightening the eyes (giving light to our spirit eyes).*" VS. 10, "*More to be desired are they than gold, even much fine gold; sweeter also than honey dripping from the honeycomb.*" I want to be wise; I want joy; and for my spirit eyes to be enlightened. His Word is more to be desired than fine gold and is sweeter than honey from the honeycomb. Desire the Word, taste and see that it is good!

JUNE 25
HE BECAME POOR AND WE BECAME RICH

2 Corinthians 8:9 (MSG)

"Rich as he was, he gave it all away for us—in one stroke, he became poor and we became rich."

Up until the last moment before He died, Jesus could have called it all off but in one stroke, He took on our sin and endured incredible pain so that we could be made right. When tuning the harp, the tortuous thumb screw has to be tightened by the harpist in order for the strings to produce a perfect sound. The Father sometimes works with us in much the same way...He hears off key, discordant sounds out of us so He plucks our heart strings with anguish and pain and then leans over to listen. If all He hears is still discord and harshness, He plucks some more. He tenderly waits for our stubbornness to melt and our will to be blended with His own. He is long suffering and never ceases until we are humbled and blended to become one in Him. The sounds that come out of us may never be perfect, but they can be in harmony. We are thankful for His fine tuning process in us and grateful that He endured His own incredible pain. The Bible tells us that all of our sin was poured into Him and in exchange, His righteousness was poured into us. In that process, He became poor and we became very rich!

JUNE 26

YOU ARE ALL I WANT IN HEAVEN OR ON EARTH

Psalms 73:25-26 (MSG)

"You're all I want in heaven! You're all I want on earth! When my skin sags and my bones get brittle, God is rock-firm and faithful." (LB) Psalms 73:26: "My health fails, my spirit droops, yet God remains. "You are the strength of my heart; You are mine forever!"

It has been said, "The enemy doesn't mind you talking about your faith as long as you don't live it." Faith can change any situation, no matter what it is. Lifting my heart to God in a moment of genuine faith in Him can quickly alter any circumstance. God is still on His throne. He can turn disaster and defeat into victory in a split second, if I trust Him. I don't want to wallow in self-pity and grief but I need your help; I hurt. Strengthen me that I may respond rightly to You. I don't want to be whimpering and weak but I do pray that You will use my life experiences for your glory. Psalms 73:21-24 (MSG), *"When I was beleaguered and bitter, totally consumed by envy, I was totally ignorant, a dumb ox in your very presence. I'm still in your presence, but you've taken my hand. You wisely and tenderly lead me, and then you bless me."* VS. 28, *"I've made Lord God my home. God, I'm telling the world what you do!"* You are not only all I need, and You are all I want in heaven or on earth; You are rock-firm and faithful!

JUNE 27
SEEK THE LORD

<u>Luke 11:9</u> (NKJV)

"Seek and you will find ..."

Oswald Chambers says: "Seek if you have not found. 'You ask and receive not, because you ask amiss.' If you ask for things from life instead of from God, you ask amiss. The more you focus on yourself, the less will you seek God. Seek, concentrate and you will find." We look at our creature comforts, our passions and pleasures and draw far too much satisfaction from them. Thus, sometimes they are removed so we can direct our attention and thoughts to Jesus. Our identity lies not in our accomplishments but in our relationship to our Lord. Regardless of yesterday, God can rearrange tomorrow in our favor if we are faithful to Him. Some relationships will never be fixed. Turn to the One who loves you. He is not limited by the past; He is only limited by your lack of faith and trust. Seek the Lord. *"You will find Him if you seek Him with all your heart and soul."* <u>Deuteronomy 4:29</u> (NKJV).

JUNE 28
DO NOT JUDGE OTHERS

<u>Hebrews 11:31</u> (NKJV)

"By faith the harlot Rahab did not perish with those who did not believe, when she had received the spies with peace."

We read in <u>Joshua 2:1</u> (NKJV), *"So they came to the house of a harlot named Rahab and lodged there."* In the ancient world there were two kinds of prostitutes ... those who engaged in sexual acts at the shrine of a god as an act of pagan worship and the others were simply those who sold sexual favors for money. It is useless to try to speculate which one she was; both were sinful. The scripture says the scouts went there; Rahab wasn't out beckoning them to come in. As a result of her courage and faith, we read that she and her entire household were saved when later the city was destroyed ... <u>Joshua 2:8-13</u>. Later she gets honorable mention in the Heroes of Faith outlined in <u>Hebrews 11</u>. Look at what she would have missed if she had turned them away. How many blessings do you imagine we miss because we don't respond to what we're exposed to? People cross our paths every day of our lives, some of them might be "scheduled" to change our destiny but we are oblivious to the opportunity. Rahab was a harlot, a nobody, an outcast; but because she was responsive to what God brought across her life, she became somebody known for all eternity. What can you learn from this? Hopefully, we learn not to judge others. God could have looked at what she was known as (a prostitute) but He looked at her heart and it was just waiting for an opportunity to be changed. What is He looking at in your heart today?

JUNE 29

HOW IS YOUR HEART TODAY

<u>Joshua 6:21</u> (NKJV)

"And they utterly destroyed all that was in the city, both man and woman, young and old, ox and sheep and donkey, with the edge of the sword."

Joshua's army utterly destroyed <u>all</u> that was in the city, both man and woman, young and old...<u>all but one family</u>. They were as safe as bugs in a rug, as if the blood was on the doorposts. There is not even a hint that the scouts did anything wrong in making Rahab, the harlot, the promise that she and her family would be safe, even though God had commanded the Israelites to <u>destroy all</u> the Canaanites. We are so amiss when we cluck our tongues over things that do not add up for us. *"God does what He sees needs doing ..."* <u>2 Samuel 10:12</u> (MSG). Your life is all about Him, not about you, you just need to let Him be in charge. This harlot was an exception to the rule; He can do that when He wants to. God can make exceptions. Rahab's life had been a mess but her heart was ready for change; her statements of faith in <u>Joshua 2:8-11</u> prove it. We need to respond to our life challenges as she did with courage and faith and be grateful for her example. Anyone can respond well, given the right environment. Acting in faith is called obedience. Have you had to move forward recently in something that needed added courage and strength? Knowing and speaking God's Words of faith are your best assets.

JUNE 30
SPREAD GOD A BANQUET OF PRAISE

<u>Psalms 50:8, 13, 15</u> (MSG)

"This is God, your God, speaking to you. If I get hungry, do you think I'd tell you? All creation and its bounty are mine. Spread for me a banquet of praise; serve High God a feast of kept promises. And call for help when you're in trouble. I'll help you and you'll honor me."

I spread you a table of praise; I praise my High God, magnificent in splendor! Would you feast or would you be apt to famine on my "kept promises?" You keep every promise You make to me; help me to keep those I make to You. I enjoy trying new recipes so help me create new praises and spread them before You as carefully as I set my table for guests. I spread a banquet of praise to you my Savior, King, Redeemer, God of the Angel Armies, Jehovah! I submit to you, whatever it takes to change me from what I am to what you want me to be. I am who You say I am. Oswald Chambers: "Beware of looking back to what you once were when God wants you to be something you've never been." People continually worry their lives away, trying to figure out why they suffer, why their life is so full of burdens and troubles. How different life would be if they would stop indulging in thinking only of themselves and what is wrong in their life but instead lift their daily experiences to God and praise Him. It is so much easier to praise Him than to try to reason out what worries you. Psalm 50:14-15 (MSG) says "*spread me a banquet of praise; serve High God a feast of kept promises. Call for help when you're in trouble, I'll help you.*"

JULY 1
WE CAN EXPERIENCE HIS HIDDEN SECRETS

Psalms 25:14a (NKJV)
> "*The secret of the Lord is with those who fear Him.*"

On the surface, God's dealings with His own children sometimes appear to be harsh and hidden. In faith, we look for "the hidden," for God's secret... that which is not seen on the surface. God may give us gifts that are wrapped in most unattractive paper—

we are to ignore the outside—because inside are treasures of <u>love</u>, <u>kindness</u> and <u>wisdom</u>. We are to receive what He sends and trust Him for the valuables inside because in time, we will experience His hidden secrets. If you have Christ as your Master, you can master any circumstance. Your situations can not only shape you but provide you with added resources for "what's next." Two years ago today I wrote in my journal regarding the loss of my husband: "There's no rug being hooked; no car being assembled; no candle in the making…all lay silent, just as he left them. All is totally silent except the screaming pain in my heart, can you hear it Lord? I know that You are using him for far better purposes today; thank You for that. Now, help me today, Lord, to make something for You out of what You have given me." Your love is not hidden; it is a revealed secret in my heart. You have awakened my spirit, help me to respond.

JULY 2
LEARN SOME NEW ABC'S

<u>Psalms 15: 1-5</u> (MSG)

"God, who gets invited to dinner at your place? How do we get on your guest list? Walk straight, act right, and tell the truth. Don't hurt your friend, don't blame your neighbor; despise the despicable. Keep your Word even when it costs you, make an honest living, and never take a bribe. You'll never get blacklisted if you live like this."

Oswald Chambers: "One life wholly devoted to God is more value to God than 100 lives simply awakened by His Spirit. God brings us to a standard of life by His grace and we are responsible for reproducing that standard in others." So often our lives do not tally with what the Lord has revealed to us, let the Son of Man arise in your heart! I try to find some new ABC's before I go to sleep at night, such as: **A** – I Admire you; **B** – I Belong to you; **C** – You Care for my soul; **D** – You are my Deliverer; **E** – You are Everything; **F** – You Favor me; **G** – Great is my God; **H** – Hallowed be Your Holy Name; **I** – I'm in You; **J** – You are Jehovah; **K** – King of Kings; **L** – Lord of Lords; **M** – Master of everything; **N** – No one like You; **O** – Omnipotent; **P** – Powerful; **Q** – You are a Quiet Spirit; **R** – You are Radiant; **S** – You are the Star of Bethlehem; **T** – I am Trusting You; **U** – You are unique; **V** – Victory through You; **W** – You are Wonderful; **X** – You are Extra- ordinary; **Y** – Yield to You; **Z** – Zealous for You! Just praise and give glory to God. Praising answers a lot of prayers. Praise when *"we walk straight, act right, tell the truth and keep our word"* both to God and to your neighbor!

JULY 3
THE ISSUE OF FORGIVENESS

Matthew. 6:14 (NKJV)

"For if you forgive men their trespasses, your heavenly Father will also forgive you."

You need to forgive for your sake. When you forgive, you set someone free…and that someone is you. If you wait until you "feel" like doing it, it will never happen. Forgiveness is a matter of choice; and it's a hard choice. You may even know that the person will turn around and do this again but you're not the Judge. When you walk in un-forgiveness, know this: There's more damage to the vessel in which un-forgiveness is stored than there is in the vessel into which it is poured. You need to be resolute when God speaks to you in

His Word; first to listen and then to do what He speaks. Act in faith immediately on what He says. Don't hesitate or you'll "reason" yourself out of it. Take the step necessary and make it impossible for you to reverse your decision. Walk in forgiveness and your heavenly Father will also forgive you.

JULY 4
CELEBRATE TODAY

Philippians 4:4-5 (MSG)

"Celebrate God all day, every day. I mean, revel in him! The Master is about to arrive. He could show up any minute!"

We have such a need in our land to "celebrate God all day, every day." A lot of celebration will be going on today and we are thankful for those who have come before us and defended our freedoms so that we may worship God in spirit and in truth. Brave men and women today our living in adverse situations so that we may have peace and enjoy life, family and friends here at home. Many have made plans today to picnic or cook out and enjoy fireworks later. But nothing could possibly compare to the great celebration when *"The Master arrives and He could show up any minute."* Think about it today as you go your way...He could intercept our plans with His own at any time. Psalms 91:16 (MSG), *"I'll rescue you, and then throw you a party. I'll give you a long life, and then give you a long drink of salvation."* Firecrackers can light up the sky, but Jesus can light up your life! Celebrate Jesus today, all day!

JULY 5
GOD'S NATURE IS TO LOVE US

Isaiah. 43:4 (LB)

"You are precious to me and honored and I love you."

God loves me not because I am loveable but because it is His nature to do so. Then He seems to say: "Love as I have loved you. I will bring any number of people around you whom you cannot even respect and you must exhibit My love to them as I have exhibited it to you." God has loved me to the uttermost and He sends me forth to love the same way. I get huffed because people are disagreeable...but I have to know how disagreeable I've been to Him. Keep going to the Word. Life includes a lot of discipline and we all go through many areas of training. Ignore what you see and what you feel...God's Word is the way it is. You have brought me through much heartache and sorrow, Lord; now bring me "into the knowledge of You." Teach, help, train, and encourage me to love others as you love me.

JULY 6
WE ALL GET PERPLEXED, PUSHED AND PERSECUTED

2 Corinthians 4:8-9 (NKJV)

"We are hard-pressed on every side, yet not crushed; we are perplexed, but not in despair; persecuted but not forsaken; struck down, but not destroyed."

Grow stronger. You must stop thinking like a victim. Stop expecting others to rescue you, feel sorry for you, or to reduce your stress levels...you're not helpless and your situation isn't hopeless. Invest your energy in what you can change, which is your attitude and your approach. It takes more energy to hang onto old habits and beliefs than to embrace new ones. When everything changes in your life, learn to adjust. You may not like the changes but you can learn a way to flow through them. *"We are perplexed but we don't give up and quit...we get knocked down but we get up again and keep going."* 2 Corinthians 4:8-9 (LB). Psalms 66:12 (NLT) states, *"... we went through the fire and the flood but in the end you brought us to a place of wealth and abundance."* Find a person who has gone through great conflict and you'll find a person at rest. Be encouraged! Psalms 91:15 (MSG) states, *"Call on me and I'll answer, be at your side in bad times!"* An untested person has no idea how to handle a crisis, much less a setback. When tragedy hits, our hearts are overwhelmed, but faith can lift our shattered hopes when we look to the One in whom we believe. We all are perplexed, pushed and persecuted, at times. It will not destroy you, but it will improve your relationship with the only One who can make it work for your good and not against you.

JULY 7
GOD WILL INCREASE YOUR STRENGTH

Isaiah 40:29 (NKJV)

"He gives power to the weak and to those who have no might, He increases strength."

We hate giving up things we do well, so we focus on 'doing things right' but not always doing the right things. It's great to be good at something but we need to reach out and learn new things.

We should be open to change...new strategies...focus on what God wants you to do. Don't fear when you enter a new situation. Our inclination is to slow down, proceed cautiously, play it safe, buy some time, thus we stall and fall behind. Help us Lord to trust You and move with You and not to drag our feet. Don't be overwhelmed but move in confidence and believe You. It is You who activates Your Word and *"gives power to the weak and to those who have no might, You increase their strength."* Help us to respond quickly. Instant obedience is the only kind there is. Delayed obedience is disobedience. Our inclination is always to ask 'why' and to have answers before obeying. Refuse to go there! If He leads you to it, He will lead you through it. Believe He will not only help you but increase your strength!

JULY 8
WE CAN TRUST HIS WORD

Deuteronomy 31:6 (NIV)

"Be strong and courageous. Do not be afraid or terrified because of them for the Lord your God goes with you. He will never leave you nor forsake you."

We fight Satan by knowing God's Word and knowing God's will...not only knowing it but standing on it and enforcing the terms God has already declared and put in place. John 8:32 (NLT) states, *"You will know the truth and the truth will set you free."* We are to know the truth and then trust God to do what He has said He will do. When God leads us through deep difficulties, go in confidence and never take your eyes off Him. Don't survey the opposition; it could cause you to fall apart. Pausing or hesitating could allow you to be overcome. Lift your eyes to the One who can and will take you to the other side. We can trust His Word.

JULY 9
WE ARE TO MANIFEST GOD'S GRACE

2 Peter 3:18 (NKJV)

"But grow in the grace and knowledge of our Lord and Savior Jesus Christ."

Oswald Chambers says: "Are you the same miserable crosspatch, set in your own way? Then it is a lie to say that God has saved you. You cannot do a thing for your salvation but you must do something to manifest it. You must work out what God has worked in. All of the Almighty God is ours in the Lord Jesus. He will tax the last grain of sand and the remotest star to bless us if we will obey Him. If we give way to self-pity and indulge in misery, we banish God's riches from our own lives and hinder others from entering into His provision. No sin is worse than the sin of self-pity because it obliterates God and puts self-interest on the throne. If the majesty, grace and power of God are not being manifested in us, God holds us responsible as He has made His grace to abound toward us. He, in turn, wants us to then to lavish His grace on others. Study His Word and obey what you learn; it is how we are enabled to manifest God's grace in our lives by working out what He has worked in.

JULY 10
GOD WILL USE YOU

Matthew 6:26, 28b-29 (NIV)

"Look at the birds of the air; they do not sow or reap or store away in barns, and yet your heavenly Father feeds them. Are you not much more valuable than they? See how the lilies of the field grow. They do not labor or spin. Yet I tell you that not even Solomon in his entire splendor was dressed like one of these."

The lilies of the field, the sea, the stars, air, sun, and moon are all on display in God's trophy room... He sustains them as they perform their ministries. We may want so much to be "something" but what we need most is simply to concentrate on God. We busy ourselves in doing for others when the only way to "be something" is to concentrate and believe Jesus, pay attention to Him. Let Him be manifested in you. The lilies of the field simply grow where they are planted. The people who influence us the most are not those who try to talk us to death but those who live their lives like the stars in the heavens and the lilies in the field, simple and unaffected. If you want to be used of the Lord, live in a right relationship with Jesus and then He will use you where He's planted you.

JULY 11
JESUS IS THE CENTERPIECE OF OUR LIFE

Hebrews 3:1b (MSG)

"Take a good hard look at Jesus. He's the centerpiece of everything we believe."

He is the center piece in the puzzle of life. If you would take a piece of faith, love, suffering, joy, desires, rejection, contentment, truth, grace, sorrow, endurance, conflict, heartache, emotions, grief and pain... fit them around the person of Jesus, you would have the complete puzzle of life itself. Everything fits in and within Him. In Him we live and move and have our being. I go with you, dear Jesus, I need you! I would like to pick and choose the pieces of the puzzle but I would probably omit the very ones You will use to make me more like You. I'd probably choose faith, joy, contentment, truth and love and someday, our life will certainly be like that, but we're not home yet. Pour Your Spirit into me today so you may disclose You to me and I won't disappoint and embarrass You. God is looking for just one man even, one God-ready woman ... Lord, help me to be ready for You today.

JULY 12
JOINT VENTURE AGREEMENT

2 Corinthians 4:8-10 (RSV)

"We are hard pressed on every side but not crushed; perplexed, but not driven to despair; persecuted but not forsaken; struck down, but not destroyed; always carrying in the body of the death of Jesus so that the life of Jesus may be manifested in us."

Our Joint Venture Agreement with the Lord should include this statement found in Joshua 24:15 (NLT), *"...as for me and my family, we will serve the Lord."* When entering a Joint Venture Agreement of life, part of that agreement is we will be pressed on every side (at times) but doesn't mean these things will crush us because God's Heavenly Police are on patrol and will make a way for you even in the worst scenarios. We are all perplexed by unfairness, things that simply don't add up...in our spiritual walk... 2+2 will not always tally out, but keep walking, God has a plan. We will be persecuted but we'll never be forsaken because His part of the Agreement is that He will never leave or forsake us. We get struck down but it is not fatal, you are not destroyed, just wounded. You can be overthrown but not overcome! Now get this, it's the most important part of the Agreement..."we will always carry in our body the death of Jesus so that the life of Jesus may be manifested (or revealed) in us. We don't even want to go there; we just want a fix. We all go through valleys and we think we can't stand it, but it is there that the life of Jesus comes to the surface and it is in that time, He helps us the most. We want deliverance without the struggle and life is not like that. Too many times we surrender to defeat or else we give up and become bitter over what we think it not right. In a Joint Venture Agreement, the cost is always spelled out. God has nothing worth having that can be easily gained. Heaven has nothing cheap for sale. The cost of your redemption cost God everything. Anything worth having will cost you plenty. Hard times and difficult situations are class rooms for learning and developing Godly character. When they come on us, we are to go forward toward them in confidence, know God is already there. Stand firm, you will not be overcome!

JULY 13
THE BITTER BECOMES SWEET

John 18:11 (NIV)

"Jesus commanded Peter, "Put your sword away! Shall I not drink the cup the Father has given me?"

166

Peter had just hacked off the ear of the high priest's servant as Jesus was being arrested. Jesus was willing to drink the bitter cup of heartache and sorrow that was to follow. God may use many strokes of heartache and disappointing circumstances in order to get you into the best image. He can visualize what you need in order to receive His gifts in the right spirit. If your soul is indifferent, you will not receive the bitter gifts and will let them pass by; hence nothing good will ever come of them. God's intent behind any sorrow is to let His love be manifested in blessings your human heart can never imagine. When you don't receive pain, you become dry inside and often begin to question and wonder why you are experiencing such trauma. Open your heart to suffering, it will accomplish more good than you can imagine. In the Old Testament, the people found their drinking water was bitter but when the prophet threw a branch into the water, the bitter water became sweet. Whatever God brings into your life, receive it, as His plan is always good; the bitter will become sweet when filtered through His love.

JULY 14
CALL UPON THE LORD

Psalms 107:28-29 (NIV)

"Then they cried out to the Lord in their trouble, and he brought them out of their distress. He stilled the storm to a whisper; the waves of the sea were hushed."

"In the battle, do you feel alone? Remember at 'Wit's End Corner' is just where God's power is shown. Are you standing at Wit's End Corner? Then you're just in the very spot to learn the wondrous resources of Him who fails you not," Antoinette Wilson. When we cry to the Lord in our distress, He brings us out! He can calm the storms that blow over you just as He calmed the waves of the sea. A closer look sometimes reveals what we perceived as a storm is more akin to showers of blessings. You worry and fret as if you are Captain of your life. Do you think that all the commotion and uproar of this life is evidence that God has left His throne? Well, He hasn't. Our Jehovah is still Master. Feelings of hopelessness and fear will wither your heart and sear you against sensing His Presence and blessings. It also causes you to exaggerate your troubles and makes them harder to bear. His encouragement is to, "*Cry out to Me in your trouble*," and He will answer you!

JULY 15
THE PEOPLE SUNG AND DUG

Numbers 21:17 (NKJV)
> "*Spring up, O well, sing about it!*"

God told Moses to gather the people together and He would give them water. And the people begin to sing. They stood on the burning sand and sang a song of praise as noted in Numbers 21:17 (NKJV), "*Spring up O well, all of you sing to it,*" and as they sang and dug, gurgling water came up, an underground stream that had been there all the time. In their thirst, they would have passed over it had they not sung and dug...they left off whining and complaining and found water in the wilderness and streams in the desert. Nothing pleases God as much as praise. Trials in our life are blessings in disguise and oh how we squirm and complain while waiting for God to accomplish something. Praise Him with everything in you for what is right and praise Him for what isn't, because He will make it right. He does all things well, in time; our part is to praise Him regardless.

JULY 16
GOD HAS CHOSEN YOU

Isaiah 48:10 (NKJV)
"I have chosen you in the furnace of affliction."

Genesis 26:24 (NKJV)
"Do not be afraid, for I am with you."

God has chosen me, whatever state I find myself, He has chosen me for it. If it's the Valley of Tears, then He is standing by. Whatever my trial, He is with me; His Presence never leaves. He is my comfort and safety. Poverty and devastation may walk through my door but God lives in my house. Sickness may penetrate my body but Jesus lives within me. My heart burns with pain but His Word is like a soft rain to put out the fire. Afflictions, heartache and pain are a part of the life He has chosen for me. I will experience nothing that doesn't fulfill some part of His plan. My purpose and communion with Him transcends time and any circumstance I encounter. Do I always respond rightly? No, but that doesn't change His Word that says, *"All of His Words are right; everything He does is worthy of our trust,"* Psalms 33:4 (LB). I want to fulfill His joy in me and experience what He has chosen for me. I want to be willing to do what Oswald Chambers recommends: "Put yourself in the place where God's almighty power will come through you." That

169

"place" is not of my choosing, it's His choice, but I do have the promise that is He is with me.

JULY 17
FOR HE IS LORD OF LORDS AND KING OF KINGS

Revelation 17:14 (NKJV)

"They will make war against the Lamb but the Lamb will overcome them for He is Lord of lords and King of kings and those with Him are called, chosen and faithful."

What a wonder You are...Lord God Almighty! I look at my creature comforts, passions and pleasures and draw far too much satisfaction from them. Sometimes You remove them so I will direct my attention and thoughts toward You. My identity lies not in my accomplishments but in my relationship with You. Thank you, Jesus for what You want to disclose to me today about You. Regardless of yesterday, You will rearrange tomorrow in my favor, if I am faithful. Some earthy relationships will never be fixed but my choice is to turn to the One who does love me. You are not limited by my past; You are only limited by my lack of faith and trust in You. A hundred years from now, we will all be alive, either in heaven or in hell, but every one of us we will all be living according to our relationship with Jesus. He is King of kings and Lord of lords! Use today to be strengthened in Him.

JULY 18

ABIDE IN ME

John 15:4 (MSG)

"Live in Me. Make your home in Me just as I do in you."

God will not make you obedient; He will not make you think like He does. We are the ones who need to bring every thought captive to the obedience of Christ. Adrian Rodgers said, "Bible study will give you knowledge of God; obedience lets you know God." Obedience and abiding is my job and it's what lets me see what needs to be done. The people who started the Salvation Army had the compassion to do so when they saw pup after pub in London with steps so little children could step up to the bar and order drinks. Now the organization ministers to 3 million people in 91 countries. How much do you care? What we read in Scripture is, Abraham entered into what God was doing for him and that was the turning point. He trusted God to set him right instead of trying to be right on his own. Sometimes you see that the job is too big for you, that it's something only God can do and you trust Him to do it, knowing you could never do it for yourself no matter how hard and long you worked. Trusting-Him-to-do-it is what gets you set right with God, by God. It only happens in your life when you are "living (abiding) in Him" and being obedient to what He is speaking into your life.

JULY 19
YOUR BROOK MAY EVAPORATE SOMETIME

1 Kings 17:7 (NIV)

"Sometime later the brook dried up because there had been no rain in the land."

Elijah had followed the Lord's directive to go the Kerith Ravine when He said, "You will drink from the brook and I have ordered the ravens to feed you there." All was well until slowly the brook began to dry up. Sometimes we experience disaster slowly and sometimes it comes suddenly and unexpectedly. Temptation is to wonder if we heard God rightly. Adversity causes us to look at our circumstances; faith causes us to put God between us and the problem so we're looking at Him instead of the circumstance. The brook dwindled to a thread of water; the birds flew away, now what? It wasn't until every scrap of evidence that God was with him was gone that he received any further direction from the Lord. Mostly, we don't stick around long enough to receive further instructions. Once the food and water was gone, we would have devised some plan of our own, asked God to bless it, and been on our way. We are too impatient to wait for God's deliverance. And what is the result? Many steps have to be retraced, many tears of repentance and much time wasted. It took time for the brook to dry up and it took time for God to lead him to Zarephath (his next assignment), where a widow was awaiting his help. Usually, we get "fixed" when we assist someone else. So the next time, you run dry, look for someone who needs your help. Just know we all experience the evaporation of the brook at some point in our lives, but God always has something new ahead.

JULY 20

GOD IS IN EVERY PART OF YOUR LIFE

Psalms 121:7-8 (MSG)

"God guards you from every evil; he guards your very life. He guards you when you leave and when you return, he guards you now, and he guards you always."

Psalms 121:7-8 (NKJV)

"The Lord shall preserve you from all evil. He shall preserve your soul. The Lord shall preserve your going out and your coming in from this time forth and even forever more."

"One of the bad habits we pick up early is separating our lives, things and people, into the secular and sacred. We think the secular is what we're in charge of: our jobs, our time, our entertainment/ social life. The sacred is what God's in charge of: worship, Bible, heaven, hell, church and prayers. We set aside a sacred place to honor God and keep Him there, leaving us free to have the final say in everything else! Absolutely everything takes place on Holy ground. The way we make our money and the way we spend it; the way we feel and act in our hearts and home; the politics we embrace; the catastrophes we endure; the people we hurt and the people we help—nothing is exempt from the rule of God and nothing is hidden from the rule of God and nothing escapes His purposes," Eugene Peterson. God is an intricate part of everything that concerns our life. He doesn't run ahead of you and slip into a phone booth and change into His Superman suit just before you walk through the church doors. Our tendency is to take Him to church and tell him to stay there. He truly "sees you when you're sleeping; He knows when you're awake; He knows when you've been good or bad" and loves you anyway! He is in every nook and cranny of your life and wants to be a part of all of it. Nothing is unusable by God...everything, everybody, and every mess can be remade. He will preserve your life every time you go out and every time you come in, His Word says so!

JULY 21
THE INSIDE/OUTSIDE OF YOUR LIFE

Job 1:1 (NKJV)

"Job was upright, blameless, feared God and shunned evil."

That scripture describes what was on the inside of Job (it is so important to want to be bigger and better on the inside than on the outside). In VS. 2-3...He had 7 sons, 3 daughters, 7,000 sheep, 3,000 camels, 500 yoke of oxen, 500 female donkeys and a very large household. He was the greatest man in all the land. That was what was on the outside. God was impressed *with what was on the inside and pointed out to Satan in* VS.8, *"Have you considered my servant Job, that there is no one like him in all the earth, a blameless and upright man who fears God and shuns evil?"* Does God even mention one thing that Job had on the outside? No! Because God's interested in what's on the inside. VS. 9-11, Satan doesn't mention anything but what he had on the outside (his possessions); because that's his domain and it's exactly how he operates in our lives (through worldly possessions). Satan believes Job is big on the inside because of what he has on the outside and says in VS.11, *"You stretch out Your hand and touch all that he has and he'll curse you to your face."* We see it every day as people turn away from God because it; and that's where losses come from... Satan exercises his powers of evil in this world and people blame God. Job lost every outside thing he had, including his children. When you get stripped of your outside possessions, what do you look like inside? It would be great if God would be impressed and see us as upright, blameless, fearing Him and shunning evil! Read the Book of Job and learn how to do this.

JULY 22

INSIDE/OUTSIDE (CONTINUED)

Acts 8:18 (NKJV)

"Simon the Sorcerer said to Peter, Give me this power that on whom I lay hands may receive the Holy Spirit..."

Here's how we tend to live our life..."*give me." The son said to the Father, give me the portion of goods that belong to me,"* Luke 15:12. The hope of every parent alive is that the child will outgrow this someday. The baby in the cradle reaches out so you will give to them; before they can even speak, they have the "give me" syndrome. So much so that children today grow up and take from the parents. A man goes into marriage so that a woman will "give him" what he needs. A woman does the same thing. In counseling, when the outside and the inside needs are not being fulfilled, the most frequent phrase is, "He/She is not meeting my needs biologically, physically, or spiritually." We all want to be recognized. We're ambitious. Simon the Sorcerer wanted to receive the Holy Spirit because he wanted to feel significant and be recognized. Please listen: Only God can make you happy. We look to people; it's not there. Psalms 139:23 (NKJV), *"Search me, O God, and know my heart."* Pride and insecurity are what stop you from searching and growing. We become un-teachable, unreachable, unsearchable when we stop searching for God and listening to Him. Be willing to be as the Prodigal and say to the Lord, *"Make me like one of your hired servants;"* i.e., fit for the Master's use. And what are the results? God blessed the latter days of Job more than his beginning. In fact, He doubled everything except his children. Why would He double the livestock and not his sons and daughters? (Half of his sons and daughters are already in heaven)! According to Job 1, *"he would rise early in the morning and sanctify them and offer burnt offerings according to the number of them all."* Job had his inside/outside life in order. That was his story and he stuck to it! He got double for his trouble. How about you? Don't you want to be bigger on the inside than what is seen on the outside?

JULY 23
LEARN TO BE BOLD

Isaiah 41:23 (NKJV)

"For I the Lord your God will hold your right hand saying to you, 'Fear Not, I will help you."

One of the attributes of a true Christian character is to encourage and lift up people and to not be afraid to do it. Andy Stanley said he brought a Bible, put it in a plastic bag, walked into a Beauty Salon and shyly/hesitantly put it on the counter in front of the beautician, his friend. Her customer said, "What's in the bag?" She took it out, "Oh, a Bible, want me to mark some verses for you?" The next customer, who came in, picked up the Bible and read out loud the marked verse! The third customer was a staunch 80 year old woman who commented on the underlined verse and then later asked the beautician if she'd like to receive Christ and the two of them went back into the closet where they kept towels and supplies and the woman accepted Christ. Andy said, "I was timid and hesitant; these women were BOLD and God worked!" We need to know He will do what He says He will do..."*Fear not, I will help you.*" Help us today to be bold to the opportunities He provides.

JULY 24
THE WORD OF THE LORD

John 6:63 (NKJV)

"*It is the Spirit who gives life, the flesh profits nothing. The Words that I speak to you are Spirit and they are life.*"

John 6:63 (MSG), "*The Spirit can make life. Sheer muscle and willpower don't make anything happen. Every Word I've spoken to you is a Spirit-Word, and so it is life-making.*" 1 Thessalonians 2:12 (LB), "*That your daily lives should not embarrass God but bring joy to Him who invited you into His holy Kingdom to share His glory.* VS.13 (RSV), "*When you received the Word of God which you heard from us you accepted it, not as the Word of man but as what it really is, the Word of God, which is at work in you believers.*" (LB), "*It changed your lives when you believed it.*" We are to live and move and have our being in Him and His Word. Don't try to separate Him in "churchy" and secular activity; He is in all of your life. God is in you; He's with you when you walk through the grocery store just as much as when you walk through the door of the church. You might wish He wasn't with you in some of the places you go, but He's there! You only have one life and it's all lived out with Him in it. How can you be so utterly unbelieving when God is in and around everything?   In tribulation, slander, misunderstandings, devastation, God is there.   Begin and end your day in His Word.   It will change your life when you believe the Bible was actually written for you!

JULY 25
SPEAK A WORD OF PRAISE

Psalms 50:8,12 (MSG)

"This is God, your God speaking to you…spread for me a banquet of praise…"

If God says He wants to be praised, how much more we stand in need of it! If you're thinking of it, don't be selfish and take people for granted…tell them! It is so much easier to find fault, you have no problem spitting that one out! Our Words are so influential. Even what you think drops down into your own heart and eventually into your spirit.   Think of how much good that can be for you, then consider the damnation it is to yourself when you're condemning someone else.   Don't want to praise someone because it could cause pride? Jesus hailed Nathaniel with, *"Here's a true Israelite in whom there is nothing false."* Believe it, more people die of broken hearts than ever die from swelled heads. Give someone a shout of praise today. If you shock them to death, at least they'll die happy! Speak God's Word into someone's heart today, it could mean everlasting life to them. God says it fulfills His joy when you do!

JULY 26

BE BLESSED BY THE LORD

Psalms 84:5 (MSG)

"And how blessed all those in whom you live, whose lives become roads you travel. VS. 10, *One day spent in your house, this beautiful place of worship, beats thousands spent on Greek island beaches. I'd rather scrub floors in the house of my God than be honored as a guest in the palace of sin."*

You need to love more people than just those in your church family. Your neighbor may be hard to love indeed as they usually don't love you, serve you, or even appreciate you. Jesus said to love them without expecting anything in return. Don't just be concerned with only your agenda. We are to be salt (putting flavor in their lives) and we are to be a light (dispelling darkness). We need to invest our lives in what God values. And, we need to have an interest in *"all those in whom you live, whose lives become roads you travel."* It easier to do when we've spent time in His Word and in His house..."*one day spent there beats thousands spent on Greek island beaches."* Scrubbing the floor of His house is better than being an honored guest in a palace of sin. Worshipping God enables and equips us to not only tolerate our neighbor but to love them. Do this and be blessed by the Lord.

JULY 27

ARE YOU GETTING IN ON THE BEST

2 Corinthians 4:10-12 (MSG)

"...we're not sure what to do, but we know that God knows what to do; we've been spiritually terrorized but God hasn't left our side; we've been thrown down but we haven't broken. ...what Jesus did among them, he does in us—he lives! Our lives are at constant risk for Jesus' sake, which makes Jesus' life all the more evident in us. While we're going through the worst, you're getting in on the best."

If I allow it, something at every turn will rob me of victory and peace of mind. When under attack, I need to exhibit faith in the power of Almighty God to deliver. Faith can change anything, no matter what. It is still Your throne, O Lord; and You can turn it all into victory in a split second. I trust you and will abide by your decision in knowing how best to demonstrate Your love and Your power and how to bring glory to You. My faith is in you, God-of-the-Angel Armies. *"Because when all is said and done, the last word is, "Immanuel--God-With-Us,"* Isaiah. 8:10 (MSG). In the darkest part of my life, God works. Do I have faith to see but I'm not yet seeing? There may be a great occurring in my life when things seem to be the darkest. There may be no evidence but I know God works in the night, as *"to You, the night shines as bright as the day,"* Psalms. 139 (LB). All I have to remember is that yes, He lives..."what He did among them, He does in us, He lives! You have lifted, redeemed and empowered me to live out my life according to how You view it. You went through the worst, so that I might get in on the best.

JULY 28
WRITE DOWN HIS ANSWERS

Philippians 4:6 (LB)

"Don't worry about anything; instead pray about everything; tell God your needs and don't forget to thank him for his answers."

We need to keep tabs on what we're asking God for. That's why it's good to write out your requests. When you were in school, sometimes you got a "star" for good performance, but sometimes your name stayed on the blackboard for a long time with nothing. If a farmer plants a crop, he frequently checks to see if anything is coming forth. When a hunter shoots his game, he goes to see if he hit or missed what he targeted. You observe your children to see if they've progressed in what you're trying to teach them. Shouldn't you do the same thing with your prayers? Under the influence of the Holy Spirit, every prayer gets answered in some way. Pray in faith and according to God's will in the Name of Jesus and prayers will be answered. Sometimes we may not discern the approach...sometimes it's not what we expected but it was God's answer to what you requested. Give God time to act. It takes time for us to honor God with our faith and still remain confident and be accepting of His decisions. It takes time for Him to develop character and steadfastness in us. His reasons for "delays" are always in our best interests because He knows what's best for us at all times. Keep records and when you know He has answered, record that as well. It is so important to thank Him for His answers. Turn to the One who loves you, the One who has no limitations.

JULY 29

TO THE WIDOW, WIDOWER OR DIVORCEE

Isaiah 54:2 (RSV)

"Enlarge the place of your tent, and let the curtains of your habitations be stretched out; hold not back, lengthen your cords and strengthen your stakes. VS. 4-7, *"Fear not, for you will not be ashamed; be not confounded, for you will not be put to shame; for you will forget the shame of your youth and the reproach of your widowhood you will remember no more. For your Maker is your husband, the Lord of hosts is his name; and the Holy One of Israel is your Redeemer, the God of the whole earth he is called. For the Lord has called you, like a wife forsaken and grieved in spirit, like a wife of youth when she is cast off, says your God. For a brief moment I forsook you, but with great compassion I will gather you."* VS. 10, *"For the mountains may depart and the hills be removed, but my steadfast love shall not depart from you and my covenant of peace shall not be removed, says the Lord, who has compassion on you."* VS. 17, *no weapon formed against you shall prosper and you shall confute every tongue that rises against you in judgment."*

Hebrews 12:12-13 (LB)

"So take a new grip with your tired hands, stand firm on your shaky legs and mark out a straight smooth path for your feet so that those who follow you though weak and lame, will not fall and hurt themselves but become strong."

If you have been ravaged by divorce or suffered the loss of your mate, I can tell you that it is worth your time to not only read these verses, but to memorize them. The Word of God is a powerful asset in helping you cope with the rejection and misunderstanding of people who once were your friend but when tragedy came, tucked tail and ran. "For your Maker is your husband. The Holy One of Israel is your Redeemer; the God of the whole earth He is called." I wrote in my margin of my Bible by this verse, "I hob-nob with the Elite!" God loves you with a steadfast love and His compassion is all over you. Nothing that is formed against you will come to fruition and every slanderous tongue spoken in judgment about you, you yourself can confute! So just get a firm grip with your tired hands and stand firm on even those shaky legs, focus your eyes on Jesus, let Him set the pace, mark the path and follow hard after Him. There will be those who will rise and fall because of how you respond. You can do this. Trust me, I know.

JULY 30
DESIRE HIM

Psalms 73:25 (MSG)

"You're all I want in heaven! You're all I want on earth! When my skin sags and my bones get brittle, God is rock-firm and faithful."

Our Heavenly Father knows how needy we are and our greatest need is His Presence. If we ask for things from life instead of from God, we ask amiss. The more you realize "yourself," the less you will seek from Him. Do you seek Him with your whole heart? Seek, concentrate and you will find. "Experience is a gateway (an opening), not an end. Beware of building your faith on experience. You can never give another person what you have found but you can make him homesick for what you have." Oswald Chambers. Die to self is genuine brokenness. When self is crushed, it afflicts the heart and conquers the mind. Don't be part of the problem by being immature, be part of the solution. Pray, walk and talk God's Word and believe in His Presence. Don't try to take the leading role in your relationship with Him, it won't work. That's His role and He will not give it to you. Try saying, "You're all I want in heaven and you're all I want on earth" over and over to yourself and out loud today and it matters not whether you are young or old, you will find He is rock-firm and faithful! You will also find that, "He performs the Words of His servants." Speak His Word; it's as powerful as if He is speaking it.

JULY 31
YAH, THE LORD, IS MY STRENGTH AND SONG

Isaiah 12:2 (NKJV)

"Behold God is my salvation, I will trust and not be afraid; for YAH, the Lord, is my strength and song; He also has become my salvation."

"Great faith is exhibited not so much in doing, as it is in suffering" Charles Parkhurst. John 18:11 (NKJV) states, *"...shall I not drink the cup the Father has given me?"* Jesus asked the question and I need to inquire the same. The cup is bitter at times and others, sweet, because You have stirred the contents with Your own finger. I have the tendency to gulp the sweet, and gag on the bitter. But You in Your loving kindness have proportioned and predetermined the contents of my cup. *YAH, the Lord, is my strength and song; He has become my salvation.* Teach me, Lord, Your way. It lies within me to do almost anything to avoid pain; yet it is my best teacher, the conduit to You. The things that are most precious to me today come by way of tears and pain. Hard times and difficulties challenge my energy but also bring out the strongest qualities of the soul. It is the <u>weights</u> that keep a grandfather clock ticking. It is God's choice to use opposition as a means of showing Himself strong; and in doing so, *He has become my salvation.*

AUGUST 1
USE YOUR VOICE FOR JESUS

<u>Luke 7:28</u> (NKJV)

"For I say to you, among those born of woman, there is not a greater prophet than John the Baptist."

So many of you live what you consider to be a mundane life, you see yourself as being almost inconspicuous, non-existent when it comes to having special talent or abilities. Mediocrity seems to be your measuring stick. You need to take a second look at what Jesus has given you. For one thing: He's given you a voice, and speech itself can give you a great life! John the Baptist was just "a voice crying in the wilderness." John never performed a miracle but he used his voice to be "a witness to the Light" and it caused others to think about the One he spoke of. You can have a GREAT life if you just do what he did, speak of Jesus to someone, say some Words, and share a simple truth about Christ. You don't know it could be that something you say would be the very thing that causes someone to first think about Jesus and then later come to know Him as Savior. That is NOT mediocrity, that's greatness where it really counts—God's eternal kingdom! Jesus evaluated it like this: *"Among those born of woman, there is no one greater than*

John the Baptist." Here's the truth: God didn't make ANY mediocre people, use your voice to speak His Words today!

AUGUST 2
HAVE FAITH IN HIS WORD

<u>Judges 6:17-18</u> (NKJV)

"Then he said to Him, If now I have found favor in Your sight, then show me a sign that it is You who talk with me. Do not depart from here, I pray, until I come to You and bring out my offering and set it before You."

It's the truth that fact is more interesting than fiction could ever be, and the Bible proves it. The Lord had just told Gideon that he would defeat all of the Midianites as if they were one man and Gideon asks for a sign to prove it. Then he asks the Angel of the Lord to wait while he prepares an offering of a young goat and makes a loaf of bread from a half bushel of flour (want to think of how long that might have taken?) When he presented it, the Angel stretched out the tip of the stick he was holding and touched the meat and the bread and it was instantly burned up. That seems to have changed the whole scenario for Gideon and as a result, he obeyed, and God granted him victory over the Midianites. Gideon's faith was genuine but it was imperfect. Faith gained through signs is credited to feelings instead of trusting what God has spoken. Greater blessing is experienced when we believe without experiencing any emotion or feeling. Originally, God had told him that He would give him victory over his enemy but he wanted to see proof of it before proceeding. Are we like that? We need to believe what God has spoken is the way that it is.

AUGUST 3

THE EAR-MAKER HEARS AND THE EYE-SHAPER SEES

Psalms 94:8-12 (MSG)

"...Do you think Ear-Maker doesn't hear, Eye-Shaper doesn't see? Do you think the trainer of nations doesn't correct, the teacher of Adam doesn't know? God knows, all right—knows your stupidity, sees your shallowness. How blessed the man you train, God, the woman you instruct in your Word. VS. 18-19, If God hadn't been there for me, I never would have made it. The minute I said, "I'm slipping, I'm falling," your love, God, took hold and held me fast. When I was upset and beside myself, you calmed me down and cheered me up."

Just remember God makes no mistakes. The Eye-Shaper sees all and He is looking for people who are willing to serve out their life in hidden obscure places from the sight of all others, yet in full view of heaven. The day will come when they will be rewarded. The Ear-Maker hears every Word of encouragement you speak to a hurting spirit. Let God bless and instruct you in His Word, it is His delight to do so and certainly to your enrichment. If you are in conflict, stand where you are and let the Lord uphold you. Stand firm and true to Him. God brought you here to this place for a purpose; He has chosen you for this experience. *"The minute I said, I'm slipping, I'm falling, your love, God, took hold and held me fast."* Whether you're in the fight or just on lookout, the *"teacher of Adam knows how prone we are to be stupid and shallow"* but He also knows how to deliver you.

AUGUST 4
YOU'RE IN TRAINING

Hebrews 12:1-3 (MSG)

"...Strip down, start running—and never quit...Keep your eyes on Jesus, who both began and finished this race we're in. Study how he did it. Jesus Christ never lost sight of where he was headed—that exhilarating finish with God—he could put up with anything along the way: Cross, shame, whatever. And now he's there, in the place of honor, right alongside God. When you find yourself flagging in your faith, go over that story again, item by item, that long litany of hostility he plowed through. That will shoot adrenaline into your souls! VS. 6-11: God is educating you, that's why you must never drop out. He's treating you as dear children. This trouble you're in isn't punishment; its training, the normal experience of children. Only irresponsible parents leave children to fend for themselves...While we were children, our parents did what seemed best to them. But God is doing what is best for us, training us to live God's holy best. At the time, discipline isn't much fun. It always feels like it's going against the grain. Later, of course, it pays off handsomely, for it's the well trained who find themselves mature in their relationship with God."

Our period of "training" is often tedious and painful, but nothing compared to *"that long litany of hostility Jesus plowed through."* He knew, *"later, it pays off handsomely!"* And the very best part is having a thriving and *"mature relationship with God."*

AUGUST 5
RECEIVE THE GRACE OF GOD

2 Corinthians 6:1 (KJV)

"We...beseech you that ye receive not the grace of God in vain."

What is the grace of God but the overflowing favor of God flowing into our undeserving lives? It's like His faithfulness, it's new every day. The grace you received yesterday needs to be renewed today. I draw on your grace now. Let circumstances do its thing. May I be aware that past hurts plague and stunt my relationship with everyone I know. Every bit of sorrow in my life is traced to unbelief...not believing the past is past and forgiven by You. The present is available with power, what am I doing with it? The future is bright because of Your total grace and faithfulness, which never changes with my moods. You stand firm and rock solid. You, Yourself made believing a condition for receiving and as Giver of all and everything; we look to You, Jesus. We ask a thousand times, "how can that possibly be?" There's only one answer, it can only "be" by the grace of Almighty God. He's the Giver, we're the receiver; help us not to receive His grace in vain.

AUGUST 6
SOME THINGS I CAN'T CHANGE OR REARRANGE

Luke 22:32 (NKJV)

"But I have prayed for you that your faith should not fail..."

Use me, Lord, let it be You. Mostly, I try to take the leading role in our relationship with You and that doesn't work. That's Your role and You will not give it to me. You give the instructions; I need to follow; even when I don't understand them. Why should it take You so long to do stuff? Unanswered questions create trust in You and keep my faith growing. You have a plan and a purpose; I just need to believe that what You're doing is best. If I'm waiting, it's for me to reach a new level of maturity so You can release a new level of blessing. You will not make me think like You. I have to do it myself. It's up to me to bring every thought into captivity and obedience to You. There are some things I can't change or rearrange, and circumstances will change, You don't. Trust in Jesus, whatever is happening. The good news is, *"You pray for me that my faith should not fail."* Thank you, Lord!

AUGUST 7
GOD CAN DO ANYTHING

Matthew19:26 (NKJV)

"But Jesus looked at them and said to them, With men this is impossible, but with God, all things are possible."

Prayer alone does not bring down answers from Your throne, but the earnest prayer of one who believes, gets answers. Faith is the communication link between heaven and earth. It links you to God and clothes you with the power of Jehovah God. Faith is what assures you that each of His attributes will be used in your defense, helping you to defy the gates of hell and walk on the necks of your enemy. Everything is possible to one who believes. Good advice: don't be discouraged when "flesh acts like flesh," because it happens! Don't be part of the problem by being immature, be part of the solution. Pray, walk, and talk God's Word and believe in His power and desire to deliver you. Complete gentleness comes only through endurance and when self is crushed, it will afflict your heart, but it will also conquer your mind. Just remind yourself…"*with men this is impossible but with God, all things are possible."*

AUGUST 8
DON'T BE CRITICAL

Matthew 7:1-3 (MSG)

"Don't pick on people, jump on their failure, and criticize their faults— unless, of course, you want the same treatment. That critical spirit has a way of boomeranging. It's easy to see a smudge on your neighbor's face and be oblivious to the ugly sneer on your own."

If I observe a speck in someone else's eye, it means I must have a beam in my own. Each and every time I judge, I only condemn myself. Stop measuring others; there is always a fact to be considered that I know nothing about. God may give me a "spiritual spring cleaning" and when He does, there is no pride left as no dirt gets missed! It is so true: *"That critical spirit has a way of boomeranging;"* as it comes back to me! I could never despair over anyone after becoming aware of what lies within me apart from the grace of God. Peterson goes on to say in VS. 5, *"Wipe that ugly sneer off your own face and you might be fit to offer a washcloth to your neighbor!"*

AUGUST 9
LISTEN FOR A WORD BEHIND YOU

Isaiah 30:21 (NKJV)

"Your ears shall hear a Word behind you saying, this is the way, walk in it, when you turn to the right hand or whenever you turn to the left."

We need to hear what the Lord is speaking into our lives and we do that by having listening spiritual ears, as we learn to recognize His voice. We will have all eternity to enjoy our victories but only one life in which to win them. We think our service is "what we do;" Jesus calls service what we are to Him, not what we do for Him. In other words, our relationship to Him is more important than anything else and if we are responding to what He speaks into our lives, we'll enjoy a close relationship. Sometimes that is perfected more when things don't change than when they do; we need him more when life doesn't add up than when it does. We need to wait to hear that voice behind us when healing doesn't come, pain doesn't stop, families fall apart, wicked get their way, the good die, comfort is not to be found, and sin seems to reign. What we do is to persevere until we're done! And, don't forget to keep listening; continue to believe you will receive what God has promised you.

AUGUST 10
THE LORD IS MY STRENGTH

Exodus15:2 (NKJV)

"The Lord is my strength and song, and He has become my salvation."

Psalms 68:28 (NKJV), *"Your God has commanded your strength."* Deuteronomy 33:25 (NKJV), *"...as your days, so shall your strength be."* Ephesians 3:16 (NKJV), *"...that He would grant you according to the riches of His glory to be strengthened with might through His Spirit in the inner man."*

The strength He gives is continuous for He is a source of power I cannot exhaust. The Lord is my strength to go up; the Lord is my strength to go down, the Lord is my strength to sit still. The Lord is the strength I simply do not have. *"The Lord is my strength and song and has become my salvation."* He hasn't just become my salvation in redeeming my soul, but He salvages and saves me from that which would devour my spirit and destroy my body now. God is my salvation both in this life and the next. Use every Word of that verse to gain strength...do it in song. Raise your voice in a song of praise; He loves it and you will be strengthened by doing so.

AUGUST 11
GOD WILL ATTEND TO THE VOICE OF MY PRAYER

Psalms 66:18-20 (NKJV)

"If I regard iniquity in my heart, The Lord will not hear. But certainly God has heard me; He has attended to the voice of my prayer, Blessed be God, Who has not turned away my prayer, nor His mercy from me!"

Nothing lies beyond the reach of prayer except that which is outside the will of God Almighty. In Your Name and by Your Word, may Your will be done in our lives. Who am I, God that You would hear me but I am your servant who needs and loves you. You know me just as I am. Let circumstances do its thing; I draw on your grace now. The past is past and forgiven by You. The present is available with power...what am I doing with it? The future is bright because of Your total faithfulness. "You yourself made believing a condition for receiving and as Giver of all and everything, You set Your own terms for the gifts we receive," Samuel Hart. You can ask a thousand times a day, how can that be, and there is only one answer...God! God will not turn away from me. Prayer with faith brings the omnipotence of God right to me! He will attend to the voice of my prayer.

AUGUST 12
EVERY OPPORTUNITY COMES WITH ADVERSITY

Exodus1:12 (NKJV)

"But the more they afflicted them, the more they multiplied and grew."

There certainly is a measure of security in playing it safe; nothing lost, but nothing is won either. True, you are completely safe in the boat, but wouldn't it be better to almost drown than to NEVER experience God's working power in your life? Adversity is like yeast; when the heat is turned up, it rises, the warmer it gets, the more the dough rises to the top. Every opportunity God gives you comes with something that will come against you, and it's up to you to rise above it. When the Israelites were in Egypt, the more they were afflicted, the more they multiplied and grew. Bad times will strengthen your faith, sometimes more than good ones do. The harsher the Egyptians made the lives of the Hebrews, the more they flourished. VS. 14, *"they made their lives bitter."* Later God had them eat something bitter with the Passover meal so that they might remember the bitterness of this time in Egypt. God did deliver them out of their troubles and He will deliver you!

AUGUST 13
HIS GRACE WILL ALWAYS BE ENOUGH

2 Corinthians 12:9 (NKJV)

"And, He said to me, "My grace is sufficient for you, for My strength is made perfect in weakness."

People that you put your trust in will let you down, if it hasn't happened yet it will, as it happens to everyone because, as a general rule, they are more interested in their agenda than yours. But people aren't the ones who determine your destiny or the outcome of what concerns you. We have the Father's assurance that He will perfect that which concerns us. People saying it doesn't make it so; God saying it does! The safest place in the world to be is in the will of God Almighty. Align your plan with God's purpose and ultimately you will win. We "feel" weak and we are weak; but He says that His strength is perfected in our weaknesses. Strong people operate in their own strength and abilities and sometimes accomplish things, but mostly for their own glory and edification. Those who depend on the Lord will see Him manifested and glorified. 1 Corinthians 10:12b (MSG), *"Forget about self-confidence, it's useless. Cultivate God-confidence."* Every one of us were born maimed and with flaws, but lovely in God's sight. It's okay; His grace is sufficient and will always be enough!

AUGUST 14
COME TO JESUS

Revelation 22:17 (NKJV)

"And the Spirit and the bride say, "Come!" And let him who hears say, "Come!" And let him who thirsts come. Whoever desires let him take the water of life freely."

Lord, because I don't sense it, doesn't mean You do not love me. At 5:00 a.m., with no sleep, I do not feel very loved. Your love isn't measured by what I "feel." Spirit and flesh are not in the same realm or category. Regardless of my feelings, Your Word says, "let him who hears (that's me) say, 'Come;' whoever is thirsty (me), let him come and whoever wishes (me) take the water of life freely." Over and over throughout the day, I can come to You, Your arms are open; the invitation is 24/7, just come. Come just as I am regardless of the state of my mind and heart, come and experience how wide, long, high and deep is His love for me. John 6:37 (NIV), *"All that the Father gives me will come to Me and whoever comes to Me, I will never drive away."* Listen for Him today and hear Him say to you, "Come!"

AUGUST 15
DON'T BE AFRAID OF FACES

Jeremiah1:8 (NKJV)

"Do not be afraid of their faces, for I am with you to deliver you, says the Lord."

How many times we are faced with hostile, menacing and demeaning faces! Go steadily on with what you have been told to do as the promise is the Lord will deliver you. He will guard your life and if you try to do it yourself, you will remove yourself from His deliverance. I need to be passionate about You and to follow you will all my might what You speak into my heart…not to just do the job but do it well, even when confronted by hard looks in a hostile environment. I just need to be mindful that this is life. You are the One who determines the length of our days and what they hold is your determination, not mine; but how I respond to it does determine the quality of my life. Help me not to be intimidated and fearful of hard, cold looks from anyone as this is part of my learning experience, but to focus on the promise that You are facing the same stare I'm looking at and You are with me to deliver me. If you are fearful, then do it afraid; the promise of deliverance is the same.

AUGUST 16
IN EVERYTHING, GIVE THANKS

1 Thessalonians 5:18 (NKJV)

"In everything give thanks; for this is the will of God in Christ Jesus for you."

Absolutely everything that happens in our lives has been allowed by God. Your attitude toward those things is one of the most important choices of your day. Paul was chained and in prison when he wrote this, so he evidently had not let his circumstances determine his attitude. Knowing and believing what God says is so powerful in your life. Satan doesn't get concerned over your sins as he knows God will forgive you; or your depression because God will drive it away; or your lack as he knows God will provide. What concerns him is when you discover the truth and power of God's Word because he knows it is the most powerful weapon you have to wield against him. Be accepting of your circumstances and situations, even what seems wrong which comes against you; trust and love the Lord, seek Him and His Word and hold the thought that this is the will of God for now. Love, trust and give Him thanks for all things...this is your attitude choice for today. VS. 24: *"He who calls you is faithful, who also will do it!"* Believe in Him and His Word.

AUGUST 17
I DON'T WANT TO MISS YOUR GLORY

Psalms 106:21 (MSG)

"They traded the Glory for a cheap piece of sculpture—a grass-chewing bull! They forgot God, their very own Savior..."

How many times Lord, have I done the same thing...traded the Glory for a cheap piece of something worth nothing! You are King and Lord God of it all; don't let me miss Your Glory! Deep and abiding is Your love. I want to focus on responding to You. I want to draw from all the love You have, and then give it out. Holy Spirit, empower me, guide me for outreach, but You do know how much I need your grace, God to cover me, grant it according to your working power within me. I need and want overcoming faith. Life is hard, Lord, but you allowed these things by Your hand and it is Your hand that will deliver. We want deliverance; You want the processing of it. God has nothing for me worth having that is easily gained as there is nothing cheap in the heavenly market. Difficult times are school days to gain faith and character. The powers of earth and Hell have to obey You. So, *"I need not fear even if the whole world blows up and the mountains crumble and fall into the sea"* as stated in Psalms 46:2 (NLT). My hope is in You; I need Your help, Jesus, as I don't want to miss Your glory!

AUGUST 18
TURN TO THE WORD

Psalms 119:169-175 (MSG)

"Let my cry come right into your presence, God; provide me with the insight that comes only from your Word. Give my request your personal attention; rescue me on the terms of your promise. Let praise cascade off my lips; after all, you've taught me the truth about life! And let your promises ring from my tongue; every order you've given is right. Put your hand out and steady me since I've chosen to live by your counsel. I'm homesick, God, for your salvation; I love it when you show yourself! Invigorate my soul so I can praise you well; use your decrees to put iron in my soul."

The future cannot be lived out ahead of its time. Learn to wait well. Psalms 62:5 (NKJV) states, *"My soul, wait silently for God alone, for my expectation is from Him."* God will work at the perfect moment, if we will let Him. Trust Him completely to do it His way and in His time. Psalms 62:8 (NKJV), *"Trust in Him at all times, you people, pour out your hearts before Him. God is a refuge for us."* We are to fix our eyes trustingly and consistently on Jesus and the encouragement we find in His Word.

AUGUST 19
BELIEVE HIS SPOKEN WORD

<u>1 Corinthians 3:21</u> (LB)

"For God has already given you everything you need...He has given you the whole world to use, and life and even death are your servants. He's has given you all the present and all the future. All are yours, you belong to Christ and Christ is God's." <u>1 Corinthians 2:13</u> (LB) *"The spiritual man has insight into everything and that bothers and baffles the man of the world who can't understand him at all. <u>VS.16</u>, "How could he? He has never been one to know the Lord's thoughts or to discuss them with him or to move the hands of God by prayer. But strange as it seems, we Christians actually do have within us the very thoughts and mind of Christ!"*

We may not "feel" like God has given us everything we need to live out our lives as our bodies scream for divine intervention, but His Word says that He's given us all the present and all the future and that the spiritual man has insight into absolutely everything, as we belong to Christ and Christ is God's! Invade our spirit with divine understanding of the scriptures; let us follow hard after you, and believe Your spoken, inspired and Holy Word.

AUGUST 20
FOCUS ON YOUR "WHAT'S NEXT"

<u>Hebrews 12:1b-2</u> (NKJV)

"...let us lay aside every weight, and the sin which so easily ensnares us, and let us run with endurance the race that is set before us, looking unto Jesus, the author and finisher of our faith,

who for the joy that was set before Him endured the cross, despising the shame and has sat down at the right hand of the throne of God."

The key is to let Jesus be the focus of our life, not our circumstances. He truly is the finisher of our faith. He has done everything necessary for us to endure. Look at what He did. He focused on what was set before him (the coming joy) and not on His present agony which He was enduring at the time. He knew the suffering of the cross was going to be His crown...the "what's next" would be His reward. VS. 2-3 (MSG), *"...he never lost sight of where he was headed—that exhilarating finish in and with God—he could put up with anything along the way: Cross, shame, whatever. And now he's there, in the place of honor, right alongside God." When you find yourself flagging in your faith, go over that story again, item by item, that long litany of hostility he plowed through!"* Our sufferings can never compare to the torture Jesus endured on our behalf. VS. 4 (NKJV), *"You have not yet resisted to bloodshed, striving against sin."* You can do this as you focus on Jesus, your "what's next," is your reward!

AUGUST 21
FAITH IS...

Hebrews 11:1 (NKJV)
"Now faith is the substance of things hoped for, the evidence of things not seen."

"Faith is the substance of things hoped for, the evidence of things not seen" is not a definition of faith as we have been told

201

repeatedly. Rather, it is a <u>description</u> of what faith does. Faith is the "substance of things hoped for;" faith treats the things you hope for as reality (being real). Evidence means "proof." Faith proves that what is unseen is real. Such is our reward at the return of Jesus. We have not seen the return of Christ, but we certainly believe in it, just as surely as if we were watching it happen! We have no visible "proof" but by faith, we can see it happening. The proof or evidence is backed up by His Word. Everything we know about spiritual truths is simply taking what God has said in His Word as being truth. Every single one of the people of faith listed in Hebrews 11 believed that what was then "a hope" would truly happen and would become a reality. Heavens things are just beyond what we are looking at, at earth's level.

AUGUST 22
YOU KNOW ALL ABOUT ME

<u>Psalms 139:1-12</u> (LB)

"O Lord, you have examine my heart and know everything about me. You know when I sit or stand. When I am far away, you know my every thought. You chart the path ahead of me and tell me where to stop and rest. Every moment, you know where I am. You know what I am going to say before I even say it. You both precede and follow me and place your hand of blessing on my head. This is so glorious, so wonderful to believe. I can never be lost to your Spirit! I can never get away from my God. If I go up to heaven you are there; if I go down to the place of dead you are there. If I ride the morning winds to the farthest ocean, even there your hand will guide me; your strength will support me. If I try to hide in the darkness, the night becomes light around me. For even darkness

cannot hide from God: to you the night shines as bright as day. Darkness and light are both alike to you.

God's eye is on me morning, noon and night. There are 3 billion people that are loved, analyzed, studied closely and I am one of them! You know my every thought, in advance. You are acquainted with all my ways, every phase of my life. Before a Word is on my tongue, You know it. You are both behind and before me. If I ride the morning winds or if I lift up dawn wings and fly to the place of sun rise and settle down on the back side of the seas where the sun sets, even there Yahweh's right hand guides and grasps me firmly. I am overwhelmed when reminded of my shortcomings, while God is looking at my potential. We gain confidence when we discover God's will and start cooperating with it.

AUGUST 23
MY AIM IN LIFE IS TO KNOW YOU

Hebrews 3:1b (MB)
"Take a good hard look at Jesus. He's the centerpiece of everything we believe"

I am here, not to know myself, but to know You. Everything that comes into my life is a circumstance to let me know You. The Holy Spirit wants me to know and realize all of it is a means of securing knowledge of You. You are here. Your Presence is with me. I do not ever want to allow any circumstance to come between me and You. So often the sun is dimmed by clouds, and that is a perfect picture of our unbelief. But if I put my faith in You between me and the circumstance, then I'll see the circumstance through You. (I'll be looking at You rather than the situation I'm facing). Never think that a circumstance is haphazard, everything that is dumped on me is a means of securing knowledge of Jesus. The work of the Holy Spirit is determined that I will realize Jesus is Lord in every part of life; and He will bring me back again and again until I do realize it. My aim in life is to know You. I am not here to "realize" me, but to know You. I am to see and realize You before I analyze any circumstance. *"You are the centerpiece of everything we believe in."*

AUGUST 24
YOU ARE PRECIOUS TO GOD

Isaiah 43:4b (LB)
"You are precious to Me and honored and I love you..."

You are who God says you are, not what others say you are. If God didn't give you a name...it's not yours! Only believe what God says about you. God can break the power of every negative thing that is said about you or that attaches itself to you. You are a saint, not a sinner; not a loser, but a winner. People may try to label you, but you need only answer to the name God calls you. He says, *"You are precious to Me and honored and I love you."* You can change the direction of your life when you realize God loves you and wants to spend time with you. You may be unworthy and feel undeserving but that doesn't change how God loves you. We need to be close enough to Him to know what He is speaking into our lives. We should be able to sense His breath! You know that would please Him as He says, *"You are precious to Me."* How many people do you know that says that to you? Think about it: He's the God of all heaven and earth and He waits for you to come to Him. Since childhood, you've sang, "Jesus Loves Me;" live it out now in your daily walk and you'll find it is more than a childhood song, but a great way to live!

AUGUST 25
KEEP GOING UNTIL YOU'RE GONE

Deuteronomy 33:25b (NKJV)

> "... As your days, so shall your strength be..."

We need to live and learn that we're never too old to serve. Deuteronomy 34:7 (NRSV) states, *"Moses was 120 when he died; his eye was not dim, nor his natural forces abated."* Job 42:12 (NRSV) states, *"The Lord blessed the latter end of Job more than his beginning."* Noah was 500 years old when he built the ark. It ain't over until God says it's over and you're not done until God says you're done. You need to live out every moment God grants you. If you can breathe, pray; if you can speak, encourage someone; if you have wisdom, share it. Look at what God accomplished in just one day! Give Him the days you have left. God is the God of plenty when life gives you less. So, you have an impossible situation... He specializes in them! If you're a Super Senior, don't you dare fold your hands with, "I've served my time, let someone younger do it." God will let you know when you're finished but until then, we need to live in the spirit of Caleb who at the age of 80, sprattled his legs, raised his arms and claimed his mountain! Keep going until you're gone!

AUGUST 26
HAVE YOU LOST YOUR SOUL MATE

Psalms 46:1 (LB)

"The Lord is my refuge and strength. He is a present help in time of trouble."

We are so prone to run from trouble... don't, head straight for it. God is there to meet you. Your goal is to know God Himself, not joy or even peace, nor even blessing, but to know God, God Himself. Over and over He may remove your friends in order to bring Himself in their place. We faint and fail and become discouraged... you know it, Lord! In the year the one who represented all God was to me died---did I give up everything? Did I become ill? Was I disheartened... or, here's the choice; did I seek the Lord? It must be God first, God second and God third in my life until I am faced steadily with God and no one else is of any account whatsoever. If you have lost your soul mate, be reconciled to your God. In the entire world, there is none like Him; there is no one like my God! I Kings 8:23 (NKJV), *"O Lord God of Israel, there is no God like you in heaven above and on earth below—You who keep your covenant of love with your servants who continue wholeheartedly in your way."*

AUGUST 27
WAIT ON THE LORD

Habakkuk 2:3 (NKJV)

"Wait for it, for it will surely come to pass."

Before God gives you more, He will observe what you do with what you have. When God speaks a Word into your life, you need to realize that it takes time to take root and sprout. We could all use a backward glance at times...what does your track record look like? How true have you been to what has enabled you to have what you have now? The more God gives you, the more accountable you are to Him. If you have trouble handling the criticism of a few people now, how in the world do you think God would make you the manager of a large group? You say you want something but are you willing to pay the price it takes to acquire it? Whatever you're going through today, have peace in knowing that there is nothing the evil one can do to preempt God's plan for you. Psalms. 37:34 (NKJV) states, *"Wait on the Lord and keep His way and He shall exalt you to inherit the land when the wicked are cut off, you shall see it"*. Wait, I say, on the Lord.

AUGUST 28
GOD KNOWS WHAT'S GOOD FOR YOU

Psalms 145:10 (MSG)

"God's in charge—always. Zion's God is God for good! Hallelujah!"

The mind of God is behind all things, strong and growing. Get it in your mind that God is there. Then, once you have established the idea, you need not ever to question it. You needn't ever go to this one or to that one questioning, "Is God in this?" Isaac may never have wanted to leave the house again alone with his Dad, but Abraham didn't for a minute question if God was in it when he raised the knife to kill his only son. God's in charge—always. His response to the scene was to make Abraham's family more numerous than the sand on the seashore and the stars in the sky. When we are willing to trust what He says and believe in His promises, then He is free to work in our lives. I don't know about you but I'd much rather be a living sacrifice than to be tied to the altar and become a dead one. "God has His finger on your pulse and is extremely sensitive to even the slightest change. He will come to save you when the perfect moment has arrived," Streams. God is God for good (and He knows what's good for you)— Hallelujah!

AUGUST 29
I'M HOMESICK, GOD, FOR YOUR SALVATION

Psalms 119:169-175 (MSG)

"Let my cry come right into your presence, God; provide me with the insight that comes only from your Word. Give my request your personal attention; rescue me on the terms of your promise. Let praise cascade off my lips; after all, you've taught me the truth about life! And let your promises ring from my tongue; every order you've given is right, put your hand out and steady me since I've chosen to live by your counsel. I'm homesick, God, for your salvation; I love it when you show yourself! Invigorate my soul so I can praise you well; use your decrees to put iron in my soul."

Living life one day at a time is not easy; we want to reach out and get ready for what is to come and not to come! Trying to do that is so painful and so unnecessary because there is nothing we can do to control tomorrow. The future cannot be lived ahead of its time. Don't let that ever be my vision...this is Your life to be lived out. I don't want to miss Your plan because I know You have one. I scream out my selfish woes, but You do what You want with this soul and body in what's left to live. If I have completely entrusted You with something, help me to keep my hands off of it. You can do a better job than I can and You don't need my help. Psalms 62:5 (NKJV) states, *"My soul waits silently for God alone, for my expectation is from Him."*

AUGUST 30
TODAY IS YOURS, LORD

Psalms 119:137 (MSG)

"You are right and you do right, God; your decisions are right on target. You rightly instruct us in how to live ever faithful to you."

You've already been in my today and are here waiting for me. Today is Yours; I hold it open before you. You do it as it pleases you. *"You have made me a polished arrow,"* Isaiah 49:2 (RSV). You called me from my mother's womb and you've hidden me in Your quiver. Living the Christian life is difficult but that doesn't cave me in; however it may cost me a few hours in waiting. The Psalmist says, "Be still before the Lord and wait patiently for Him." I am the one caught in a *frenzy; God is never in a hurry.* He has all the time in the world to *"do what is right, His decisions are always right on target;* and He is willing to instruct me in how to live faithfully in Him."* He is already here in my today waiting to do what His Word says. God will work at the perfect moment if I will let Him. I just need to trust Him completely to do it His way and in His time. Psalms 119:166 (MSG), *"For those who love what you reveal, everything fits—no stumbling around in the dark for them."* VS. 158.

"I follow your directions, abide by your counsel; my life's an open book before you." This day is Yours, read every Word of my heart, Lord!

AUGUST 31
GOD'S HOUSE

Psalms 84:2 (LB)

"I long, yes even faint with longing to be able to enter your courtyard and come near to the Living God. VS. 5: Happy are those who are strong in the Lord, who want above all else to follow your steps. When they walk through the Valley of Weeping, it will become a place of springs where pools of blessings and refreshment collect after rains. VS. 10: A single day spent in your house is better than a thousand anywhere else. I would rather be a doorman in the Temple of my God than live in palaces of wickedness."

I need to long for, yes even faint with longing to be able to enter the courtyard and come near to the Living Lord...my own designated place of worship. It is a sanctuary for my hungry soul. It is there I realize not myself, i.e., what's going on with me, but to know Him. Everything part of and every phase of my natural life is to know Jesus. He is in charge of it all. Everything that comes into my life is a circumstance meant to let me know Him. The Holy Spirit wants me to realize all of it is a means of securing knowledge of Jesus. What I learn in His house enforces what I've read in His Word ...walking through the Valley of Weeping brings me to pools of blessing and refreshment. It is better to spend one day in His house than a thousand anywhere else. Thank you, Lord, for a place to meet with others who desire to come near to the Living God!

SEPTEMBER 1
SAVE YOUR CRITICAL COMMENTS FOR YOURSELF

Galatians 6:1-3 (MSG)

"Live creatively, friends. If someone falls into sin, forgivingly restore him, saving your critical comments for yourself. You might be needing forgiveness before the days out. Stoop down and reach out to those who are oppressed. Share their burdens, and so complete Christ's law. If you think you are too good for that, you are badly deceived."

When we look at another's sin, we might say, "I know I'm bad, but certainly not that bad." If I view someone else's sin in that way, I become a Pharisee and violate something very important about my own relationship with Jesus... which have you noticed has become suddenly a strange silence? God graciously reminds me that there is no sin of which I am not capable of doing. It is only His restraining hand that keeps me from being as bad as I could be! Mother Teresa has said, "Bless those who curse you, think what they would say if they knew the truth ... the real me." The fall or failure of another person can be spiritually devastating. Saying or even thinking, "I told you so," reveals pride, self-wisdom and insight and shows there is something very wrong and sinful going on in my own heart. 1 Corinthians 10:12 (NKJV), *"Let him who thinks he stands, take heed lest he fall."* It is so true, *"you might need forgiveness yourself, before the days out!"*

SEPTEMBER 2
HOW SUBJECT ARE YOU TO CHANGE

Acts 4:13 (NKJV)

"Now when they saw the boldness of Peter and John, and perceived that they were uneducated and untrained men, they marveled. And they realized that they had been with Jesus."

If the Holy Spirit can transform Saul into Paul, changing the purpose of his existence, He can transform you. If you do your part, He will gladly do His. Just one touch from Him can change your life and cause you to talk, walk and accomplish His will, not yours. You can change what you hear and He will change the way you hear it. You can change what you say and Jesus will change the way you say it. You can change your appearance and He will change your behavior. In Acts 6:2, Stephen went from waiting on tables to a flaming evangelist in VS. 10. He can change your vision, instead of looking down, you can look up (Acts 7:55). The Holy Spirit can give you discernment just as he gave Philip the perfect moment to meet and witness to the Ethiopian as in Acts 8:29-30. On many of Paul's journeys, he didn't try to witness until the people were ready. You don't need to trust your own judgment, allows the Holy Spirit to give you discernment. Paul went from being a murderer to being a "brother." The Apostles couldn't believe the transformation as they heard him preach as found in Acts 9:20. You can never change another person but you can let the Holy Spirit change you and your purpose for living. *"And they realized they had been with Jesus;"* that's how we become different. How subject are you to change?

SEPTEMBER 3
MAKE MY CALLING SURE

<u>Acts 10: 14-15</u> (NKJV)

"But Peter said, Not so, Lord! For I have never eaten anything common or unclean. Again a voice spoke to him again the second time, What God has cleansed you must not call common."

Because of this vision, Peter had to change his opinion of tradition. Peter had despised the Gentiles but after this encounter on the roof top, where God told him <u>three</u> times that what He had cleansed, Peter was to kill and eat, Peter responded. As a result, God opened up a great ministry for him to those he had formerly despised. The Holy Spirit will show you through an inward knowing that what He reveals in your heart will happen. Sometimes He reveals the future enough so we may prepare for what lies ahead. Later when Peter was in prison, continual prayers without ceasing were offered for him until he was delivered. It was so miraculous that he thought he was dreaming. Peter responded to his calling and you need to respond to yours. Sometimes it calls for breaking more than tradition. Every page in the book of Acts is separating those whom He has called to do specific things. May our prayer be, "Lord make my calling sure, quicken me and I will call upon your Name. I can't do this without your help, Holy Spirit."

SEPTEMBER 4
INTERNALIZE THE WORD

Acts 15:28 (NKJV)

"For it seemed good to the Holy Spirit and to us to lay upon you no greater burden than these necessary things."

The key to life is internalizing the Word of God which never fails to expose sin and to supply the power to overcome sin. Allow God to be your Partner in decision making. Don't make plans and then ask God to bless them...let Him be in the decision making process. Allow Him to be your Teacher, Guide, Counselor and Advisor. Be willing to let Him change your direction. Acts 16:6-7 (NKJV), *"They were forbidden by the Holy Spirit to preach the Word in Asia...they tried to go into Bithynia, but the Spirit did not permit them."* Later, Paul received the Word that he was to go to Macedonia and help them. Let the Holy Spirit lead you, He never makes a mistake. The key lies in internalizing the Word of God because it never fails to give us the right direction as well as the power needed to overcome the barriers and sin that come against us.

SEPTEMBER 5
BLESS GOD EVERY DAY

Psalms 145:1-3 (MSG)

"I will lift you high in praise, my God, O my King! And I'll bless your name into eternity. I'll bless you every day, and keep it up from now to eternity. God is magnificent; he can never be praised

enough. There are no boundaries to His greatness. VS. 13, *God always does what He says and is gracious in everything He does."*

We want joy, peace, health and blessings... our goal should be to want Jesus. He is the centerpiece of our life. It is in and through Him that the supernatural becomes possible. There is nothing you can do about the past but there is something you can do about this day. When you are doing acts of love and service to others, you yourself will experience healing and recovery. What you do lives on in others, so that it never ever really dies but goes on from age to age. You can do nothing better for yourself than to help someone else. When you lift up others, you lift up Jesus. Bless Him every day and keep it up from now into eternity!

SEPTEMBER 6
GOD'S IN CHARGE

Psalms 146:10 (MSG)

"God's in charge—always. Zion's God is God for good! Hallelujah!"

The storms we face by physical elements bring us in conflict with the spirit elements. It is there our faith finds the best soil and grows the fastest. "Strong trees aren't found in the forest but out in the open field, where they are beat on from storms and winds, where they blow, bend and are twisted into giants. Toolmakers seek them for handles because of their strength. The same is true of our spirits. The strong person of faith has had the winds of hell come against them, suffered greatly, experienced tears, sorrow, conflicts and hardships" Streams in the Desert. Don't run from your storms, run into them. God is already there to strengthen you and to bring you through them with a faith that all the demons of hell cannot come against. Learn from sorrow and pain and learn from His heart. We can be encouraged in His Word because our "*God is in charge—always. Zion's God is God for good" and we can all shout Hallelujah!"*

SEPTEMBER 7
GREAT IS OUR GOD

Psalms 147:3-6 (MSG)

"He heals the heartbroken and bandages their wounds. He counts the stars and assigns each a name. Our Lord is great, with limitless strength; we'll never comprehend what he knows and does. God puts the fallen on their feet again... VS. 11: He's not impressed with horsepower; the size of our muscles means little to him. Those who fear God get God's attention; they can depend on his strength. VS. 15-18, He launches his promises earthward how swift and sure they come! He broadcasts hail like birdseed – who can survive his winter? Then he gives the command and it all melts; he breathes on winter—suddenly its spring!"

Yeah Lord, You do all these things. You are complete. Everything we do is known to you. Even when it seems like the world is grinding to dust and very few people care and nothing moves, You launch your promises earthward and how swiftly they come! The One who has counted the stars and given each a name has named you and one day will give you a new name in glory. Our Lord is great and limitless in strength and as humans, we will never comprehend all that He does. God puts the fallen on their feet again... *He feeds both cattle and crows and sees every sparrow that* *falls. He scatters frost like ashes and broadcasts hail like birdseed.* *He breathes on winter and suddenly its spring!* Great is our God, there is none like Him. <u>Psalms 145:3</u> (MSG), *"God is magnificent;* *He can never be praised enough. There are no boundaries to His* *greatness."*

SEPTEMBER 8
YOU ARE A RIVER OF LIFE

<u>John 7:37b-38</u> (NKJV)

"If anyone thirsts, let him come to me and drink. He who *believes in me as the Scripture has said, out of his heart will flow* *rivers of living water."*

God never puts anything in you that He doesn't want to flow out of you... you are a river of life. "A river touches places of which its source knows nothing... out of us will flow rivers that will bless to the uttermost parts of the earth. We have nothing to do with outflow, this is the work of God... A river is victoriously persistent, it overcomes all barriers. For a while it goes steadily on its course, then, it comes to an obstacle and for a while it is baulked, but it soon makes a pathway round the obstacle. Or a river will drop out of sight for miles and presently emerge again broader and grander than ever... The river of the Spirit of God overcomes all obstacles. Never get your eyes on the obstacle or on the difficulty. The obstacle is a matter of indifference to the river which will flow steadily through you if you remember to keep right at the Source," Oswald Chambers. There is a river of life coming out of all who believe in Christ. Not only will you be satisfied, but you will become a river so that others may drink and be satisfied.

SEPTEMBER 9
LET THE HOLY SPIRIT DIRECT YOU

Acts: 16:6b-7 (NKJV)

"...they were forbidden by the Holy Spirit to preach the Word in Asia...they tried to go to Bithynia but the Spirit did not permit them."

The Holy Spirit is your Teacher, Guide, Counselor and Advisor. Let Him be your Partner in decision making. Let Him be in charge and/or change your direction. Paul was forbidden by the Holy Spirit to preach the Word in Asia and Bithynia but later was told in a vision to go to Macedonia to help the people there. Because he and Silas followed God's direction, everywhere they went people were being saved, healed and God's Spirit was at work. He wants to do the same with you. The Jews were so jealous of Paul and Silas' preaching that they stirred up mobs and riots against them. The Bible says this of them, Acts 17:6b, *"These who have turned the world upside down are now here too."* The quickest way to turn your world upside down is to turn yourself right side up! He will even change your understanding. You need to know the ways of God more perfectly in order to be more sensitive to your relationship with Him. God never makes a mistake when He changes your direction or understanding; trust Him to lead you and He'll do it perfectly.

SEPTEMBER 10
LET THE HOLY SPIRIT CHANGE YOU

Acts 20:28 (NKJV)

"Therefore take heed to yourselves and to all the flock, among which the Holy Spirit has made you overseers, to shepherd the church of God which He purchased with His own blood."

If God has called you to shepherd a church, the Holy Spirit will show you how to take that responsibility and will empower you to do it. It's always such a relief when He takes over...takes charge. Paul's farewell to this church came straight from his heart; he knew the Holy Spirit would give all the leadership they needed to succeed in shepherding the church which He had purchased with his own blood. But he warned them in Acts 10:29, *"For I know this that after my departure savage wolves will come in among you not sparing the flock."* Shepherding a church requires insight into the diverse strategies that will challenge you and the church. Paul well remembered a time in his life when he was driven to take the lives of those of whom he now preached the gospel! Paul had to learn about the One who had *"made him an overseer to now shepherd the church of God."* The Holy Spirit had totally changed him and his insight. God will and wants to do the same for you!

SEPTEMBER 11
A DAY WE WILL NEVER FORGET

Some of us will never forget as we watched the attack being made on the Twin Towers in New York by enemy aircraft, September 11, 2001. In our home, we were watching as we saw the unbelievable effect of the first hit and then saw the next approaching plane with its impact. It seemed as if all the people in the United States were stunned and could hardly believe what was happening. Even today as we listen to the incredible stories of the First Responders and how so many gave their lives to save the lives of people they had never known or will ever know this side of eternity, we are forever amazed and grateful. A lot of people made a lot of promises then that are not being kept today. It was a "wake up call" certainly as we never know what a day will bring and we need to humble ourselves before the Keeper of the Universe and have our lives right before Him. Enemy planes came, unsuspected, undetected and brought much destruction. Almighty God in heaven is still giving us time, but there is a Messenger coming and these are His Words: Malachi 3:1-3 (NKJV) *"Behold, I send My messenger, and he will prepare the way before Me. And the Lord, whom you seek, will suddenly come to His temple, even the Messenger of the covenant, in whom you delight. 'Behold He is coming,' says the Lord of hosts. But who can endure the day of His coming? And who can stand when He appears? For He is like a refiner's fire and like launderers' soap. He will sit as a refiner and a purifier of silver."* Jesus is scheduled to come again and it will be just as undetected as the enemy planes. You need to be ready.

SEPTEMBER 12
REJOICE IN THE LORD

Philippians 4:4 (NKJV)

"Rejoice in the Lord always. Again I will say, rejoice!" VS. 12 (MSG), *"I know what it is to be in need and I know what it is to have plenty. I have learned the secret of being content in any and every*

situation, whether well fed or hungry, whether living in plenty or in want."

Regardless of what is going on in our own world, we can always rejoice in something going on in God's world. Psalms 102: 25-27 (NKJV) states, *"You laid the foundation of the earth and the heavens are the work of Your hands. They will perish, but You will endure; yes, they will all grow old like a garment; like a cloak You will change them, and they will be changed. But You are the same, and Your years will have no end."* God's work is forever and has no ending; our lives are brief, and 1 Peter 1:17 tells us how we are to *"conduct ourselves during this time of our temporary residence."* We spend so much of our day thinking of how we would like to change our circumstances, our health, finances, or relationships and it's almost like trying to catch an overturned bottle from spilling its contents. Instead of trying to change the circumstances, turn every unfilled thought into praise to the Lord who truly knows how to effect change. Rejoice in the Lord always; and do it now!

SEPTEMBER 13
PAUL WAS WILLING TO BE BOUND

Acts 21:19-11 (NKJV)

"...a certain prophet Agabus came down from Judea. And when he had come to us, he took Paul's belt, bound his own hands and feet and said, Thus says the Holy Spirit so shall the Jews at Jerusalem bind the man who owns this belt..."

Agabus took Paul's belt and bound his own hands and feet and said that the owner of this belt will be bound with it and be delivered

221

into the hands of the enemy. Paul's response was that he was not only willing to be bound but to die for the Name of Jesus. The Holy Spirit gives spiritual understanding instead of panic in temporal situations. Over and over, Lord, you bring us through stress when our tendency is to bail out in defeat. We are so quick to cry out rather than to draw from the strength from within. We cringe at the thought that our weakest moment is actually the height of our spiritual depth. We think our victory is in our successes, when our victory is in our weaknesses. We abhor the thought of "being bound" and yet Paul says he was not only willing to be bound but to be hand carried to those who would try to kill him. How many times, Lord, do we have to be bound and delivered to learn who it is that delivers us?

SEPTEMBER 14
GOD CAN INCREASE YOUR INFLUENCE

Acts 23:1-3 (MSG)

"Paul surveyed the members of the council with a steady gaze and then said his piece: 'Friends, I've lived with a clear conscience before God all my life, up to this very moment.' That set the Chief Priest Ananias off. He ordered his aides to slap Paul in the face. Paul shot back, 'God will slap you down! What a fake you are! You sit there and judge me by the Law then break the Law by ordering me slapped around!'"

God can change every part of your life and your world. He can change your insight, wisdom, understanding, decisions, direction, and in this instance for Paul, change your influence. Paul looked at the Chief Priest after he had ordered him slapped in the face and

Paul said in VS. 3 (LB), "*God shall slap you, you white-washed pig pen!*" Later, he did apologize and said that he was sorry as he didn't know he was a Chief Priest as he certainly didn't act like it. Some of the council against him was made up of Pharisees and others of Sadducees and they were split right down the middle and were divided. Vs. 9-10, "*We don't find anything wrong with this man! What if a spirit has spoken to him or maybe an angel? What if it turns out we're fighting against God?*" God can cause even your enemies to defend you. Later, Paul was about to be torn apart and God spoke to him and told him not to worry about any of the uproar...that He was sending him to Rome and that he would give his testimony there God changed Paul's direction and then greatly increased his influence. Does this make you ask yourself, "How far does my influence go?" We all have influence over someone!

SEPTEMBER 15
SOLD OUT FOR CHRIST

Acts 20:24 (NKJV)

"*But none of these things move me, nor do I count my life dear to myself, so that I may finish my race with joy, and the ministry which I received from the Lord Jesus to testify to the gospel of the grace of God.*"

Paul was only one person, true, but he was sold out for Christ. How prone are you to keep one foot for yourself and slide all over the place with the other? Forty of the priests and elders made an oath that they would not eat or drink until Paul was dead but what had God said? God had told him that he would give his testimony in Rome. The plot thickens in a scheme to kill Paul, but he is safely delivered. What God says is the way it will be. Before any of this, Paul had spoken what God had revealed to him. Acts 20:25 (MSG) says, *"What matters most to me is to finish what God started: the job the Master Jesus gave me of letting everyone I meet know all about this incredibly extravagant generosity of God."* How would you have liked to have been the one chained to Paul in prison...you would have heard Jesus for breakfast, Jesus for lunch and guess what...Jesus for dinner! Paul only had one theme, one aim, one subject in mind, he was sold out for Christ. He was only one man but one man totally sold out for Christ! Saul was so completely changed that he was renamed, Paul. If Jesus were to rename you today, what do you suppose He would call you? Would it have anything to do with you being "sold out for Christ?"

SEPTEMBER 16
HE KNOWS THE WAY THAT I TAKE

Ephesians 1:3-5a (NKJV)

"Blessed be the God and Father of our Lord Jesus Christ who has blessed us with every spiritual blessing in the heavenly places in Christ, just as He chose us before the foundation of the world that we should be holy and without blame before Him in love, have predestined us to adoption as sons by Jesus Christ..."

God has a prearranged plan for your life; there is nothing that will deter you from keeping the appointments He has made for you. We see heartache and resentment, injustice and deceit, unfairness and lies; but God sees the end results. God works in, through and during whatever we are experiencing; trust Him, He's not done yet. Many times Paul was desolate, lonely and totally forsaken but he knew he had the ever-present Holy Spirit interceding in his behalf. We get discouraged but most likely will never be jailed or flogged. Paul dropped out of sight and for two years, little was even seen or heard from him. Sometimes he was in smelly dungeons with little or no food or even light, but when they brought him out, it was like he picked up in mid-sentence of what he was saying when they threw away the key! The harder life was, the stronger he became through the Holy Spirit. We walk freely, go wherever we please, live in relative comfort and ease and have the promise of what we don't have, God will provide; yet we complain and blame. We need to live in the knowledge that God chose us before the foundation of the world to be His and has been so gracious and generous in dispensing His gifts of grace and love. He not only knows "the way that I take," but "where I'm going next."

SEPTEMBER 17
GOD CAN CHANGE YOUR TURMOIL

Acts 27:9b-10 (NKJV)

"Paul advised them saying, 'Men I perceive that this voyage will end with disaster and much loss, not only of the cargo and ship, but also our lives."

We read about a "northeaster" (a heavy wind of typhoon strength) that struck the ship as Paul was on his final journey to Rome. Paul, even though he was the prisoner, had advised against setting sail before they ever left port. It was unheard of that a storm would last for two weeks but they were without food and had thrown overboard all their cargo, even needed items for the boat. Paul stood in the eye of the storm and told them, Vs. 21 *"Men, you should have listened to me, but take heart, no one will lose their life, only the ship.*" He was basing this on what he had been told that he would go to Rome and then an angel said, "*You will go to Caesar and all these men with you*" VS. 23-24. Nothing or no one will alter God's unchanging and prearranged plan for your life. Circumstances and situations; storms of the body or the soul must come under the control of the One who plans your life. God may allow us to flounder and struggle our way through when that's what we want to do, but make no mistake..."*We need not fear even if the whole world blows up and the mountains crumble into the sea...the nations rant and rave in anger—but when God speaks, the earth melts in submission and kingdoms totter into ruin*" Psalms. 46:2, 6 (LB). If you are in the midst of a storm, God is capable of changing your turmoil!

SEPTEMBER 18
GOD CAN CHANGE YOUR CONFLICT INTO VICTORY

Acts 27:5 (LB)
   "*But Paul shook off the snake into the fire and was unharmed.*"

Paul was called, appointed and anointed of God, but He can and will do the same things for you. God can handle any conflict that comes against you, as surely as He delivered Jesus from the conflicts He endured here on earth and raised His dead body to life again. On this particular missionary journey, Paul had told them that they would lose the ship but none would lose their life and that's exactly what happened. Once safely ashore, Paul built a fire and in doing so, a snake came out and fastened itself on his hand. Those around him thought he must be a murderer and then they decided he was a god! Paul continued his role of seeing to the need of others by healing the sick and praying for them. The natives responded by giving the crew everything they needed to be on their way. Once in Rome (just as God had said he would be in <u>Acts 23:11</u>), Paul maintained his innocence and appealed to Caesar. His victory speech in <u>Acts 27:23-31</u> never changed and is as true today as it was then. Had Paul been acquitted years before, look at the people he would never have reached. God changed his conflict into total victory and God received all the glory, Today, Lord, please change my hearing, vision, speech, and actions until I am aware of how you can change all conflict into victory when I am obedient to you.

SEPTEMBER 19
SURVIVE YOUR PAST

<u>Micah 7:19b</u> (LB)

"You will tread our sins beneath your feet; you will throw them into the depths of the ocean." (NKJV) *"...who will haul all our iniquities into the deepest sea?"*

God's promise is to pitch, haul, or throw all our sins into the depths of the sea when we come to Him in true repentance, so why in the world do we keep digging up the past? Lord, save me from me; You know that I can self-destruct in minutes! I need to look at what lies ahead to a life lived with all the love You offer. <u>Ephesians. 2:7-8</u> (MSG) states, *"So overflowing is his kindness toward us that he took away all our sins through the blood of his Son, by whom we are saved; and has showered down upon us the richness of his grace—for how well he understands us and knows what is best for us at all times."* You need to acknowledge His forgiveness and live in the wisdom He offers; as you can survive your past and be stronger because of it, because of Jesus.

SEPTEMBER 20
BELIEVE WHAT THE PSALMIST ABOUT YOU

Psalms 92:12-15 (LB)

"But the godly shall flourish like palm trees and grow tall as the cedars of Lebanon. For they are transplanted into the Lord's own garden, and are under his personal care. Even in old age they will still produce fruit and be vital and green. This honors the Lord and exhibits his faithful care. He is my shelter. There is nothing but goodness in him!"

Do you see yourself as a transplanted tree in the Lord's own garden under his personal care? The Psalmist says, *"even in your old age, you will produce fruit and be vital and green."* That may not be what you see when you're looking in the mirror but that's what you look like to Him because, *"this is what He sees when He's looking at you and it's what honors Him and exhibits His faithful care."* Spend enough time with Him until you can see what He's looking at. Wait upon the Lord…tarry long enough for Him to speak to you. You cannot have a "drive-through" relationship and expect to hear from Him, much less experience His glory. Believe what God says about you, lack of belief has got to be the greatest detriment in Him fulfilling His plan for your life. Believe what the Psalmist says and he says that He is your shelter and there is nothing but goodness in Him!

YOU CAN DO THIS

1 Peter 1:13-16 (HCSC)

"Therefore, with your mind ready for action, be serious and set your hope completely on the grace to be brought to you at the revelation of Jesus Christ. As obedient children, do not be conformed to the desires of your former ignorance. But as the One who called you is holy, you also are to be holy in all your conduct; for it is written, Be holy, because I am holy."

Any time you read *therefore*, you always want to look at what came before it. Peter was pointing out that as believers we have received through God's provision, our salvation; so therefore we are to prepare or get our minds ready for action. You *"gird up the loins of your mind"* (KJV) much like an athlete would gather up the flowing part of his garment and get ready to race...be prepared for some serious and strenuous action! When you talk about being holy, you're talking about something serious and Peter says to be serious. Don't be a "squatter" on your knowledge that you're saved, going to heaven, and just sit waiting for it to happen. It takes a lot of guts to discipline your mind, which is the most unruly body part you have except for your tongue. You need to be calm, collected, well-balanced, self-controlled and obedient. None of us were born with any of it; we have to learn these traits by doing them. Have the favor of God and *"be obedient and do not be conformed to the desires of your former ignorance."* Get rid of your pre-conversion life styles. You didn't used to know better, now you do; so put it in practice! We may never duplicate His holiness, but we can strive to do so. Instead of screaming, "I can't be holy!" Grit your teeth and give it a try. You would never have learned to walk, if you had given up when you first failed. You can't do it on your own but if you ask Him for guidance and depend on Him each day, He will help you. God isn't impressed with our perfection, but He is impressed when we try. Aren't you impressed when you see your children trying? You can do this!

SEPTEMBER 22
HIS JUDGMENTS ARE IMPARTIAL

1 Peter 1:17 (HCSB)

"And if you address as Father the One who judges impartially based on each one's work, you are to conduct yourselves in fear during the time of your temporary residence."

Peter points out that "the One" you're addressing as "Father" is the Supreme judge. It's wonderful that we can address Him and come to Him. When He spent time with His disciples, He encouraged them to spend time with our compassionate Father as He is loving, caring, attentive and always judges impartially, without favoritism, each one of us individually. He doesn't judge by outward appearance, nor is He influenced by anything that so often sways our judgments. He always knows everything about anything; He knows the facts and truth. He knows everything about you. Psalms 119:168, (LB) *"Everything I do is known to you."* He knows what you do and why you do it. His judgment is impartial. We are to be infused with fear and that's not being scared to death but to have reverence, awe and respect for Almighty God. Think these hard times are never coming to an end? Look at the scripture, this is, *"during your time of temporary residence here."* We are here as earthlings for a brief pilgrimage; just like the Israelites, we're on a journey to a new land; our promised land is heaven, next stop. This journey and our whole life should be made in light of eternity which is just ahead!

SEPTEMBER 23
WE ARE A SERMON IN THE FIELD

2 Corinthians 4:16-17 (LB)

"Though our bodies are dying, our inner strength in the Lord is growing every day. These troubles and sufferings of ours are after all quite small and won't last very long. Yet this short time of distress will result in God's richest blessing upon us forever and ever!"

"Let's look at the sermon of the fields. You must die in order to live. You must be crucified, not only to your desires and habits that are obviously sinful but also to many others that may appear to be innocent and right. If you desire to save others, you cannot save yourself, and if you desire to bear much fruit, you must be buried in darkness and solitude. My heart fails me as I listen. But when the Words are from Jesus, I remind myself that it is my great privilege to enter into *"the fellowship of sharing in his sufferings"* (Philippians3:10) and I am therefore in great company. I also remind myself that all suffering is designed to make me a vessel suitable for His use. His Calvary blossomed into abundant fruitfulness, and so will mine. Pain leads to plenty, and death to life—it is the law of the kingdom. Do we call it dying when a bud blossoms into a flower?" Streams in the Desert. The sermon of the field is that you must die in order to live. We are all like a seed sown in the field; unless a grain dies and is buried in the ground, it

231

cannot yield any fruit. If you asked a grain of wheat, "do you want to be obscurely buried in the dirt for weeks?" The answer would probably be, "Not!" But when given the choice of being obscure or of bearing an abundant harvest, even a grain of wheat yields to its Master. When we are willing to let our flesh die, and yield to will of our Maker, we will bear an abundant harvest as we become a sermon in our field.

SEPTEMBER 24
YOU WERE REDEEMED

1 Peter 1:18-19 (HCSB)

"For you know that you were redeemed from your empty way of life inherited from the fathers, not with perishable things like silver or gold but with the precious blood of Christ, like that of a lamb without defect or blemish."

You were redeemed from your empty way of life to a new life in Christ by the precious blood of Jesus. You can redeem miles earned on a credit card for an airline ticket or you take coupons to the store and exchange one thing for something you want. We can take our coupon, our life of sin and exchange it for a life that is covered by the blood of Jesus. That exchange cost Jesus His life. The cross represents all the cash registers and ticket counters across all of heaven and earth when He allowed His blood to be spilled all over them so that we might not die in our sin. We were redeemed by the precious blood of Christ like that of a lamb without defect or blemish. When the Israelites offered an animal in sacrifice, it had to be without blemish. Jesus was the perfect sacrifice for our sins, since He was sinless, He could do that. That exchange of His life for ours was a priceless gift and is so perfectly described as being "precious." You've known some of these scriptures forever and sometimes just "read over them." You need to digest them, let them get into your innards as they will strengthen your devotion to Him and put another layer of gratefulness around your heart for God's great gift of redemption!

SEPTEMBER 25
I WILL BLESS YOUR NAME EVERY DAY

Psalms 145:1-2 (MSG)

"I lift you high in praise, my God, O my King! And I'll bless your name into eternity. I'll bless you every day and keep it up from now to eternity."

This is the verse of scripture that I had just copied in my journal, as my husband and I did our devotions together on the lanai, November 13, 2008, when I realized Louie (my late husband) was again on his knees proposing as he did EVERY anniversary of our marriage. Years have gone by, You are still here Lord, help me to grasp this as another opportunity to grow. It is a new era that I wouldn't have chosen, but it is Your choice, Let me hear, experience Your disclosure, and to fill my mind with Your Word, renew it within my spirit; and cleanse my heart. You have given me reason and knowledge of You and never intended for me to forego using either of them. Help me to discover Your will and Your intent behind all this and draw on Your power to use the gifts You've given me... using common sense to trust You and abide in You. You are the centerpiece of all I believe in. *"I will lift You high in praise and* bless Your name into all eternity and do it from now to eternity." I will bless Your Name every day and lift you high in praise!

SEPTEMBER 26
ASK HIM WHAT HE'S THINKING

Jeremiah 29:11 (ML)

"For I know the thoughts I think concerning you, says the Lord, thoughts of peace and not of hurt, to give you a future and a hope."

When you pray, why not invite God's thoughts as you speak? We pray for a hundred things we want and need; God knows all of it before we ask. Ask Him what He's thinking about as you make your requests, what He has in mind. Scripture tells you that He's actually given you a portion of His thoughts and mind. He speaks a Faith language...worry, defeat, anxiety are not in His vocabulary. When your baby was born he/she babbled and you couldn't understand a thing, but finally the little one spoke your language and actually said words you understood. Stop babbling to God and pray in His language. Speak His Words of faith, hope, grace, love, trust and listen for His thoughts as you are speaking. Never ask for anything? He tells you to ask that you may receive, but pray spirit Words (life-changing, life-making Words) and you'll see your disappointments as His appointments. You'll start to understand His purposes. Life's most severe jabs are nothing more than God staking your claim to an ordained victory. Satan may whisper, "Just look at what God's done to you now;" but you just watch God show up and show off! *"For I know the thoughts I think concerning you says the Lord."* God will never make plans for the past; He always will take you forward.

Stop living your days in what has happened and look to what's next. And, when you pray, ask Him what He's thinking.

SEPTEMBER 27
JESUS WAS CHOSEN BEFORE THE FOUNDATION OF THE WORLD

1 Peter 2:20 (HCSB)

"He was chosen before the foundation of the world but was revealed at the end of the times for you." KJV: *"Who verily was foreordained before the foundation of the world, but was manifest in these last times for you."*

God chose a fixed time in eternity past to redeem your soul. Christ was "chosen before the foundation of the world"...just as God had always planned. Before God chose to form the foundation of the world, they chose a plan that man would be redeemed through the death of Jesus. It was determined and appointed beforehand, before even time began; God's eternal purpose was to provide salvation of your soul. Peter says, *"so that at the end of time"*—the last days (a time it seems in which we now live) God's redemption through Christ was for all who would believe. It is in His resurrection that we have our faith and hope. We should never lose our awareness of the high cost of our salvation and as we acknowledge it, it should motivate and move us to live as the redeemed. Arthur Blessitt physically walked a wooden cross around the world; it took him 40 years. He was beaten, put in prison and suffered many hardships. He faced ridicule and scorn, but his message today is always one of praise and thankfulness for God's chosen plan before the world began for the salvation of souls to be revealed at the end of time. Today, there is still time for God to redeem your soul.

SEPTEMBER 28
FEED YOUR SOUL

Isaiah 55:2-3 (LB)

"Why do you spend your money on foodstuffs that don't give you strength? Why pay for groceries that don't do you any good? Listen and I will tell you where to get good food that fattens up the soul. Come to me with your ears wide open. Listen for the life of your soul is at stake. I am ready to make an everlasting covenant with you to give you all the unfailing mercies and love that I had for King David. VS. 6, Seek the Lord while you can find Him. Call upon Him now while He is near."

God, if only we were as concerned with the health of our soul as we are of our bodies! Far too many hours of our day are spent on preparing and consuming foodstuffs that give little or no strength and groceries that do more harm than good; while our soul is starved instead of being fattened. If we fed ourselves more in your Word, we'd find that it shows us what is right; what is not right; and how to stay right. Help us to know and realize You want to make an everlasting covenant with us of Your unfailing mercies and love...much like the one You had with King David. If we seek after You, we will find You; we know You are near as You are never far from anyone of us.

SEPTEMBER 29
GIVE THANKS

1 Thessalonians 5:18 (NKJV)

"In everything give thanks, for this is the will of God in Christ Jesus for you."

Attitude is everything and one of the most important choices of your day. Most of our attitudes are founded on what are circumstances are at the moment. Paul was in prison when he wrote this so when he wrote to give thanks for everything, it was a choice he made, but certainly not based on the circumstance he was experiencing. Mostly, we let how good we feel determine our thanksgiving! Believing and knowing what God says is our power point in life. Satan doesn't get concerned over your sin because He knows God will forgive when we confess; your depression doesn't bother him too much as He knows God can drive it away; or, if you have a lack, he knows God will provide. What scares him to death is for you to discover the truth of God's Word because he knows your ignorance of it is the most important weapon he can use against you. You have the choice every day of enforcing the power of what God speaks into your life as being your rule in everything you do. You can do this when you give thanks for all things, as it is God who loves you and ultimately brings out what is the good and perfect will of the Father for you.

SEPTEMBER 30

LOVE AND CARE FOR ONE ANOTHER

1 Peter 1:22 (HCSB)

"By obedience to the truth, having purified yourselves for sincere love of the brothers, love one another earnestly from a pure heart."

Once you yourself have learned obedience to the truth, then you are enabled to love others earnestly and from a pure heart. (MSG) states, *"Now that you've cleaned up your lives by following the truth, love one another as if your life depended on it."* Wouldn't that be life changing? If your life depended on how you love others? Think about it! The list of things to change immediately would be unending! When you were saved, you experienced a cleansing that is still in effect. You didn't do it; God did it; and because God purified you, you are to live in a state of being cleansed, daily. And, if you are to care for others as you care for yourself, you are to earnestly seek one another's best interests "from a pure heart" with your whole being. One Pastor recently who has been in the ministry 54 years said that more Christian people are bruised and offended by people in the church than ever are by people of the world. The time you spend in letting the Word of God get inside of you will bring about change in the way you live and how you treat and respond to others. Have the courage to live the way Jesus would want you to live by sincerely and earnestly doing and caring for others as if you was doing it for yourself.

OCTOBER 1
GOD'S WORD IS LIVING AND ENDURING

<u>1 Peter 1:23-25a</u> (HCSB)

"Since you have been born again—not of perishable seed but of imperishable—through the living and enduring Word of God. For all flesh is like grass and all its glory like a flower of the grass. The grass withers and the flower fails but the Word of the Lord endures forever."

Everyone born again experiences new life and this new life doesn't come from any physical aspect such as perishable seed, but through that which is imperishable...the living and enduring Word of God. Our lives are brief and quickly fade away. Peter says, *"...like the grass of the field that withers and the flowers that fail, but the Word of the Lord endures forever."* Ask yourself, "What is my strongest motive to live according to His Word?" Pray for God to deliver you from the sins that tempt you the most...you can't be delivered from something you won't admit to. Increase your time of study in His Word and gaze into His face. You have His promise that as you do, you will experience His glory reflected back inside of you. Every day...on the street, in your kitchen, standing in line at the checkout, wherever and whatever you're doing, do it *"through the living and enduring Word of God."* God can certainly accomplish His purposes without you, but He has chosen to use you. Preach the Word wherever you are, and if necessary, use Words!

OCTOBER 2
WE ARE GIFTS TO GOD THAT HE DELIGHTS IN

Ephesians 1:11-12a (LB)

"Moreover, because of what Christ has done we have become gifts to God that he delights in, for as part of God's sovereign plan we were chosen from the beginning to be his, and all things happen just as he decided long ago. God's purpose in this was that we should praise God and give glory to him for doing these mighty things for us..."

We were chosen from the very beginning to be His and He is the One that keeps us from falling; we are kept by His power and not by our own strength. We are sustained and protected so that we can persevere and be able to stand before Him and become "gifts to God that He delights in." We all make mistakes but God doesn't give up on us as easily as we do Him. He holds onto us and is long-suffering; He shapes, convinces and convicts us of our sin. He will send people in your life to hold you accountable; He is faithful. We need to learn as we go along what pleases Him, *"what He delights in"* and be open to His direction as He leads us. Just because He tells you something one time doesn't mean it is a lifetime direction; we need to be aware of any changes He might want to make, so we need to be closely walking with Him each day. A thing might seem good, look good, but we need God's unction. His Spirit is active and ever new and we need to be mindful and watchful for *"His purpose and give praise and glory to Him for doing these mighty things for us."*

OCTOBER 3
ONE DAY AT A TIME, SWEET JESUS

<u>Exodus15:2</u> (MSG)

"The Lord is my strength and song and has become my salvation."

Your Spirit is creative and unique. I need to look for Your unexpected, unusual Presence in everything. You're not always in the 'spiritual box' I create but in every ordinary experience of my life whether I acknowledge it or not. You are perfect and every manifestation of Your Spirit reflects power and glory. Help me to keep my eyes on You, The Master, more than the manifestation. No matter the calamity that befalls me, it can't be soul destructive because I belong to You. You want me to go about each day without fear and anxiety, totally trusting and submitting to You. The more submissive I am, the more indifferent I'll be to the circumstances around me. I won't be constantly trying to figure out what to do next or be affected by the disturbing news swirling about. How can I say, "I trust You with everything," when there is this one thing, I'm not trusting You with? Over and over, daily, I surrender when there is no other way out. It would please You so much more if I willingly submitted before coming to my wit's end. There's no deals cut; You see through all my faked and feigned obedience. Sometimes I manage to submit to spiritual issues but the flesh raises its ugly head and still wants to look good...demands to have its own way. Submitting today doesn't clear tomorrow's calendar! *You are my strength and song and have become my salvation!*

OCTOBER 4
WHAT WERE YOU CALLED TO DO

1 Peter 2:21 (HCSB)

"For you were called to this, because Christ also suffered for you, leaving you an example, so that you should follow in His steps."

Peter is talking about how people can put up with suffering in their lives because they are conscious of God's presence and plan and in doing so, find peace with God. Even those who suffer unjustly and do what is good and right are sometimes treated cruelly, but if you endure, it will bring favor with God (VS. 19-10). What do you do with the Words, *"For you were called to this?"* Are you doing what God called you to do? Are you one of those who think that "calling" is for ministers and missionaries? Have you ever reconciled yourself that your circumstances, relationships, health issues, sufferings and unjust situations are a part of your journey here? Is it possible you "were called" to have what you are experiencing? Here's a truth: If you don't recognize any other call on your life, let me tell you of at least one... you were called to imitate Jesus...*"He left you that example, so that you should follow in His steps."* We are to copy or trace exactly what He did. Did you ever hold something up to the light and trace it? You may not have gotten a perfect duplicate but got a very good likeness. That's what we are to do with Him, hold Him up to His Light and get the best likeness possible. He not only was the model and example but left us instruction sheets, in case we have trouble. It is just like putting anything else together, when all else fails, read the manual. Every Christian is called to be like Jesus.

OCTOBER 5
WE NEED A GUARDIAN OF OUR SOUL

<u>1 Peter 2:25</u> (HCSB)

"For you were like sheep going astray, but you have now returned to the Shepherd and Guardian of your souls."

How much experience have you ever had with sheep? As a little girl, I can remember that sometimes little lambs were brought into the house and kept behind our wood burning stove when it was bitter cold outside, just to keep them alive. Sheep need constant care and do not do well on their own at all. Jesus said that He was the Good Shepherd and that we are His sheep because He knew how much we need a Guardian. People all have very "sheepish" instincts. Before knowing Christ, we were all like sheep going astray, moving farther and farther away from our Shepherd. Nothing you read about sheep is very favorable or smart...they will graze themselves right over a cliff; they are totally dependent, easily separated, scattered and led astray, needing help 24/7...recognize any of that in yourself? Peter says, *"We all like sheep have gone astray and need to return to the Shepherd and Guardian of our souls."* <u>Psalms 34:7</u> (LB) states, *"For the angel of the Lord guards and rescues all who reverence Him."* We all need a Guardian, One who is an Authority Figure that loves guards and rescues our soul when we go astray.

OCTOBER 6
GOD IS BIGGER THAN YOUR LIFE

Psalms 37:5 (NKJV)

"Commit your way to the Lord, trust also in Him and He will bring it to pass."

Once we submit to the control of the Lord, placing every matter of our life into His hands, Satan rises up against us. As long as Paul was doing what the Devil wanted, life was fine, but when he changed, all hell broke loose and he was under attack relentlessly. If you yield completely to the Lord, Satan will concentrate on you. He will cause you to doubt the things you KNOW; you'll begin to look at fear instead of faith. You will think, "How bad can this get;"...instead of focusing on the fact that God has promised to get you through your crisis. When hard times come, doubts arise and you have a whole new crew to deal with as Satan will do anything to keep your focus diverted away from Jesus. You aren't the first to submit to fear. Ezekiel 22:14 (NKJV), *"Can your heart endure, or can your hands remain strong in the days when I shall deal with you? I the Lord have spoken and will do it."* Noah was *"moved with godly fear"* in Hebrews 11:7. David said in Psalms 119:120 (NKJV), *"My flesh trembles and I'm afraid of my judgments."* Habakkuk 3:16 (LB) says, *"My belly trembled; my lips quivered, rottenness entered my bones and I trembled in myself..."* These men were gripped by fleshly fear but also stood in awe of God Almighty. You have nothing to fear but fear itself, submit to the control of the Lord; He is bigger than your fear, and He's bigger than the one who comes against you!

OCTOBER 7

WHAT IS MAN THAT WE SHOULD BE AFRAID OF HIM

Isaiah 51:11 (NKJV)

"I, even I, am He who comforts you. Who are you that you should be afraid of a man who will die, and of the son of a man who will be made like grass?"

Why is it that we are so afraid of man and what he might do to us? God says a man's life is brief and that he will soon die like grass in the field! Yet, even as Christians, we tend to be more concerned as to what men think than we are of the One who made us. God Almighty should be the One we stand in awe of; when God begins to move in your life, nothing can stop His shaking. Judgments will begin at the house of God...and these all now lie at the door. For years, faithful men of God have pleaded for God's own to repent and return to their Creator and for the most part, we see life going on...business as usual. God's promises are not pie-in-the-sky fantasies or fables. You can rely on Him. Life isn't found in memorizing scriptures or perfecting a presentation, but rather in submitting yourself to the Lord. Tell someone what Christ has done for you; give of yourself and give others hope. Let them know that hopelessness can always be replaced with hope! Be an encourager; let them know that they can have their own relationship with the One who said, *"I, even I, am He who comforts you."*

OCTOBER 8
THE FIVE R'S OF HIS WORD

The Bible was given to us by the inspiration of God and is useful to each one of us as it prepares us for living. There are five ways to get God's Word in your life.

- Receive it: Luke 8:13 (NIV), *"...receive the Word with joy when you hear it."*
- Read God's Word: Revelation 1:3 (NKJV), *"Blessed is he who reads and those who hear the words of this prophecy."*
- Research God's Word: Psalms 101:2 (NRVS), *"...study it day and night."*
- Remember God's Word: Psalms 119:11 (NKJV), *"Hide it in your heart."* Memorize it!
- Reflect on God's Word: 2 Timothy 2:7 (NLT), *"For the Lord will give you insight."*

With knowledge comes increased responsibility! Joshua 1:8 (NKJV), *"Don't let this Book of the Law depart from your mouth."* Be a doer of the Word—knowing it is not enough. John 13:17, (NKJV), *"Once you know these things, you will be blessed if you do them,"* We aren't saved from sin's grasp by knowing the commandments of God because, we can't and don't keep them. God destroyed sin's control over us by giving Himself as a sacrifice for our sins. You need to receive, read, research, remember, reflect and then always respond to God's Word!

OCTOBER 9

YOU KNOW HOW I AM; HELP ME TO DEPEND ON HOW YOU ARE

<u>Psalms 27:4-5</u> (LB)

"The one thing I want from God, the thing I seek most of all is the privilege of meditating in his Temple, living in his presence every day of my life, delighting in his incomparable perfections and glory. There I'll be when trouble comes. He will hide me. He will set me on a high rock."

Jesus what a wonder You are! You are so precious; so kind and true. You shine like the morning star. Invade my life today with Your living, loving Presence. Motivate me to speak, acknowledge and live for You. Your Holy Spirit is power and God my Father is in control. Your love is a blanket over me. I praise you and worship You; Holy are you, O God. Your purpose and plan are good. I praise the Name of Jesus! In Your time, You make all things beautiful. You scheduled every day of my life before I began to breathe. I own nothing but your promises. I may think I have something, but everything that bears my name belongs to You. Help me, Lord, to relinquish my so-called possessions; even my next breath is yours. Just "Color me gone!" Have Your way; You know how I am; help me to depend on how You are!

OCTOBER 10
SIN SAPS YOUR STRENGTH

Psalms 32:4b (LB)

"My strength evaporated like water on a sunny day until I finally admitted all my sins to you and stopped trying to hide them. I said to myself, 'I will confess them to the Lord.' And you forgave me. All my guilt is gone."

What relief we have when we confess our sins and God clears the record. As long as we do not confess, God does not cover our sins; but the moment we confess, He covers them..."*then all my guilt is gone.*" Guilt will wear out your mind, sap you spirit and body of strength and you will feel like "your bones being worn away." There is a definite link between spiritual distress and physical disorders. *"My strength evaporated like water on a sunny day."* You will be like a tree without sap in a land without moisture; you'll have no strength and no energy. First, the Psalmist admitted the sin to himself, then he uncovered it; next, he repented and confessed it. How pleased You are, Father, when we finally get it right! We know how grieved we are when our own children make mistakes and hurt themselves or others and many times we don't even know about it. But we are in Your face, always; *"everything we do is known to you,"* Psalms 119:168 (LB). Thank you Father, you see and still forgive!

OCTOBER 11
SEEK HIS FACE AND HIS HEART

Psalms 27:8 (KJV)

"When you said, seek ye my face, my heart cried unto thee, Thy face Lord will I seek!"

The Lord so appreciates it when we seek Him, His face, His nearness. You may not be able to move too much on earth with your Words, but you can move all of heaven!! So, reach out to the unseen, the eternal, and the heavenly. Difficulties are sent in order to reveal what God can do!! Any Valley of Trouble can become a Door of Hope. We don't have to "see" the physical answer but we do need to be aware of the spiritual aspects of our trouble and sense Your Presence. We flitter and flail, but You remain sure and strong. There is a time of testing and establishing during which we must stand still until the new relationship becomes ingrained in us that it becomes a permanent habit, like a surgeon setting a broken arm by splinting it to keep it from moving. God, too, has His spiritual splints He puts on His children to keep them quiet and still through difficulties. 1 Peter 5:10 (NKJV), *"...after you have suffered awhile, He will restore you and make you steadfast."* Jeremiah 17:7 (NLT) , *"Blessed is the man who trusts in the Lord and has made the Lord his hope and confidence."* Seek His face and His heart; Isaiah 43:4 (LB) says, *"You are precious to me and honored and I love you."*

OCTOBER 12

THE EYES OF THE LORD RUN TO AND FRO THROUGHOUT THE WHOLE EARTH

2 Chronicles 16:9a (NKJV)

"The eyes of the Lord run to and fro throughout the whole earth to show Himself strong on behalf of those whose heart is loyal to Him."

The eyes of the Lord run throughout the whole earth searching for one who will be willing to be nothing so that He can be everything. There is no limit to what God can do through you, providing you do not seek your own glory. You need to lose all sense of self-sufficiency; 1 Corinthians 10:12b (MSG) says, *"Forget about self-confidence, it's useless; cultivate God-confidence."* Have confidence in the One who can be what you would like to be. Many of us have worn heart monitors and they serve a purpose, but they can only monitor the body. The Lord monitors the Spirit and the heartbeat of the soul. There is no way you can benefit someone else unless you have endured immense pain. Your own hard circumstance that is pressing so hard is His tool to shape you for His work. Don't push away His instrument or you'll miss His purpose and intended result; and ultimately His glory. Philippians 1:30 (MSG) says, *"There's far more to this life than trusting Christ; there's also suffering for Him and the suffering is as much a gift as the trusting,"* It's so true, *"The eyes of the Lord run throughout the whole earth searching for those who will endure and yet remain loyal to Him."*

OCTOBER 13

YOU'RE BLESSED WHEN YOU'RE AT THE END OF YOUR ROPE

Matthew 5:3 (NKJV)

"Blessed are the poor in spirit, for theirs is the kingdom of heaven."

Matthew 5:3 (MSG)

"You're blessed when you're at the end of your rope. With less of you there is more of God and His rule."

"Blessed are the paupers in spirit" which is the first lesson to receive in the kingdom of God. The bedrock in Jesus Christ's kingdom is poverty, not possessions, and carries a sense of total futility. It takes a long time to believe or even want to be poor; but the verse says blessed are the poor (paupers) in spirit and it is the place where Jesus will begin to work. The world regards material blessings, money and personal recognition as a sure sign of being blessed. Your greatest blessings are found in God's promises and His gift of eternal life. I am a pauper and destitute for You, Jesus. I am blessed when I'm dangling at the end of my rope; because less of me means there is room for more of You. *Blessed are the poor in spirit for theirs is the kingdom of heaven!*

OCTOBER 14

GOD COMMANDS YOUR STRENGTH

Psalms 68:24 (NKJV)

"Your God has commanded your strength..."

God daily measures out and then enforces the amount of strength that you need. He has a plan for you each day, and you need to make a plan that parallels with His. God has promised to deliver you and will continue to deliver you until you're gone. He wants you to empty out into someone, everything He's put in you. Let Him touch your heart and your lips that I may Isaiah 50:4b (NKJV), " be able to speak a Word in season to one that is weary." 2 Corinthians 2:14 (NKJV) says, "Now thanks be to God who always leads us to triumph in Christ, and through us diffuses the fragrance of His knowledge in every place." God will command your strength so that you will triumph and in doing so, will allow you to leave His fragrance, showing He's been there! Regardless of the situation, God's Word contains the dynamite of the Holy Spirit. It explodes within you when the circumstance of your life causes it to do so. When God reveals some truth of His Word, you have to decide whether you will accept the upheaval that will come in your circumstance if you obey. And, as you obey, God commands your strength!

OCTOBER 15
SUFFERING IS AS MUCH A GIFT AS TRUSTING

Philippians 1:29 (MSG)

"There's far more to this life than trusting in Christ. There's also suffering for him. And the suffering is as much a gift as the trusting."

Regardless of the crisis, we should have total confidence in You. We do to a point. Then we revert to panic prayers as if we don't even know You. We get to our wits end showing we haven't the slightest reliance in Jesus or God and His rule in this world. God's been dealing with corrupt people since the beginning of time. He told Ahaziah, King of Judah in 2 Chronicles 21:16-20, *"You're going to come down with a terrible disease of the colon and die a painful humiliating death and two years later, he was totally incontinent and writhing in pain and died."* One day we will realize the joy we could have given Jesus if we would have trusted Him no matter what. When we pray and nothing happens, we go scrambling elsewhere for answers and solutions. In a crisis, we reveal who we have placed our trust in…we could be at the beginning of finding God's wisdom. Don't succumb to panic, He will bring you into truth; and that could be the place you will learn that *"suffering is as much a gift as trusting."*

OCTOBER 16
YOUR WILL BE DONE

Matthew 26:42 (NKJV)

"Oh, My Father, if this cup cannot pass away from Me unless I drink it, Your will be done."

Jesus was willing to drink the bitter cup of death, as it was God's will. Before He suffered His agonizing death on the cross, He knew how hard it would be but he also knew that God's will is the most glorious thing in the world. His will is the continual working of His omnipotent power for our benefit with nothing to prevent it, as we are surrendered and believe. All of Satan's schemes backfire and result in our good. Jesus said, "Shall I not drink the cup the Father has given me?" And because He did, we have eternal life. It's a fascinating life in the center of His will. Even the sins that

Satan hurls against us are useless when God gets through processing them. Nothing that is not a part of God's will is allowed to come into the lives of those who trust and obey You. Nothing haphazard ever gets dumped into your life. Fill every heart that is lifted to you today, dear Jesus. Because you died of a broken heart, You are close to those whose hearts are breaking. You gave us the example, when You were hurting the most; You turned Your face to the Father and showed us how to be accepting of the Father's will being done.

OCTOBER 17
WHAT HE DID AMONG THEM, HE DOES IN IS...HE LIVES

<u>2 Corinthians 4:14</u> (MSG)

"...what Jesus did among them, he does in us--he lives! Our lives are at constant risk for Jesus' sake, which makes Jesus' life all the more evident in us. While we're going through the worst, we're getting in on the best!"

Paul is telling the Corinthians that he has been surrounded and battered by troubles but is not demoralized...he wasn't sure what to do but he knew God knew what to do; that he had been spiritually terrorized but God had never left his side. He recounted how Jesus had been tortured, mocked and murdered but what He did among them, He does in us...He lives! And as long as we know He is alive, we know He loves and lives within us in the same resurrected power that brought Him up out of the grave. He lives to ever make intercession for us before the throne of Almighty God. What we need to grasp is that He lives! He lives within our body and our life! As long as we live, our *"lives will be at a constant risk for Jesus' sake,"* but that's okay because in the process, it *"makes Jesus' life all the more evident in us!"* <u>We</u> may be surrounded and battered by troubles and not know what to do but we know <u>God knows what to do</u>; and when *"we're going through the worst, we are indeed getting in on the best!"* Read <u>2 Corinthians4:10-12</u> (MSG).

OCTOBER 18
GOD IS WHO HE SAYS HE IS

Beth Moore gives five statements of faith: "God is who He says He is; God can do what He says He can do; I am who Christ says I am; I can do all things through Christ; and God's Word is alive and active in me!" Say them over and over; so many times you could say them backwards in your sleep! Enforce these truths in your inner Spirit! To get what God has, you have to do what God says, and He can do anything He says He can do. If a moment of fear can render you a whole season of failure, then a moment of supernatural faith can totally reverse it! We so shy away from anything called supernatural but that's exactly where God works. God is not stirred by my needs, but He is stirred by my faith. We all have a bearing on our own future by the words of our mouth, as that's what gets lived out in our lives. Our thoughts (meditation of our heart) usually wind up being lived out in our actions. Your Words are seeds and we plant them all the time. You sow and God gives the harvest, as He is the Source of supply. Your actions are seeds, i.e., you cut someone off in traffic, you sow a seed; you let someone get in line ahead of you, that's a seed. You reap what you sow. When you let go of something dear to you; God will let go of something He wants to give you. There is only one proof that you have faith and it's called obedience. You break the devil's hold over you every time you obey and do what God says you can do. Remember you are who God says you are and He will always encourage and affirm you. The devil will always remind you of what you are NOT. The most important step of faith is to know that <u>God is who He says He is</u>!

OCTOBER 19
IS GOD IN THE EVIL OF THIS WORLD

<u>Psalms 103:19</u> (LB)

"The Lord has made the heavens his throne; from there he rules over everything there is."

Do you believe that God is in the evil of this world? This verse says that <u>He rules over everything there is</u> and there IS a LOT of evil! If He knows and sees all the sin, why doesn't He step in and stop it? God has been dealing with sin and sinful people from the beginning of creation. He rules, He reigns, and He is Sovereign Almighty God now and forever. Doesn't look like it? Well, let's look at someone who had a lot of evil come against him. Joseph's brothers hated him and cast him in a pit and later sold him into slavery. They didn't just sell him to anyone but actually sold him to the highest, most important household in all of Egypt. Through acts of sin, he was wrongfully accused and jailed; but there he was made Overseer of the whole jail. The Butler may have forgotten him, but God didn't and had him brought to Pharaoh, who later made him the highest official, other than himself, in all of Egypt. Step by step God ruled over every evil that came against Joseph. He was able to tell his brothers later that what they meant for evil, God meant for good, because God does rule over everything there is! When evil and sin pile up against you, be encouraged, God is bigger than either of them; and He knows exactly how to deliver you, just as he delivered Joseph. Evil runs rampant today, but God has dealt with evil before!

OCTOBER 20
THE GOODNESS OF THE LORD IN THE LAND OF THE LIVING

Psalms 27:13-14 (NKJV)

"I would have lost heart, unless I had believed that I would see the goodness of the Lord in the land of the living. Wait on the Lord; be of good courage, and He shall strengthen your heart."

The first time I ever heard anyone quote this verse was my Pastor as he stood in the kitchen of the home of someone whose young son had just taken his life. It was so appropriate and so true. Yes, in times like that and so many others, we have to concentrate on not only the other living family members but earnestly look for the goodness of the Lord, even when our heart is breaking. In our brokenness He comes to encourage and strengthen us as we lean on Him. He does come; even when it feels like our life has taken wings and flown away. A loved one may be taken away but God goes with him; He also remains with you to comfort you. He is with us through the really hard days of adjustment and difficulties because *"He is the Lord in the land of the living."* He is with those living in the emergency room, the delivery room, the rehabilitation center, the nursing home, the unemployment line, through divorce court; in the jail cell... He is with us as we live through our every experience. If we believe that He is truly with us and we turn to focus on Him, He will hold us together even when we think we're falling apart. He is with us until we're done... then, He's there too!

OCTOBER 21
YOUR LIVING WILL SPILL OVER INTO THANKSGIVING

Colossians 2:7 (MSG)

"You know your way around the faith. Now do what you've been taught. School's out, stop studying the subject and start living it, and let your living spill over into thanksgiving!"

We are not to rejoice in successful service but rather rejoice in the fact that you know God and He knows you. It is a snare to rejoice in that God has used you. Don't ever be impressed with yourself. 1 Corinthians 10:12 (MSG), *"You are just as capable of messing it up as they were. Don't be so naïve and self-confident. You're not exempt. You could fall on your face as easily as anyone else. Forget about self-confidence, it's useless. Cultivate God confidence."* So, *"Now do what you've been taught, schools out, stop studying the subject and start living it."* It is not possible to measure what God will do through you if your relationship is right. Rivers of living water will pour through you when you're rightly related to Him; it doesn't matter where you are, God put you there. As God teaches you and you learn your way around the faith," *your "living will spill over into thanksgiving"* as God uses you. What God does through you is what counts, not what you do on your own for Him.

OCTOBER 22
OUR GOD IS GREATER

<u>John 16:33b</u> (NKJV)

"In the world, you will have tribulation; but be of good cheer, for I have overcome the world."

You are Sovereign God Almighty, our Savior, and our Defender! God will sometimes allow barriers to come into our lives. When that happens, we need to stay focused on Him and He'll show us how to maneuver around them or else, He will remove them. Get your eyes off the problem and on to the One who has already overcome it. God is great enough to put someone in position instantly. It might take us years in schooling but God can download a lifetime of living in us in an instant. It is God who works in us and if we're receptive, God can do it all—anything! Mostly, we aren't "instantly" made heroes or judges. We go through valleys and tunnels but before we know it, He brings us out into light as God is greater than that which comes against us. We all come up against barriers that from all appearances stop the flow of our life and we seem to disappear and are not seen anywhere for a time. Then, almost magically we reappear stronger and better than ever. Reversals come but they also go; because greater is He that is in us than he that is in the world!

OCTOBER 23
YOU ARE CONTINUALLY WITH ME

Psalms 73:23-24 (NKJV)

"I am continually with you, you hold me by my right hand. You will guide me with your counsel and afterwards receive me to glory."

When I trusted You as Savior, You promised to always be here with me. If I feel that is not true, it's just a feeling, not reality. Over and over You tell me that You are always here. *"I am with you and will watch over you wherever you go,"* Genesis 28:15. Since Your Presence is continually with me, *"I need not fear even if the whole world blows up and the mountain crumble and fall into the sea,"* Psalms. 46:2. Regardless of what else I may lose in this life, I can never lose You or my relationship with You. Thank you, Jesus! Pierce my ear with Your voice and let me hear it above all the others. *"Morning by morning you awaken my ear to hear as the learned,"* Isaiah 50:4. I belong for You and can never be another's. Keep my lying tongue from whining and asking for deliverance, except as You are wanting to give it, in Jesus Name, I pray. Thank you for keeping Your promise of always being here with me!

OCTOBER 24
CONDUCT YOURSELVES HONORABLY

1 Peter 2:12 (HCSB)

"Conduct yourselves honorably among the Gentiles, so that in a case where they speak against you as those who do what is evil, they will, by observing your good works, glorify God on the day of visitation."

As believers, we face intense pressure to act as though we are of the world. This is not a time to do finger pointing; it's a time to encourage and support one another and to conduct ourselves honorably among those who wouldn't know Christian behavior from a fence post. To act honorably is to walk excellently in a moral upright manner as we interact with unbelievers. You understand an unbeliever a lot better than they understand you because you used to respond very much as they do now. Unbelievers attack believers, it's what they do. They may speak slander, criticize, make false accusations; in short, it's where they are and how they are. As believers, if we can respond rightly, it's entirely possible they will *"observe your good works and glorify God on the day of visitation,"* or the day He returns. This brings out the "who you are" in this scripture... you are to be the one that is to excel, and in doing so, bring glory to God!

OCTOBER 25
GOD LEADS HIS DEAR CHILDREN ALONG

Matthew 28:20b (NKJV)
"Lo, I am with you always, even to the end of the age."

You are a God of miracles. You always act on behalf of Your people. You did this as you led the Israelites out of Egypt, and when Jesus walked in ministry here on this earth. That's what You do, You lead Your dear children along and You were doing it on 9/11/01. A man by the name of Stanley looked out his window of the Twin Towers in New York City just in time to see a plane headed straight at him; he dived under his desk. It was the only thing in the room left standing... his Bible laid untouched on top of that desk, and it was the only thing left in the room. Another man by the name of Brian was on another floor of the building. Everything was confusion; people didn't know what to do to try to escape as they were cut off. Some tried to ascend to be picked up by helicopters; some tried to descend. Brian could hear Stanley calling for help but there was a wall between them. He didn't follow the others out but stopped to see if he could help the man crying out. Stanley had a nail driven in his palm and it was very difficult for him to climb, but finally Brian was able to reach him and to help him up over the wall. Later when they were eventually rescued, Brian was bleeding too and he took his blood stained hand and put it over Stanley's and said, "I've always wanted a brother, now we're blood brothers." It was nothing short of a miracle they were ever found. So many lives slipped into eternity that day but God performed many miracles as He led His dear children along!

OCTOBER 26
YOU GIVE ME EVERYTHING I NEED

2 Thessalonians 1:2 (MSG)

"Our God gives you everything you need, makes you everything you're to be."

2 Thessalonians 2:15-17 (MSG)

"Keep a tight grip on what you were taught, whether in personal conversation or by our letter. May Jesus himself and God our Father who reached out in love and surprised you with gifts of unending help and confidence, put a fresh heart in you, invigorate your work, enliven your speech."

You give me everything I need; make me everything I was meant to be. Thank and praise you, Father, for what is right in my life and help me through what is not right. You created me first and foremost to know you and to live in rich communication with You. Rather than trying to evaluate Your way with me, help me to accept it thankfully. You are King of Kings, yet You live within me and walk with me... How awesome You are! Thank You for being Perfect, Holy and True. You continually surprise me with Your gifts of unending help. As I tighten my grip on what I've been taught, you refresh my heart, invigorate my work and enliven my speech. I'm usually surprised at Your greatness, Your miracles but You know what You're doing. I know nothing except You are Everything! *"Diffuse through me the fragrance of Your knowledge in every place,"* 2 Corinthians 2:14 (NKJV). Thank you, Father, for giving me everything I need and never stop enabling me to become everything I was meant to be.

OCTOBER 27
WE START AND END WITH YOU

John 6:63b (MSG)

"Every Word I have spoken to you is a Spirit Word, so it is life-making."

The whole human race was created to glorify God and to enjoy Him forever! Sin switched us all onto another track, but that hasn't altered God's plan and purpose in the slightest. God's love is powerful and He can give us a "singleness of heart for Him." He not only introduces us to His love but the very nature and attributes of Almighty God lives within us. We need to maintain an open mind and Spirit to receive what He freely gives. Don't muddle it with our own intentions but rely on the tremendous creative purpose of our Great God. Praise You, Lord God Almighty for Your good plan and for your work of grace in our lives. We want to reflect and bring honor to You; the aim of our lives is to do Your will. We start and end with You. Nothing deterred you from Your purpose. You didn't linger on the mountain top where You were appreciated; nor did your hurry through the villages where You were persecuted. Neither gratitude nor ingratitude turned You away from the Cross that awaited You. Your purpose was to glorify the One Who sent You. Our purpose also is to do the will of the Father and to glorify Him. Help us to realize every day that we started with You and we will end with You; and that every Word You have spoken is a *"Spirit Word and so it is life-making!"*

OCTOBER 28
THE GIFT OF EMPTINESS

1 Kings 17:7 (NKJV)

"And it happened after a while that the brook dried up, because there had been no rain in the land."

We need to understand and experience the fact that God gives the gift of emptiness. That's hardly what any of us want. We want to be fulfilled always! We want to feel full...whether it is your body (stomach) or your spirit (soul), we want to be satisfied! It is in the insecurities in our lives that we become spiritually established. Elijah's experience at the dwindling brook is a perfect example. You can absolutely believe that at some point, *"your brook will dry up"*—it is the history of your yesterday or a true prophecy of your tomorrow.

Then you will need to differentiate between trusting in the gift or trusting in the Giver. Gifts sometimes are for a season; our Giver is eternal. Delays, changes, heartache, and tears are interludes in our lives but are not the finale. Elijah found that when the stream dried up (his earthy source); he received help from the God who made heaven and earth. *"It happened after a while that the brook dried up;"* it happens, its life, and it leaves you feeling empty. Your earthly resources too may fail you, but your God will not. Should you experience the gift of emptiness, turn to the One who gave it to you!

OCTOBER 29
ENJOY THE BEST OF JESUS

Romans 16:20 (MSG)

"...before you know it the God of peace will come down on Satan with both feet, stomping him into the dirt! Enjoy the best of Jesus!"

If you think that Satan has come down on you with both feet, stomping you into the dirt, believe the way it really is and hang in there! Before you know it, God will stomp him into the dirt! Far too many believers are content to live like those who work in the coal mines who never see sun or daylight. Doom and gloom seem to hang over them at every turn; they live out a dungeon mentality and rarely seek a way out, accepting dejection and defeat. Satan seems to have a bulldog grip on their lives. VS. 19b, Paul says, *"I want you to be smart; making sure every "good" thing is the real thing. Don't be gullible in regard to smooth-talking evil. Stay alert..."* Look for the pure love and light of Jesus as your Source, the One who can light up your life as well as your path. Psalms 139:12 (LB) *"To Him the night shines as bright as the day; darkness and light are both alike to Him."* Struggles of life are discouraging but you can climb to new heights with His help and encouragement and really *"enjoy the best of Jesus!"*

OCTOBER 30
THE LORD IS SEARCHING FOR YOU

2 Chronicles 16:9 (NIV)

"For the eyes of the Lord range throughout the earth to strengthen those whose hearts are fully committed to him."

God is looking for those who will continually trust Him with their lives. The world watches to see what God will do through a life fully committed and God Himself watches to see who will be nothing so that Christ can be everything...never hindering Him but always allowing Him to work. There is no limit to what God can do through you providing you do not seek your own glory. George Mueller said that he lost his love for money, prominence, power, position and worldly pleasures and found that God alone was His all in all. "I found everything I needed and desired nothing else; I care only about the things of God. He revealed the truth to me of Himself and has become an inexpressible blessing. From the depths of my heart, God has become an infinitely wonderful Being." If your heart is fully committed to Him, be assured that the eyes of the Lord are continually searching you out, to strengthen and encourage you.

OCTOBER 31
WE ALL NEED WISDOM

<u>Proverbs 3:7a</u> (NKJV)

"Do not be wise in your own eyes."

God educates us by means of people who are better than we are; don't begrudge their relationship with the Lord, learn from it and be attuned to anyone who can bring you closer to Him. *"Do not be wise in your own eyes."* <u>Proverbs 2:2</u> (MSG) *"Tune your ears to the world of Wisdom; set your heart on a life of Understanding."* <u>VS. 6-14</u>: *"And here's why: God gives out Wisdom free; is plainspoken in Knowledge and Understanding. He's a rich mine of Common Sense for those who live well. He keeps his eye on all who live honestly, and pays special attention to his loyally committed ones. Lady Wisdom will be your close friend, and Brother Knowledge your pleasant companion. Good Sense will scout ahead for danger; Insight will keep an eye out for you. They'll keep you from making wrong turns or following bad directions."* God's Words are full of wisdom and insight and are available for the taking. We all need Wisdom, Knowledge, Understanding and Good Sense to keep us from making those wrong turns and following after bad directions. So says the Lord and we can depend on His Word!

NOVEMBER 1
HE CAN BRING YOU OUT OF YOUR CAVE

<u>1 Samuel 22:1</u> (NKJV)

"David therefore departed from there and escaped to the cave of Adullam."

David went from being exalted as King to being hounded and hidden in a cave. His life fell apart. We can all relate to similar times in our own lives. We all "do time" when it's learning time. You all have experiences in which you learn where your help comes from and learn about yourself...your strengths and your limitations. It is where God can do some of His best work. It's also where your worst inadequacies are confirmed and where God sends His power to help you out. For all David knew, he was going to die in his cave. This is as good as it gets! When you get in a situation you cannot fix, trust God. Never let your sense of security be based on you. God will help you even at your lowest point. Trust God, and then trust God! He can bring you out of your cave! Begin to know Him now and finish never!

NOVEMBER 2
JESUS IS IN ME AND WITH ME

Ephesians 3:20 (NKJV)

"Now to Him who is able to do exceedingly abundantly above all that we ask or think..."

Oswald Chambers says: "We look for God to manifest Himself to His children: God only manifests Himself in His children." Yea, Lord, I want to know you! Know how to live before You and not hurt You and not disappoint You. If I completely give this life to You, I have no further claims on it. You be manifested in me. I can stop the struggle...83 years and I've done very little right. My only hope is You, Jesus. I praise You and thank You for being the wonderful Savior You are. Help me to walk before and after You, love You, and always be obedient and submissive. Romans 4:19-20

(NIV),"...*Abraham faced the fact that his body was as good as dead ... but he didn't waiver in unbelief regarding the promise of God ... but was strengthened in his faith, being fully persuaded that God had power to do what He had promised.*" You have promised that You will be with me. You are able to do immeasurably more than I can ever ask or imagine. Help me to stop looking for outer manifestations and look for you, Jesus, within me, as You are here!

NOVEMBER 3
THE SPIRIT MAKES INTERCESSION FOR US

Romans 8:26-27 (NKJV)

"Likewise the Spirit also helps in our weaknesses. For we do not know what we should pray for as we ought, but the Spirit Himself makes intercession for us with groaning's which cannot be uttered. Now He who searches the hearts knows what the mind of the Spirit is because He makes intercession for the saints according to the will of God."

How we as humans, sinful as we are, can pray to a Holy God and get answers is a mystery; and even though we can't explain it, we do know it happens. We cannot even express the longings of our hearts and often they are more of a groan rather than a request; but a groan is interpreted by the One who hears it. The Holy Spirit understands the groan as, *"The Spirit makes intercession for the saints according to the will of God."* He hears, understands perfectly and receives our prayer and then separates whatever is in error before bringing it before the Father. When we are troubled and really burdened, we can take comfort in knowing that Jesus ever lives to make intercession for us. We can fully trust Him and be so thankful for the Words of comfort as well as His embrace.

NOVEMBER 4
GOD CAN DO ANYTHING

Acts 12:5 (KJV)

"Peter was kept in prison, but the church was earnestly praying to God for him."

Wicked King Herod and the Jews were ready to draw Peter's blood and what happened as the church prayed? The prison doors opened and Peter was free, for one thing. For another, as an indication of God's judgment, Herod was "eaten by worms and died." The power of prayer is unequaled and is a supernatural weapon to be used boldly and with divine confidence. God isn't looking for great people but He is looking for people who are willing to prove the greatness of our great God! We should never limit God and don't ever try to think you know what He can do. Look for the unexpected, because our God can do more than you can ever imagine or conceive. What will prayer do? Everything that our Almighty God can do for you! He once told King Solomon: *"Ask me for anything, I will give it to you"* 2 Corinthians1:7 (LB). The next time you find yourself imprisoned by one of lives "whatever's," ask the One who can do anything, to set you free!

NOVEMBER 5
"I HAVE TO DO WHAT I GOTTA DO"

Acts 4:19-20 (NIV)

"But Peter and John replied, "Judge for yourselves whether it is right in God's sight to obey you rather than God. For we cannot help speaking about what we have seen and heard."

Evil rulers do not deserve believer's allegiance and support. Christians should resist government when its dictates go counter to God's commands; but generally all believers are to be responsible and law abiding. Civil government is ordained of God and it is the duty of Christians to render loyal obedience in all things not contrary to the revealed will of God. Arthur Blessitt walked over 38,000 miles as he took the cross around the world;* he was 28 when he started and 68 when he finished 40 years later. As he approached one war zone (he walked through five wars), the enemy told him that if he came one more block, they would nail him to the cross he was carrying. He explained that he meant them no harm; he was simply carrying the cross around the world and continued his approach. They told him again that they would nail him to that cross. He said, "Well, you do what you gotta do; but I have to do what I gotta do." He got close enough to put his hand on one of them and said, "You look like really nice guys, you don't have to live like this, you could let Jesus come into your lives and totally change you, why don't we just kneel down here and pray?" They were totally stunned by his actions and behavior and told him, "Go! Just get out of here." Arthur could not help but speak the Wind Words God had told him to say and Jehovah God provided him safety. God's Word and Presence are as alive as He is alive, so use them today!

NOVEMBER 6

REMEMBER HOW GOD HELPED YOU AT A CRITICAL TIME

Exodus 15:26-27 (NIV)

"He said, 'If you listen carefully to the voice of the Lord your God and do what is right in his eyes, if you pay attention to his commands and keep all his decrees, I will not bring on you any of the diseases I brought on the Egyptians, for I am the Lord, who heals you.' Then they came to Elim, where there were twelve springs and seventy palm trees, and they camped there near the water."

The Israelites had traveled three days in the desert without finding water and when they came to Marah, they found that the water was bitter, and grumbled to Moses. Moses cried out to the Lord and He showed him a piece of wood which he threw into the water and it became sweet. Later, they came to Elim and found twelve springs of good water and seventy palm trees. Every one of those springs and trees became a remembrance of how He helped them in a time of crisis. To receive any benefit from adversity, we have to accept a situation and be determined to make the best of it. Anyone who experiences a great difficulty will not be easily parted from their Bible. When you write a few lines on a tear-stained page, it is meaningless to others, but you remember how God helped you when you were desperate; you will recall what God whispered to you and fulfilled His promise, years later. He says, "*If you will listen carefully to My voice and do what is right in My eyes ...*" It's like: "I will help you and bring you not to one spring but to twelve, and I will let you camp not in the shade of seventy palm trees, but in the shelter of My arms!

NOVEMBER 7
GOD REMAINS, FOCUS ON HIM

Genesis 18:14 (NIV)

"Is anything too hard for the Lord?"

When we grieve and worry over what we have lost or even from what has been taken from us, it never makes it reappear. Worrying never makes things easier and usually prevents us from moving forward to what is better. During times of any loss, focus on that which remains. Resistance only tightens the noose. Nothing disastrous will destroy you or bring only evil against you, if you will immediately take it to the Lord in prayer. When you fling yourself honestly and openly before Him, you will not only find shelter in your storm but you will find more love in His Presence than you have ever experienced, seen or known before. It is through difficulties, trials and tribulations that God gives us fresh and new insight about Himself. *Ask yourself the question "Is anything too hard for the Lord?"* If you're a believer, you know the answer. Every day we are challenged to believe that God can do anything. One of our statements of faith is, "God can do what He says He can do." His desire is to fill your deepest need. If you truly desire to know Him better and you are striving to do that, know and be prepared for "all hell to break out against you" but it is in the opposition that you learn and experience that indeed there is nothing too hard for God to do. He is so pleased when we want a closer relationship with Him and He will truly move heaven and earth to help you accomplish that purpose. Don't worry over what falls by the wayside, God could replace it, give you something better or enable you to live joyfully without it.

NOVEMBER 8
NOT EVERYONE IS GOING TO LIKE YOU

1 Peter 2:15 (NIV)

"For it is God's will that by doing good you should silence the ignorant talk of foolish men."

Those who do not understand true Christian behavior will criticize you with no real basis for that attack. They aren't being malicious intentionally, it's just they are religiously ignorant. Sometimes doing good will silence (muzzle) them but sometimes you will infuriate them. That is because they are without understanding. I like the way the Living Bible states it: *"It is God's will that your good lives should silence those who foolishly condemn the Gospel without knowing what it can do for them, having never experienced it's power."* Not everyone is going to like you or want to be with you. Well, maybe they missed an opportunity to know someone really awesome! You will have many disappointments in this life but in God, you can get re-appointed! People you care about will come against you. Galatians 6:9 (NKJV) says, *"And do not grow weary while doing good for in due season, we shall reap if we do not lose heart."* My thought is if you continue to do the right thing with the right attitude, it will eventually close the mouths of the unwise and uninformed critics.

NOVEMBER 9
YOU CAME WITH A PLAN

2 Peter 1:3 (NIV)

"His divine power has given us everything we need for life and godliness through our knowledge of him who called us by his own glory and goodness."

God has given us everything we need to look and be like Him, awesome! Read on...we obtain it through our knowledge of Him. We become more like Him as we know Him better and better. What are some of the characteristics you share with your own family members? Some of us have little "look-alikes" from the get-go! They look like us and act like us...that's scary! Some of these attributes are inherited and some are acquired. Good looks, bad manners...we can't deny but we are related! Like it or lump it! But God has given us His divine power and everything else we might need in order for us to take on His likeness. And He's done this so we can live the way we want to? He's given this to us, *"so that through them you may participate in the divine nature and escape the corruption in the world caused by evil desires"* as stated in VS. 4. Before you ever begin to breathe, God had a plan in place, something for you to do that no one else will ever do. Every person He ever made came with a plan and a set of blueprints as He has empowered you with whatever you need. You can do whatever God planned for you, and it happens as He processes you in becoming like Him, as you take on His character. It started with your salvation and will continue until you stand in His Presence in eternity.

NOVEMBER 10
WE HAVE THE WORDS OF THE PROPHETS

2 Peter 1:19 (RSV)

"And we have the prophetic Word made more sure. You will do well to pay attention to this as a lamp shining in a dark place until the day dawns and the Morning Star arises in your heart."

Even more than ever before in history, we should be giving heed to prophecy as it has been outlined to us by the prophets and is totally reliable. Every Word God has spoken will surely come to pass. What God outlined as land belonging to Israel so many years ago was well defined and the most binding real estate contract ever written came with it. Those evading Israel's territory *"would do well to pay attention to it."* Jesus is our *"Lamp shining in a dark place* (our Light Bearer) *until the day dawns and the Morning Star arises in our heart."* When we experience the return of Jesus, we will have such joy and complete enlightenment as only His Presence can provide. False teachers love to distort the scriptures to support what they believe. Man's prophecy seldom happens but what God has spoken in prophecy, we are to pay attention to it. God is moving across the land today and every message he has given to His prophets will surely come to pass. You can believe what God has inspired to be written concerning things to come... pay attention!

NOVEMBER 11

BE SUBMISSIVE AND PRACTICE HUMILITY

<u>1 Peter 5:5</u> (NIV)

"Young men, in the same way be submissive to those who are older. All of you, clothe yourselves with humility toward one another, because, God opposes the proud but gives grace to the humble."

Peter urges the younger men to be submissive to those who are older, their elders. They are to be subject to them, obedient, show honor and respect. For younger people to show honor and respect for the older generation seems to be evaporating in our society today. It is so heartwarming when you do see it, as the younger generation seems to be so much more assertive. The admonition here is that all believers are to clothe themselves in humility much as you would put on a garment and actually fasten or tie it around yourself. Humility is to display true Christian virtues and to be willing to place others' interests first. God takes a firm stand in opposing proud and arrogant people but grants favor to the humble. If you however, look out for another's interests, it could result in God looking with favor on yours. Look for ways you can lift others up; it could result in finding yourself elevated! Don't insist on having it your way. You'll have much better relationships if you show humility and respect to others. *"God opposes the proud but gives grace to the humble."*

NOVEMBER 12
TRUST HIM AND THEN...TRUST HIM

1 Peter 5:6 (NIV)

"Humble yourselves, therefore, under God's mighty hand, that he may lift you up in due time. Cast all your anxiety on him because He cares for you."

If you indeed "humble yourself" you will acknowledge God's lordship, obey Him and serve Him. Oswald Chambers: "Let Him have His way with you; if you do not, instead of being of the slightest use to God in His Redemptive work in the world, you will be a hindrance and a clog." If you will humble yourself before God, in time He will deliver you and He will judge those who oppress you. Your God stands against proud people but always blesses those who will humble themselves before Him. Oswald Chambers: "Why shouldn't we go through heartbreaks? Through those doorways God is opening up ways of fellowship with His Son. (And who in his right mind doesn't enjoy that?) Most of us fall and collapse at the first grip of pain; we sit down on the threshold of God's purpose and die away of self-pity, and all so-called Christian sympathy will aid us to our death bed. But God will not. He comes with the grip of the pierced hand of His Son and says—'Enter into fellowship with Me; arise and shine!' If through a broken heart God can bring His purposes to pass in the world, and then thank Him for breaking your heart." Don't you know that the God you love and serve always has your best interest at heart? You have no problem submitting to a police officer as it's the law of the land. It is also most important to humble yourself before God.

NOVEMBER 13
THE DEVIL GIVES IT HIS BEST SHOT

1 Peter 5:8-9a (NIV)

"Be self-controlled and alert. Your enemy the devil prowls around like a roaring lion looking for someone to devour. Resist him, standing firm in the faith..."

Peter warns against the antics of the evil one and to be self-controlled, well balanced, serious, sober, and have a sense of being vigilant, awake, alert and attentive! If you knew you were approaching a den of lions, you would do it with a heightened sense of alertness! Your adversary comes in many forms, the fiercest being the Devil. His name means slanderer or false accuser. Accuse means to, "thrust through, to inform against." He stalks his prey to swallow that person greedily; he is insidious, relentless and gives it his best shot at being destructive. Peter urges you as a believer to resist and to stand up against him and to remain firm in your faith. Rely totally on God's strength to overcome whatever he tosses your way. An animal trainer in the circus risks his life and has no guarantee that the animal won't strike back. Satan can be just as dangerous as a lion, but you have a guarantee that by totally relying on God and staying humble before Him, the Devil cannot devour you; you can come under attack but he cannot destroy you. You have His Word on it: *"...after you have suffered a little while, will himself restore you and make you strong, firm and steadfast"* 1 Peter 5:10. The Devil gives it his best shot; he misses by a mile, when you stand firm in your faith!

NOVEMBER 14
THE RIGHTEOUS VS THE WICKED

Proverbs 29:2 (NKJV)

"When the righteous are in authority, the people rejoice; but when a wicked man rules, the people groan."

People will always respond well to good government and justice. But when wicked men rule, the people groan in misery. Proverbs 11:4 (NKJV) *"Riches do not profit in the day of wrath but righteousness delivers from death."* Many times Proverbs addresses death as a time of reward or punishment. Riches cannot help you at the time of death. Only righteousness has any meaning and power beyond the grave. It is true that righteous people bring justice to ALL those who live in the city and the whole city lives in peace. Proverbs 11:10-11 (NKJV), *"When it goes well with the righteous, the city rejoices. By the blessing of the upright, the city is exalted but it is overthrown by the mouth of the wicked."* The fate of an entire city without any righteous people in it is the story of Sodom and Gomorrah. Proverbs 25:5 (NKJV), *"Take away the wicked from before the king and his throne shall be established in righteousness."* Wickedness needs to be removed from a king so that his throne can be established rightly. Those who are in authority need to surround themselves with wise godly men who uphold truth and know what God has spoken in His Word. *If a righteous man is in authority, the people prosper and rejoice but if a wicked man rules, every man groans!*

NOVEMBER 15
GOD CHOOSES WELL

Genesis 18:19 (KJV)

"I have chosen him, so that he will direct his children."

God choses those He knows will direct well; not only his own children, but direct God's children well. The rest of the verse should be a delight for us all: *"...keep the way of the Lord by doing what is right and just, so that the Lord will bring about for Abraham what he had promised him."* Abraham did what was right and just for the sake of God's people, and it resulted in God's promises being fulfilled in his own family. God still looks for people he can place in powerful and influential positions that will do *"what is right and just."* In order to be used, we often need to go through times of training and discipline in His school of stability and many fail the training sessions. God knows what you need to withstand the test or else He would never have given it to you. God knows your strength as He has already measured it to the last degree. Isaiah 30:18 (RSV), *"Therefore the Lord waits to be gracious to you; therefore, He exalts Himself to show mercy to you..."* If the Lord has chosen you for something and you are not responding rightly, He waits for two reasons: one is to be gracious to you ,and two, that He may be exalted. How gracious is our God! If He has chosen you for something, it is not only for some purpose that exalts and glorifies Him, but it will also in time be a blessing to you and your family. Don't think you can be an Abraham? He doesn't expect it; He just wants you, and you need to believe that He chooses well!

NOVEMBER 16
DON'T FRET OR WORRY

Philippians 4:6-7 (MSG)

"Don't fret or worry. Instead of worrying, pray. Let petitions and praises shape your worries into prayers, letting God know your concerns. Before you know it, a sense of God's wholeness, everything coming together for good will come and settles you down. It's wonderful what happens when Christ displaces worry at the center of your life."

What does a believer do in times of darkness...a darkness of perplexities and confusion...not of the heart necessarily, but of the mind? This does happen to faithful believers; there are times when we really don't know what to do or which way to turn. It's a time to listen to God, trust in His Name and lean on Him. Ask the Lord to help you and then do nothing. It's very difficult to do nothing; but when you're rattled, don't do a thing because you think you need to be doing something! You may be in a spiritual fog; you don't need to race ahead, but to slow your pace. The right response is to simply trust God, for when you trust, He can work. Worrying will actually prevent Him from doing His work. Worrying, fretting and being anxious will make you physically ill. Don't cower in terror, seeking a way of escape from the trial in which God has placed you. Only the peace of God will quiet your mind and put your heart at rest. *"Before you know it, a sense of God's wholeness, everything coming together for good will come and settles you down. It's wonderful what happens when Christ displaces worry at the center of your life."*

NOVEMBER 17
COOPERATE WITH GOD'S LOVE

Psalms 139:1-5 (LB)

"O Lord, you have examined my heart and know everything about me. You know when I sit or stand. When I am far away, You know my every thought. You chart the path ahead of me and tell me where to stop and rest. Every moment, you know where I am. You know what I am going to say before I even say it. You both precede and follow me and place your hand of blessing on my head."

You have examined my heart and know everything about me and you still love me! Your love is everlasting and constantly! That's hard to comprehend. I don't, or can't seem to remember that your love comes all the time from Your gaze. Help me to sense it and to respond to it. Your love flows into me continually and my need for it is as constant as the outflow of it. *"I can never get away from my God, if I ascend to heaven You are there, if I go to the place of the dead, you are there. If I take my dawn wings and fly to the farthest ocean, even there your hand will guide me and your strength will support me"* (VS. 7-10). His hand indicates his nearness; his protection and his power. It gives me pleasure in thinking: "If I lift up dawn wings and fly to the place of sunrise or settle down on the back side of the sea where the sun sets, even there Yahweh's right hand guides and grasps me firmly." I so appreciate the confidence of knowing God's love!

NOVEMBER 18

GOD PROTECTIVELY CARES FOR HIS OWN

<u>1 Samuel 2:4</u> (MSG)

"For God knows what's going on. He takes the measure of everything that happens. The weapons of the strong are smashed to pieces while the weak are infused with fresh strength. <u>VS.6-9</u>: *God brings death and God brings life, brings down to the grave and raises up. God brings poverty and God brings wealth; he lowers and he also lifts up. He puts poor people on their feet again; he rekindles burned–out lives with fresh hope, restoring dignity and respect to their lives—a place in the sun! For the very structures of earth are God's; he has laid out his operations on a firm foundation. He protectively cares for his faithful friends, step by step, but leaves the wicked to stumble in the dark. No one makes it in this life by sheer muscle!"*

God knows what's going on! He knows what's going on in your life and He is sovereign. He can bring good out of everything! Offer it all to God for His purposes to be processed. You may have to experience the very worst before you are delivered but you will be delivered. He possesses resourcefulness equal to any difficulty..."*He infuses the weak with fresh strength; He lowers but He also lifts up. He gives fresh hope and restores dignity and respect and protectively cares for those who are faithful.*" It is always safe to trust Him and His methods. *"He will always deliver His own step by step but He leaves the wicked to stumble in the dark."* It's His Word. Difficulty is the atmosphere that usually surrounds a miracle. It means an impossibility is about to become a reality. A desperate situation is a delight to our God. *"God will set things right over all the earth...He'll set His anointed on top of the world!*" (VS. 10b) God will protectively care for those who are faithful to Him. You have His Word!

NOVEMBER 19
GOD'S WORD IS A TREASURE TO BE DESIRED

1 Peter 1:3-5 (MSG)

"What a God we have! And how fortunate we are to have him, this Father of our Master Jesus! Because Jesus was raised from the dead, we've been given a brand-new life and have everything to live for, including a future in heaven—and the future starts now! God is keeping careful watch over us and the future. The Day is coming when you'll have it all—life healed and whole. I know how great this makes you feel, even though you have to put up with every kind of aggravation in the meantime. Pure gold put in the fire comes out of it proved pure; genuine faith put through this suffering comes out proved genuine. When Jesus wraps this all up, it's your faith, not your gold that God will have on display as evidence of his victory."

I love the richness of the Word; God has given us more than 32,000 promises for us to believe in and has inspired writers to write them down that we may know. You cannot know what they are unless you spend time reading them, so do it! R E A D and heed:

- **R - is to reflect**. When you go over the verses, look back over them again and again and determine the meaning. I have some notes written in the margin that are over 30 years ago and it is good to remember how God has led, instructed and taught through His Word.

- **E – is to engage.** There is a definite message for you. The Bible is as up-to-date as tomorrow's newspaper and even though written years ago, there is a correlation of what you're reading and your need for this day.

- **A – is to apply.** The Word for today was written for you to apply in your own life. My jaw drops sometimes at the truth revealed. God's Word speaks directly into my life. It truly "discerns the thoughts and intentions of my heart." Hebrews 4:12b (RSV).

- **D – is to disciple.** God's Words will accomplish what He desires and achieve His purpose for you and that purpose is to bring your life into line with His plan of making a disciple out of you, a true follower of Jesus.

Spend time studying, running references, and memorizing. Read and compare translations; so much is gained in doing so. It is better than "proved" gold. It is more than a guide for your life and a light to your path; it is as necessary as your next breath!

NOVEMBER 20
GOD SAID TO ABRAHAM, "I WILL…"

Genesis 12:1-3 (NKJV)

"Now the Lord said to Abram, 'Get out of your country, from your family and from your father's house to a land that I will show you. I will make you a great nation; I will bless you and make your name great and you shall be a blessing. I will bless those who bless you and I will curse him who curses you and in you all the families of the earth shall be blessed."

Five times in these verses, God said to Abram, "I will" and everything He said came true in Abram's life. His name means, "Father of Many." Once his father, Terah died, Abram became the leader and had the responsibility of the family clan. God's command was intensely demanding in that it caused Abram to leave his place, people, and family, when that was simply not done. Only the defeated, poverty-stricken, or landless ever left their ancestral homes. God's promise was to create a great nation through him and this would be the Hebrew people, His own chosen Israelites. God blessed Abram and Sarai beyond measure because as they obeyed, they gained His smile and blessings with a long and healthy life, plus wealth and importance (Genesis 13 & 15). His name is honored even today. We need to know what God is saying and what "He will do" for us, as His will is the key to our life. Is "His will" being done in yours or are you living by the edicts of "your will?" Abram obeyed God and received every promise God had made to him.

NOVEMBER 21
"COME; LET US MAKE A NAME FOR OURSELVES"

Genesis 11:3 (NKJV)

"Then they said to one another, Come let us make bricks and bake them thoroughly. They had brick for stone and they had asphalt for mortar. And they said, Come let us build ourselves a city and a tower whose top is in the heavens; let us make a name for ourselves, lest we be scattered abroad over the face of the whole earth."

We have the perfect contrast in <u>Genesis 12</u> of God telling the people what He would do, and then seeing what men decided what they would do. *"Come, <u>let us</u> make bricks and bake them; <u>let us</u> build ourselves a city and a tower and <u>let us</u> make a name for ourselves…"* These people wanted to become famous and to make a name for themselves; they wanted to achieve their own greatness. They were doing a pretty good job of it until the *"Lord came down to see the city and the tower which the sons of men had built"* <u>VS. 5</u>. Nothing they proposed happened. The "us" in this passage, their language, culture, values, all came from human arrogance. *"The Lord scattered them abroad from there over the face of all the earth and they ceased building the city"* <u>VS. 8</u>. Everything that God spoke into Abram's life came to pass and everything that men purposed within themselves to accomplish came to nothing. You need His input "before" you act. As believers, we create the plan and ask God to bless what we have started; God's wants it to originate with Him. We are to glorify Him; not make a name for ourselves!

NOVEMBER 22
LOVE JESUS

<u>1 John 2:15-17</u> (MSG)

"Don't love the world's ways. Don't love the world's good. Love of the world squeezes out love for the Father. Practically everything that goes on in the world—wanting your own way, wanting everything for yourself, wanting to appear important—has nothing to do with the Father. It just isolates you from him. The world and all it's wanting, wanting, wanting is on the way out—but whoever does what God wants is set for eternity."

Keep your eyes set on Jesus, not on the world and the things of the world. It is so easy to get caught up in our earthly surroundings, but things only lead to the desire to have more, and all of it "*squeezes out love for the Father.*" Having your own way, wanting everything for yourself makes you feel exalted and important, but it also isolates or puts bridges between you and the Lord. None of this goes anywhere, but if you do on this earth what God sent you here to do, you "will be set for all eternity"; that's His promise. Nothing Jesus ever said or had written is just common sense, it is revelation sense as in 2 Peter 1:19 (NIV) "you would do well to pay attention to it as a light shining in a dark place until the day dawns and the Morning Star rises in your hearts." Psalms 33:4 (LB) "*All of God's Words are right, everything He does is worth of our trust.*" We want to enjoy life; He just wants us to enjoy Him. Your relationship with Jesus is the most "important want" you will ever have, so "*don't love the world's ways and don't love the world's goods.*" Love Jesus!

NOVEMBER 23
A PRICELESS GAIN IN KNOWING JESUS

Philippians 3:8-9a (LB)

"*Yes, everything else is worthless when compared with the priceless gain of knowing Christ Jesus my Lord. I have put aside all else, counting it worth less than nothing, in order that I can have Christ and become one with Him...*"

Everything that thwarts my plans and desires causes me to talk to Jesus and that strengthens and blesses my relationship. Instead of dragging me down, disappointments are transformed into opportunities for something good. That transformation takes the strength out of the disappointment, making it possible for me to adjust to the adversity. It begins by being disciplined in little things, in minor setbacks; because it is in the little things we are drawn away from our Father's Loving Presence. When you can reframe setbacks as opportunities, you will find you have been given much more than you lost. It takes time and training to accept losses in a positive way. Paul said that compared to knowing Christ Jesus, he considers everything he once treasured to be as insignificant as rubbish. Everything that we once thought was so important could be dumped in the trash compared to knowing Him. *"I've dumped it all in the trash so that I could embrace Christ and be embraced by Him,"* Philippians3:8 (MSG). To have a thriving vibrant relationship with him is life; and everything else is worthless in comparison.

NOVEMBER 24
GOD IS GREATER THAN OUR WORRIED HEARTS

1 John 3:20 (MSG)
"For God is greater than our worried hearts and knows more about us than we do ourselves."

You can live as close to God as you choose. He does not set up any barriers between you; neither will He tear yours down. People tend to think their circumstances determine their quality of life. So we try with all our might to control what happens. We're happy when it's good; frustrated when it isn't. It is possible to be content whatever our situations. Amos 7:1 (NKJV) refers to the king's mowing's. Our King has many scythes and constantly uses them. In life, we try to stand before His scythe of pain, disappointments and even death. But just as there is no way to have a beautiful lawn without repeated mowing's, there is no way to have a balanced life of tenderness and sympathy for others without enduring God's mowing's. How many times does God compare us to grass... when grass is cut, it bleeds for a while and when God mows you, don't dread the seeming destruction, for He is sure to bring restoration. Cutting grass brings new growth to the grass just as some of the cuts we experience not only bring something new, but something better. Trust the Lord. You can live as close to God as you choose, when you realize *"He is greater than our worried hearts and knows more about us than we do ourselves."*

NOVEMBER 25
BE THANKFUL

Habakkuk 3:17-19 (LB)

"Even though the fig trees are all destroyed, and there is neither blossom left nor fruit, and though the olive crops all fail, and the fields lie barren; even if the flocks die in the fields and the cattle barns are empty, yet I will rejoice in the Lord: I will be happy in the God of my salvation. The Lord God is my Strength and he will give me the speed of a deer and bring me safely over the mountains."

Regardless of what is going on in your world, *"rejoice in the Lord and be happy in the God of your salvation."* Be thankful for what is good in your life and have a thankful attitude as it opens you up to receive spiritual blessings you would otherwise miss. God can bless your heart enough that you can actually get "glimpses" and experience a foretaste of heaven itself. These little samples of glory can not only strengthen you now but give you a hope for your future.

Psalms. 46:2 (LB) tells us *"even if the whole world blows up and the mountains crumble and fall into the sea"* we have a God who sits on top and in the midst of the turmoil... so be thankful. If all the crops fail, the fields lie barren, and there's no cattle left in the barns and when all of life seems to have gone south, we can still rejoice in the Lord and be happy in knowing we are secure in our salvation. We can trust in God as He is our strength; He can give you hind's feet, as swift as the deer and bring you safely over all your mountains! Hind's feet are the feet of a red female deer and it's the only creature God made that puts its hind feet in the exact spot of the front feet when leaping. God made you surefooted!! Be thankful to Jesus!

NOVEMBER 26
GOD'S ARM

Isaiah 53:1b (NKJV)

"And to whom has the arm of the Lord been revealed?"

To whom has the Lord revealed His mighty works? The "arm of the Lord" refers to His great works. Isaiah 50:15c (NKJV), *"Therefore His own arm brought salvation for Him"* Isaiah 40:10 (NKJV), " B*ehold the Lord is come with a strong hand and His arm shall rule for Him, behold His reward is with Him"* The Lord's strong arm brings His mighty acts of judgment and deliverance. And in Isaiah 48:14b,(NKJV) *"He shall do His pleasure on Babylon and His arm shall be against the Chaldeans."* God will defend His people against their enemies. The *"hand that laid the foundation of the earth and whose right hand has stretched out the heavens"* (Isaiah 48:13) is the same One who planned the redemption of His own chosen people but also all who will call upon His Holy Name. *"The Lord's arm is not shortened,"* Numbers 11:23 (VKJV). *"You have a mighty arm,"* Psalms 89:13 (NKJV). *"His huge outstretched arms protect you—under them you are perfectly safe; his arms fend off all harm,"* Psalms 91:5 (MSG). Shelter and comfort are In His arms!

NOVEMBER 27
MY EYES ARE UPON YOU

Psalms 141:8 (NKJV)

"But my eyes are upon You, O God the Lord; in You I take refuse."

We need to keep our eyes on You always. "You may not always look where you are going, but you will always end up going where you're looking! Your perspective determines your choices and direction in life," Bob Gass. So, we need to keep our eyes on Jesus who has *"Commanded us to love one another,"* 2 John VS. 5 (NLT). Your prayer each day should be to ask God to help you to spend this day first in loving Him and then loving others, whether you get anything else done or not. The more time you spend with someone will tell them how important they are to you. It is never enough to say, "You're so important to me," we need to show them—prove to them that they are—by investing some time with them-- the giving of yourself. It's better than a present. We are so prone to spend our time on what concerns us. None of us know how much time we even have to give; we need to take the opportunity of "now;" it is the only guarantee you have of time. "The very best use you can make of your life is to love and the best expression of love is your time, and the best time to love is now,"

Bob Gass. Proverbs 16:9 (NIV), *"In his heart, a man plans his course, but the Lord determines his steps."* If your eyes are upon the Lord, you will trust His course as He is the One who determines your steps.

NOVEMBER 28
BE CAREFUL AND WATCHFUL

1 Peter 5:8-9 (LB)

"Be careful—watch out for attacks from Satan your great enemy. He prowls around like a hungry, roaring lion, looking for some victim to tear apart. Stand firm when he attacks. Trust the Lord; and remember that other Christians all around the world are going through these sufferings too."

Peter warns us against the evil one and other translations tell us to be serious, sober, self-controlled, well balanced and have a sense of being vigilant. Be alert, awake and attentive. Peter urges us to resist and to stand up against our adversary and to remain firm, keep up a solid front in your faith and personal commitment to God. Sometimes we feel we are alone but we need to realize that people suffer for Christ throughout the whole world. Nero wrapped oily rags around the early Christians and set them on fire and used them as a torch to view his roses at night. Christians for years have been paying a heavy price and given their lives because of their faith. We are all vulnerable, we just have to resist His attacks; rely totally on God's strength to overcome. Be aware and watchful but of utmost importance is to trust in the One who watches over you.

NOVEMBER 29

TRIALS WILL MAKE YOU PARTNERS WITH CHRIST

<u>1 Peter 4:12-14</u> (LB)

"Dear friends, don't be bewildered or surprised when you go through the fiery trials ahead, for this is no strange, unusual thing that is going to happen to you. Instead, be really glad—because these trials will make you partners with Christ in his suffering, and afterwards you will have the wonderful joy of sharing his glory in that coming day when it will be displayed."

What is your response to a surprise that bewilders you? A "surprise" can stagger, amaze or even shock you! When we are completely stunned by some turn of events, we tend to fix our whole attention on it; we mull it over, can't seem to think of anything else. We search for a way over it, around it, or a way out of it. And what happens is in our effort to correct, either to make it better or right, we get completely off course. When you are totally stumped, the best thing you can do in any fiery ordeal is to try to minimize the ordeal and put your entire focus on Jesus. If you will do this, the next thing you know, the ordeal is behind you and you haven't a clue as to how you got through it. A fiery ordeal is just that as fire burns; hurts like sin; and can destroy; which is probably the intent of the one who "set" it. Suffering will improve your character, if you allow it. Does God allow some infliction with the thought, "let's-just-see-how-you-handle-this-one"... I don't think so. But if your suffering is connected to your faithfulness to Him, He will always strengthen you. Don't regard it as something unusual that is happening to you. You may think it's something foreign and only happens to you when multitudes have experienced the same or even worse. Rather than be amazed, as believers, we are to rejoice. Possibly God has allowed you to experience this as you are special; not everyone could handle it. And if you are being persecuted because of your faithfulness to Him, how great your joy will be when He returns! When you are insulted and reproached for His name, you will be blessed. And that is not being "happy" but it is having God congratulate you on your character, which is far more to be desired. Having His approval goes a long way when suffering, as you have the promise that "*afterwards, you will share the wonderful joy of His glory as trials will make your partners with Christ,*" what could be better than that?

NOVEMBER 30
WHAT DO YOU SEE

1 Peter 1:8-9 (NIV)

"Though you have not seen Him, you love Him and even though you do not see him now, you believe in Him and are filled with an inexpressible and glorious joy for you are receiving the goal of your faith, the salvation of your soul."

In time present or time past, we have not seen Jesus but we believe in Him, believe His Word and His promises. In believing, we are filled with an inexpressible and glorious joy because we are in the process of receiving the goal of our faith: which is that appointed time when we will receive the salvation of our soul...our redemption through the blood shed on the cross for our sins by the One in whom we believe. What a glorious gift; there is none other like it. "*All honor to God, the God and Father of our Lord Jesus Christ; for it is his boundless mercy that has given us the privilege of being born again, so that we are now members of God's own family. Now we live in the hope of eternal life because Christ rose again from the dead. And God has reserved for his children the priceless gift of eternal life; it is kept in heaven for you, pure and undefiled, beyond the reach of change and decay. And God in his mighty power will make sure that you get there safely to receive it, because you are trusting him. It will be yours in that coming last day for all to see,"* 1 Peter 1:3-5 (LB). What you have not "seen" in time present or past awaits you in the future. You may not physically see Jesus now, but you can "see" in His Word what lies before you!

DECEMBER 1
CALL ON THE NAME OF JESUS

Philippians 2:9-11 (NKJV)

"Therefore God also has highly exalted Him and given Him the name which is above every name, that at the name of Jesus every knee should bow, of those in heaven, and of those on earth, and of those under the earth and that every tongue should confess that Jesus Christ is Lord to the glory of God the Father."

When you find yourself totally overwhelmed, call upon the Name of Jesus; His Name is above every name whether it's in heaven, on earth or under the earth. "In the thick of battle, call upon His Name. At that instant, the battle becomes Mine; your role is simply to trust Me as I fight for you. My Name, properly used, has unlimited Power to bless and protect. At the end of time, every knee will bow when my name is proclaimed. People who have used "Jesus" as shoddy swear Word will fall down in terror on that awesome day. But all those who have drawn near Me through trustingly uttering My Name will be filled with inexpressible and glorious joy," Jesus Calling. Matthew 5:3 (MSG), "*You're at the end of your rope, you are blessed because there is less of you and more of God and His rule."* We are so limited and He is so Limitless! Call on His Name, He has unlimited power to bless and protect. Someone has so wisely said, "Don't run to the phone, run to the throne!" The one on the other end of the phone is probably a bigger mess than you are; the One on the throne can deliver you! He is mighty to save!

DECEMBER 2
WHAT DO YOU DO WITH ANTAGONISM

Revelation 2:7b (NKJV)
"To him who overcomes..."

You may or may not believe it, but your life is a war zone, whether you're talking about the physical, mental, moral, or spiritual aspects of it. You are constantly striving with the things that come against you. Your health is a balance between what is going on inside your body and what's happening on the outside. "Everything outside my physical life is designed to put me to death. This is the open fact of life. If I have enough fighting power, I produce the balance of health. The same is true of the mental life. If I want to maintain a vigorous mental life, I have to fight and in that way, the mental balance called thought is produced. Morally it is the same. Everything that does not partake of the nature of virtue is the enemy of virtue in me and it depends on what moral caliber I have whether I overcome and produce virtue. And, spiritually, it is the same. Jesus said, In the world ye shall have tribulation, i.e., everything that is not spiritual makes for my undoing, but—Be of good cheer, I have overcome the world. I have to learn to score off the things that come against me," Oswald *Chambers*. *With God's help, you can do this. You have a promise, "To him who overcomes, I will give to eat from the tree of life, which is in the midst of the Paradise of God."* <u>Revelation 2:7b.</u> All your antagonism and aggravation serves a purpose, you're going to love the results!

DECEMBER 3
YOU HAVE TODAY

<u>Philippians 3:13-14</u> (NKJV)

"Brethren, I do not count myself to have apprehended, but one thing I do, forgetting those things which are behind and reaching forward to those things which are ahead, I press toward the goal for the prize of the upward call of God in Christ Jesus."

Are you willing to live in today, or are you stuck in what happened yesterday? Perhaps you had a really good day and you feel you can relax and relish in the glory of it. Maybe it was a disaster. You should never settle for your yesterdays. Little is to be gained by wistful hopes of tomorrow because your future is based on what you accomplish today. Bob Gass: "Between the great things we can't do and the little things we won't do, the danger is that we'll do nothing. George spent his early years shuffled between foster homes until one day Maria Watkins, a washerwoman, found him asleep in her barn. She didn't just take him in; she took him to church and introduced him to Jesus. When he eventually left her home, he took with him the Bible she'd given him. Maria left her mark on his life and George Washington Carver left his mark on the world." Helping others is always a big key to your own success. What are your plans today? Yesterday with its goodness or badness is gone but you have today to make a difference in your life and in the life of someone else! You really do need to *"forget those things which are behind and reach forward to those things which are ahead!"* You have today to do it!

DECEMBER 4
TREAT EVERYONE WITH DIGNITY

1 Peter 2:17 (LB)

"Show respect for everyone. Love Christians everywhere. Fear God and honor the government."

The (MSG) Bible states it this way: *"Treat everyone you meet with dignity."* That states that we should honor everyone and respect them, recognizing their worth because all are created in God's own image. That means even though we may show no respect for others, God loves them and every last one of them need a Savior. We may hate what they do but they have a soul and God wants all people to know Him. We are to honor everyone and love the brotherhood. This refers to all people; at least have a concern for their souls. What we do reflects back on the God who made us. When your children do foolishly, don't you examine your own lifestyle to see if it somehow came from you? We all are guilty of remaining silent when God gives us an opportunity; and I flunked that one last week. I was in the hospital waiting for some tests when a bedraggled, dirty looking, oversized couple came in. They were both on their cell phones, continuously. He was carrying a heavy winter coat, even though it was 91 degrees at the time.

When I left two hours later, they were still in the lobby on their phones. You tell me what was going through my mind; clearly I was looking at the outside when Jesus was peering inside. I showed neither respect nor honor. I was puzzled and intimidated by some of their actions. I wish I could tell you that I rose to the occasion, but I did not. Hopefully given another opportunity, I will "*treat them with dignity*" and will alleviate some need in their lives. Jesus treated everyone with respect and gave of Himself, whatever it took, to meet the need of their soul.

DECEMBER 5
HE WILL REVIVE YOU AGAIN

Psalms 71:20-21 (NKJV)

"You have shown me great and severe troubles, shall revive me again, and bring me up again from the depths of the earth. You shall increase my greatness and comfort me on every side."

No matter how many troubles, twists/turns it takes, there is always one smooth path ahead for you. Even on the longest day of the year, the sun sets. So keep your focus on the path just ahead of you, and leave the outcome to Jesus. God's time for mercy will come; in fact, it has already come, if our time for believing has arrived. God doesn't concentrate on your messes; he concentrates on you, and your destiny. Ask God to either close the door or open it wider, but you keep on walking! Ask in faith and keep asking, don't cease because of a delay. There is no such thing as an unanswered prayer that is offered rightly in the right Spirit. Prayer is not getting God to do what we want Him to do; it is getting us in line with His plan for our lives. And, He has let us in on His plan as He has said that He will *"revive you again and increase your greatness and comfort you on every side."* You have His Word!

DECEMBER 6
THE LORD IS IN THIS PLACE

Genesis 28:16 (NKJV)

> *"…Surely the Lord is in this place and I was not aware of it."*

Jacob awoke from a dream and realized that he had encountered the Living God. So many times, we act as if He is nowhere around and He is always in our "wherevers." VS. 15, *"I am with you and will watch over you wherever you go."* Thank you, God. You are ready to give us comfort, insight, understanding and wisdom, wherever we are. You are the Lord God Almighty! Isaiah 41:10 (LB), *"Do not fear, for I am with you. Do not be dismayed. I am your God. I will strengthen you; I will help you; I will uphold you with my victorious right hand."* Praise and power belong to you, Lord God. You are here; you see our deepest needs and in Your Presence, we find solace and answers. Grant to us the mercy and grace You have promised to be with us all the days of our lives and give us a balance of holiness in the process. *"Surely, You are in this place,"* just help us to be aware of it!

DECEMBER 7
WORK OUT WHAT HE HAS WORKED IN

2 Corinthians 12:9 (NKJV)

> *"And He said to me, "My grace is sufficient for you, for My strength is made perfect in weakness."*

God's grace is an absolute in your life; it is as eternal as the One who gave it to you. When He died on the cross, it provided a means of salvation to all who will believe; His salvation is complete and perfect. Nothing is lacking in His provision of eternal life to those who believe in Him. If you have confessed your sins and accepted Him into your heart, you aren't being saved, you are saved. "Salvation is as eternal as God's throne; the thing for me to do is to work out what God works in. I am responsible for doing it. It means that I have to manifest in this body the life of the Lord Jesus, not mystically, but really and emphatically....Most of us are much sterner with others than we are in regard to ourselves; we make excuses for things in ourselves whilst we condemn in others things to which we are not naturally inclined," Oswald Chambers. Keep in mind his Words, *"My grace is sufficient for you and My strength is made perfect in weakness."* You do that by working out, what He has already worked in.

DECEMBER 8
HE WANTS YOU TO KNOW HIM

Hosea 6:6 (LB)

"I don't want your sacrifices—I want your love; I don't want your offerings—I want you to know me."

God created you to have fellowship with you; He requires sacrifices and offerings, but He desires us to know Him. Hosea 10:12 (LB), *"Plant the good seeds of righteousness and you will reap a crop of my love; plow the hard ground of your hearts, for now is the time to seek the Lord..."* Hosea 14:8-9 (LB), *"I am living and strong! I look after you and care for you. I am like an evergreen*

303

tree, yielding my fruit to you throughout the year. My mercies never fail. Whoever is wise, let him understand these things. Whoever is intelligent, let him listen. For the paths of the Lord are true and right and good men walk along them." How great is the Word of the Lord and the encouragement of His promise to always look after and care for us; His mercies never fail. We just need to use the wisdom and understanding He offers and then listen. When you read His Word, always do it with a listening ear and ask, "What are you saying to me?" Listening and speaking to Him is how we get to know Him. That is what He wants as He has said, *"I want your love and I want you to know me."*

DECEMBER 9
HE IS TRUSTWORTHY

Proverbs 3:5 (NKJV)

"Trust in the Lord with all your heart, and lean not on your own understanding..."

When facing a dilemma, do not lean on your own understanding primarily and do not consult anxiety-driven people. Refuse to be depressed, deflected or derailed. Think God's thoughts instead of your old thoughts. God thoughts are in His Word. He does a lot of it in His Word. Proverbs 3:6 (NKJV), *"In all your ways acknowledge Him, and He shall direct your paths."* Troubles will only seem to destroy your happiness but they definitely build up your character. A hard blow on the outside can actually be a blessing on the inside. The real trouble is what you lose when you rebel against it. Stop focusing on yourself and trust and rest in Jesus. Deep within every one of us is a place of peace where God lives, turn to Him and listen for His still small voice. Thank you, Jesus, for being with us and for being Who and what You are and for being so trustworthy!

DECEMBER 10
GOD-OF-THE-ANGEL-ARMIES

Amos 4:13 (MSG)

"Look who's here: Mountain-Shaper! Wind-Maker! He laid out the whole plot before Adam. He brings everything out of nothing, like dawn out of darkness. He strides across the alpine ridges. His name is GOD, God-of-the-Angel-Armies."
Amos 5:8-10 (MSG)

"Do you realize where you are? You're in a cosmos, star-flung with constellations by God; A world God wakes up each morning and puts to bed each night. God dips water from the ocean gives the land a drink. GOD, God-revealed does all this. And he can destroy it as easily as make it. He can turn this vast wonder into total waste. People hate this kind of talk. Raw truth is never popular."

The Mountain-Shaper/Wind-Maker brought everything out of nothing and is the same who flung the stars in place. He puts the world to bed every night and gets it up every morning! He dips water from the ocean and waters the land. He is indeed God-of-the-Angel-Armies. He is LORD and can destroy the earth just as easily as He made it; people hate to be reminded of it, but it is the way it is. He said, *"Time's up, O Israel! Prepare to meet your God!"* Amos 4:12 (MSG). Are you prepared? What do you need to do before you stand before the Mountain-Shaper? We need to spend time alone with the Lord, sitting at His feet in the sacred privacy of His blessed Presence. The Commander and Chief of the heavenly army wants an intimate relationship with you. You don't want to wait to hear Him say, "*Time's up!*"

DECEMBER 11
PROBLEMS ACHIEVE VICTORY

2 Corinthians 4:17 (NIV)

"For our light and momentary troubles are achieving for us an eternal glory that far outweighs them all.""

Our life and the world itself seem to be filled with troubles...why is that? Everyone you talk to has so many problems...family, relationships, finances, or health. "The answer is found in the Word *achieving*, for these *'momentary troubles are achieving for us'* something very precious. They are teaching us not only the way to victory, but better still, the law of victory—there is a reward for every sorrow and the sorrow itself produces the reward. It is the very truth expressed in this dear old hymn, 'Nearer my God to Thee, nearer to Thee, E'en though it be a cross that raiseth me.' It is comforting to know that sorrow stays only for the night and then takes its leave in the morning. And a thunderstorm is very brief when compared to a long summer day," Streams in the Desert. Our problems, though painful and difficult, do achieve something very precious because in, through and on the other side of them, we are taught the way to victory!

DECEMBER 12

HE WILL DO WHAT HE PROMISED!

<u>Revelation 3:11</u> (LB)

"Look, I am coming soon! Hold tightly to the little strength you have—so that no one will take away your crown."

People for centuries now have read, "Look, I am coming soon!" and believe that You coming soon. George Mueller, in his day, expected You to arrive at any moment; we still wait. It's a mystery, God, as we have no idea what time You have in mind. Waiting for us to do what you told you to do could be the key! You created us so that we could enjoy You and glorify You. You provide the joy; our part is to glorify You by living close to You. Most of our lives flow from past to present to future. The Bible says our lives should flow from a focus on <u>the future</u> into the present, forgetting the past. We all dwell entirely too much on what "has happened" we need to focus on what is ahead...and that is Jesus! *"Though the cherry trees don't blossom and the strawberries don't ripen, though the apples are worm-eaten and the fields stunted, though the sheep pens are without sheep and the cattle barns empty, I'm singing joyful praise to God. Counting on God's rule to prevail, I take heart and gain strength. I run like a deer. I feel like I'm king of the mountain!"* <u>Habakkuk 3:17-19</u> (MSG). Help us Lord to not always be wanting some visible sign that You are coming, but be convinced that You will!

DECEMBER 13
HELP US TO SEE

<u>Matthew 5:8</u> (NKJV)

"Blessed are the pure in heart, for they shall see God."

Instead of yearning for a trouble free life, rejoice that whatever you're into right now can highlight your awareness of Jesus and enable you to see Him. Keep in mind that you have an eternity of trouble free living awaiting you in heaven. God never promised to remove our struggles but He promised to change the way we look at them, when we're looking at Him and in His Word. God let Elisha's servant see a whole army of horses and chariots of fire around them; Jacob saw a ladder that extended to heaven; Saul regained his sight after his experience on the Road to Damascus. Let your prayer be, "Jesus let me see your hand today in my life." Just beneath the surface of pain is discipline, knowledge and a lot of insight into the limitless possibilities that are before you. Every one of them will strengthen you and equip you to help someone else. Open our eyes and hearts to see You, Lord!

DECEMBER 14
COMMIT YOUR WAY INTO THE LORD

<u>Psalms 37:5</u> (NKJV)

"Commit your way into the Lord, trust also in Him and He shall bring it to pass."

Commit "all" your ways into Him; trust through days of waiting and times of delays, and when it seems as if everything is full of difficulties. There will be times when you sense all have rejected you and everyone you encounter opposes you; even when you cannot understand your way or situation, *"trust Him for He will surely bring it to pass."* There is One who will never leave you nor forsake you; you will walk out of the darkness and into the light. VS.6, *"He shall bring forth your righteousness as the light, and your justice as the noonday."* He is the light that penetrates the darkness of our lives. Psalms 139:11-12 (LB) *"If I try to hide in the darkness, the night become light around me. For even darkness cannot hide from God; to you the night shines as bright as day. Darkness and light are both alike to you."* Instead of yearning for a trouble free life, know that whatever you are experiencing can also heighten your awareness of His Presence. As you commit more things to Him, you get to know Him better and you find His Words are true.

DECEMBER 15
HEAR THE WORD OF THE LORD

Hosea 4:1a (NKJV)

"Hear the Word of the Lord, people of Israel, for the Lord has a case against the inhabitants of the land."

People have changed over the years but no matter how right and wrong shifts over time, God doesn't change. And this is His plan: Philippians 2:9-11 (NIV), *"Therefore the Lord exalted Him to the highest place and gave Him a name that is above every name, that at the name of Jesus every knee shall bow in heaven and on earth and under the earth and every tongue shall confess that Jesus Christ is Lord, to the glory of God the Father."* Man may devise all kinds of sordid lifestyles but that doesn't alter what God Almighty has ordained. If there was ever a time in history when people needed to *hear the Word of the Lord*," it is now. There is little to be gained by wailing about all that is wrong; you need to recognize evil and when you see it in leadership, pray for them; but you, yourself, need to know what the Lord is saying to you every day. The only way you'll ever know that is through study and prayer. You will never help anyone else or rightly serve God unless you know what He is speaking into your own life. Don't be the recipient of God bringing a " *case" against you*." Listen for God to speak and hear His Word today.

DECEMBER 16
THERE IS NO KNOWLEDGE OF GOD IN THE LAND

Hosea 4:1b (NKJV)
"There is no truth or mercy or knowledge of God in the land."

At the time Hosea wrote this there wasn't a "little bit" of truth in the land, there was none...nothing absolute, nothing of wholeness or integrity; no loyalty, devotion, graciousness, kindness, compassion or doing good for one another. *"No knowledge of God"* doesn't mean intellectual awareness but there was no recognition of God's authority as Israel's covenant Lord. The intent is: "The people do not acknowledge Me as God." If you pick up a newspaper or walk in our marketplace today, what do you hear? You offend someone if you even mention His Name! What can you do? You can make truth, faithful love and knowledge of God a priority in your life and it will not only affect those around you, but it will let you avoid God's rebuke. You be genuine and reliable, show kindness and mercy to others. Keep your own heart and life right before God; it will count with the One whose doing the counting. Know what the Lord is saying to you. Sit down each day and spend time studying your Bible, make notes of anything that specifically speaks to you. It is surprising how many times you will be privileged to share what He has spoken into your life with someone else before the day's end. Spread *"some knowledge of the Lord"* in the land around you. If there's, *"no knowledge of God in the land;"* then you change the land about you.

DECEMBER 17
THE LAND MOURNS

Hosea 4:2-3a (NKJV)

"By swearing and lying, killing and stealing and committing adultery, they break all restraint, with bloodshed upon bloodshed. Therefore the land will mourn..."

The people of Hosea's day had turned their backs on God's Commandments. We don't need to be in a war torn country to see one murder after another happening every day, sometimes multiple times a day. All creation is affected by God's wrath, *"the land mourns"* when sin abounds and restraint is broken. The land mourns with earthquakes, drought and floods, as prophecy unfolds the theme of the undoing of creation as a result of God's judgment. What do we see in our society and environment today that corresponds with these verses? Not every natural disaster is God's judgment but He does use some physical events in the physical world as punishment. Sins against Him do bring physical harm to people and to their environment. All the earth groans under the burden of sin. Sin damages your relationship with God and with

311

others, and it will not only separate you from Him but from others, as well. Our land today mourns under the same burden but our focus is on the One who bore that sin for us and has promised us deliverance.

DECEMBER 18
GET RID OF DESTRUCTIVE BEHAVIOR

Hosea 4:14 (NKJV)

"People without discernment are doomed."

Billy the Kid lived a wild life in the Wild West. Rumor has it that he killed 21 men, one for each year of his life, as he died sometime before his 21st birthday. He made a name for himself, but not a good one. In the Wild West, it was clear as to who were the good guys and who were the bad ones. People were either outlaws or law-abiding citizens. In our culture today, it's still true but not so clearly defined. We need to be acutely aware that God sets the standard for all of us and His Word is still the same as when He first spoke His commandments. God's Word never changes nor does His meaning and purpose for your life. This chapter began with: *"Hear the Word of the Lord"* and ends with, *"People without discernment are doomed."* A personal challenge would be for you to let God's Word be your standard for right and wrong and if you have within you any destructive behavior, get rid of it!

DECEMBER 19

KEEP YOUR COVENANT WITH YOUR SPOUSE

Hosea 1:2 (NKJV)

"When the Lord began to speak to Hosea, the Lord said to Hosea: 'Go take yourself a wife of harlotry and children of harlotry, for the land has committed great harlotry by departing from the Lord.'"

VS. 1 of this chapter says *"The Word of the Lord that came to Hosea..."* God has asked a lot of people to do a lot of things but what he required of Hosea was very special. God was demonstrating his grief over Israel's infidelity by telling Hosea to "go take to yourself an adulterous wife." The description of the wife God asked Hosea to marry was known to have multiple sexual partners who paid for her affections. Not only that, but she would bear children of unfaithfulness. This marital infidelity would picture Israel's idolatry and unfaithfulness in their covenant with God. God's people were currently participating in lewd cult worship practices and courting the favor of other gods, while claiming devotion to their God. Very few transgressions in a marriage equal that of the unfaithfulness of a spouse. The pain it causes is worse than death. Marriage is a covenant relationship, one that you take before God and you need to be true to it. The betrayal and broken trust that occurs when people are unfaithful in their marriage vows is an abomination to the Lord. Keep your covenant with your spouse and with your God!

DECEMBER 20
BE FAITHFUL

Hosea 2:19-20 (NKJV)

"I will betroth you to Me forever; Yes, I will betroth you to Me in righteousness and justice. In loving kindness and mercy; I will betroth you to Me in faithfulness, and you shall know the Lord."

The Lord regards His relationship with His people as a betrothal agreement which was a strong binding commitment and the last step before the actual wedding takes place. He wanted it to be one that was righteous, just, full of loving kindness, mercy and forever" That was the intent of the Lord concerning His people and so it is to be between husband and wife; it is to be a faithful relationship. Bounding back from an unfaithful spouse is almost equal to rising from the dead. It is a far worse sin to be unfaithful to your God and Savior Jesus Christ; yet many gloss over that one! You are unfaithful to God when the things of the world become more important to you than your relationship with Him. You can see others sin; why in the world would you ignore your own waywardness? When you were raising your children, you disciplined them for their own benefit and sanity. Likewise, because God loves you, He will not ignore your unfaithfulness. Just as an unfaithful partner will get caught; God will confront you with your sin, not to punish you, but to restore you. He will show you loving kindness and mercy; He will bind you to Himself in faithfulness... all so that you will learn to know and trust in Him!

DECEMBER 21
THE WORK OF THE HOLY SPIRIT

Luke 1:34 (NKJV)

> "Then Mary said to the angel, "How can this be...?"

Mary, mother of Jesus, was a young girl when the angel appeared to her and explained that she had found favor with God and that she would conceive and bring forth a Son and that His name would be Jesus. She was amazed and did not respond in unbelief but instead asked, "*How can this be?*" She doesn't understand but is fully accepting of her role then as well as in the years to come. Becoming the mother of the Son of God happened only because of the Holy Spirit. She probably asked the same question many times in the events that followed as she rumbled over rough, hilly country roads on the back of the donkey, possibly even walking at times for miles. Again, when she finally arrived and could find no room at the Inn, no hot bath or clean sheets to accommodate her tired, swollen body; and yet again, as she gave birth for the first time amid sheep and cattle. Have you ever smelled a sheep or a cow? Going through the pangs of labor is not exactly when you want to inhale that smell for the first time! "How could any of this be?" The next time you think you're overwhelmed, think of what Mary got for her trouble and believe with her that *"With God, nothing will be impossible."* Luke 1:34-37 (NKJV). Mary learned that through the work of the Holy Spirit that "all these things could be." And, regardless of what you are experiencing, you can know answers to some of the problems that trouble you too...it all happens through the same Holy Spirit working in you.

DECEMBER 22
SEARCH FOR THE LORD

Matthew 2:1 (NKJV)

"Now after Jesus was born in Bethlehem of Judea in the days of Herod the kind, behold wise men from the East came to Jerusalem."

Jesus who created humans and the planet on which we live became a human being too and came to live for a little while on the planet He had made. It was predetermined years before that He would be born in Bethlehem, a very small village about six miles South of Jerusalem. The wise men had already traveled a very long distance seeking the Promised Messiah. Did it ever occur to you that these were actually pagans that had walked such a long distance to seek the Savior while the chief priests and scribes serving just six miles down the road in Jerusalem weren't willing or interested enough to seek Him out? These men earnestly sought the Savior. How about you, is it possible that you know this story but still do not know Him as your Savior and Lord? People then, as well as today, seek association with Jesus for all kinds of personal gain; but lasting fulfillment is only found when we seek Jesus with humility and honesty and with an open desire for no other reason than to know more of Him. Jeremiah 29: 13-14 NKJV), *"You will seek Me and find Me, when you search for Me with all your heart. I will be found by you, says the Lord...."* One scripture says, *"The eyes of the Lord range throughout the earth to strengthen those whose hearts are fully committed to Him."* 2 Chronicles 16:9 (NIV). When you earnestly seek the Lord, know that He is already searching for you!

DECEMBER 23
SEARCH FOR HIM FOR THE RIGHT REASONS

<u>Matthew 2:8</u> (NKJV)

"And he sent them to Bethlehem and said, "Go and search carefully for the young Child, and when you have found Him, bring back Word to me that I may come and worship Him also."

King Herod asked the wise men to search diligently for the young Child so that He could go and worship Him. He provided them with a piece of vital information they had been missing...the Child had been born in the nearby village of Bethlehem which gave them the endpoint of their pilgrimage. In exchange for supplying them with this, Herod asked them to do him the favor and report back to him. He had no thought of worship; this would simply provide him with an idea of the Child's current age and thus aid him in determining who would need to be killed by his murderous men. The wise men did not return to Herod with any information. VS. 16: *"Then Herod, when he saw that he was deceived by the wise men, was exceedingly angry and sent forth and put to death all the male children who were in Bethlehem and in all its districts, from two years old and under..."* This is the time of year when we celebrate the birth of the Christ Child and we need to be so thankful for the wisdom of these men as they were told in a dream to not return to Herod. Don't be so caught up in your busy plans of the day that you would miss anything He might be speaking into your life right now. Herod sought Jesus for selfish reasons; you want to seek Him for intimacy, love, and companionship. Love Him because He dearly loves you.

DECEMBER 24
EXPERIENCE GREAT JOY IN HIS PRESENCE

Matthew 2:9b-10 (NKJV)

"...And behold, the star which they had seen in the East went before them, till it came and stood over where the young Child was. When they saw the star, they rejoiced with exceedingly great joy."

How incredible is it that the same star they had seen in the East now appeared to them as they again went on their way?! Various attempts have been made to explain this but there is none except God used supernatural means in guiding not only the star, but led them to Bethlehem and miraculously stopped above the place where the Child was born. The Bible says, *"when they saw the star, they rejoiced with exceedingly great joy."* What a wonderful experience for them! When was the last time you were totally overcome with joy just to be in His Glorious Presence? With just two remaining days before we celebrate His birth, how much of it are you spending in wonder and amazement of His birth and thanking God for letting Jesus come to earth to be born of men that we might be born of God? Let Jesus fill your heart and be overcome with joy beyond measure! Take time today to just be in His Presence and sense His glory, power and un-surpassing love.

DECEMBER 25
FALL DOWN AND WORSHIP JESUS

Matthew 2:11 (NKJV)

"And when they had come into the house, they saw the young Child with Mary His mother, and fell down and worshiped Him."

The wise men fell on their knees and worshipped the Child. Today, we need to do the same thing. During this busy season, there may be a hundred other things clamoring for your attention and some of it needful, but take time to worship Jesus and do it on your knees, if you possibly can. Doing so humbles you and shows total submission. If someone sticks a gun in your back, what do you do? You raise your hands; it's a universal sign of submission or surrender in ANY language on earth. Psalms. 63:4: *"Thus I will bless You while I live; I will lift up my hands in Your name."* So raise your hands and bow your knees! While you're there, bend your heart and your ear, listening for any Word He may be waiting to speak into your life. If you will do this, all the other "things" clamoring for your attention will more likely happen if you pause, fall down and spend some time in true worship!

DECEMBER 26
GIVE GOOD GIFTS

Matthew 2:11b (NKJV)
"And when they had opened their treasures, they presented gifts to Him: gold, frankincense and myrrh."

We don't know how many wise men there were but because three gifts are mentioned, we believe there were three. The gifts they gave to Jesus were of great value; no peasant could have afforded such expensive gifts…gold, frankincense and myrrh. What kind of gifts are you bringing to Jesus today? Are you giving Him the first and the best or does He get what you have left when you've taken care of everyone else? They gave Him gifts that represented His Priestly ministry as well as His sacrificial death, and they did it joyfully.   Gold then, as well as today, was of great value; frankincense was a fragrance that came only as a result of fire; myrrh was a fragrant resinous substance obtained from certain species of balsam trees. It has been said that Queen Esther used oil of myrrh for six months before appearing before the King. They not only gave us the example of how to truly worship by bowing low, but they presented meaningful, costly gifts. You may not be able to physically lay yours at His feet, but one of the best gifts you can possibly give is yourself. Live out every day of your life in a way that honors Him and then give sacrificially to whatever and whoever takes the gospel to those who have not heard. It will not only mean life instead of death to those who hear it, but you will be blessed! God honored you by giving you the best gift ever, Jesus, His beloved Son!

DECEMBER 27
BE OBEDIENT

Matthew 2:13 (NKJV)

"...Behold an angel of the Lord appeared to Joseph in a dream saying, "Arise, take the young Child and His mother, flee to Egypt and stay there until I bring you Word, for Herod will seek the young Child to destroy Him."

God   didn't do it often, but He used angels in this way, throughout Scripture to give specific instructions. Joseph obeyed unquestionably without delay and escaped with Mary and the Baby during the night. How many times have you hesitated and paused rather than obeyed? Sometimes what He has told you to do is difficult and you wait to see if you can come up with a better plan before deciding. How many times do we miss it altogether because we don't even recognize it being from Him? If you check the Scriptures, you'll find that Joseph obeyed everything God told him to do; he might have had some problem with the scenario at first, but he did obey each time and without hesitation. In the nine months of waiting for the Child to be born, Joseph not only defended Mary but he took care of her and always did what was best for her and the Baby. It was a sign of God's approval and trust in having the angel appear to Joseph (not Mary), when He gave the instructions to flee to Egypt. How obedient are you and what is your response to the birth of the Savior of the world? Have you accepted Him as your Lord and Savior? If not, why not? This Christmas season is all about knowing and worshiping Him. Come Let Us Worship the King! Let us celebrate Jesus, God's Son! Listen and obey today!!

DECEMBER 28
JESUS WAITS

Psalms 118:24 (NKJV)
"This is the day the Lord has made, I will rejoice and be glad in it."

For some, the flurry of shopping, parties, exchanging of gifts, rushing to finish the unobtainable suddenly comes to a halt. The tinsel isn't so sparkling and the lights seem to lose some of their glow as friends and family leave to go their separate ways. Your life that was spinning out of control comes to a standstill, as you download. That's what happens if that's where your heart is. But the realness of Christmas and the joy of our salvation are not found in beautifully wrapped packages, sparkling lights and dainty desserts. Everything you share during the holidays can have a relationship to your relationship with Jesus, if done in the right spirit, and that's as it should be. Keep in mind though that when you were your busiest, Jesus was with you, giving you strength, fresh ideas and energizing your efforts so that it could all happen. If you slighted Him during those days, He's still right where you left Him; He loves you and is waiting to spend time with you today. Every day was especially designed for you to delight yourself in Him and to give Him praise and honor. It is always a good day to rejoice and be glad in the Lord! *"Therefore the Lord will wait that He may be gracious to you!"* Isaiah 30:18 (NKJV).

DECEMBER 29
WHAT ARE YOU LISTENING TO

Ephesians 4:30 (MSG)

"Don't grieve God. Don't break his heart. His Holy Spirit, moving and breathing in you, is the most intimate part of your life, making you fit for Himself. Don't take such a gift for granted."

You need to be listening to what the Holy Spirit is speaking into your life so that you don't grieve God and break His heart. What are you listening to today? Are you listening to the cries of despair and discouragement all around you or are you listening to what the Word of God has to say? You listen to ill advice; you listen to bad reports from the doctor; you listen to political schemes that threaten your very existence, when you need to be listening to the One who can make a difference in your life. If you do listen to what God is saying and spend enough time in His Word, the Holy Spirit will enable what is inside of you to be lived out of you. *"The Holy Spirit, moving and* breathing in you is the most intimate part of your life, making you fit for Himself"...do you believe that? Accepting and believing God's Word works within you is a powerful source of strength and wisdom that you desperately need. It's a wonderful gift and one we should never take for granted! Listen to what the Word says to you!

DECEMBER 30
AT THE SOUND OF YOUR CRY, HE HEARS YOU

<u>Isaiah 30:19b-21</u> (RSV)

"He will surely be gracious to you at the sound of your cry; when he hears it, he will answer you. And though the Lord give you the bread of adversity and the water of affliction, yet your Teacher will not hide himself any more, but your eyes shall see your Teacher. And your ears shall hear a Word behind you, saying, 'This is the way, walk in it,' when you turn to the right or when you turn to the left."

Over and over Jesus taught about the value of suffering and certainly lived and died proving it. We will do almost anything to avoid *"the bread of adversity and the water of affliction"* but no way can you deny its benefits. Whether it is in the body, relationships or finances, if you're a Christian, adversity and affliction will always strengthen your relationship with Jesus. *"Your Teacher will not hide himself anymore but your eyes shall see your Teacher"* is so true because it is then that *"your ears will hear a Word behind you saying, this is the way, walk in it when you turn to the right and when you turn to the left."* You don't know what you're going to do; the only thing you know is that God knows what He is doing. Each morning you wake up with a confidence in God and an utter

323

dependence on Him. *"He will surely be gracious to you, at the sound of your cry, when he hears it, He will answer you."* Live out each day in and through Him; He will lead you as you *"turn to the right and as you turn to the left."*

DECEMBER 31
WALK IN THE TRUTH OF HIS WORD

<u>1 Samuel 12:24</u> (NKJV)

"Only fear the Lord, and serve Him in truth with all your heart, for consider what great things He has done for you."

Let Jesus be first in your life, every morning, as you start your day. Live in the truth of God's Word. Your Father controls this universe. In acceptance, you find peace, not in resignation. Resignation is to surrender, give in. Acceptance is to surrender to God. Resignation lies down and says, "I can't." Acceptance rises up to meet God and says, "I can do this, God helping me." Resignation says, "It's all over for me." Acceptance says, 'Now that's over, what's next?' Resignation says, "I'm all alone." Acceptance says, "I may be alone but I belong to the Lord." In accepting the twists and turns of your life, you do experience peace with the Father who controls not only you but the whole universe and directs everything in it, as well as you. God forgives, heals and restores you when your let Him be first in your life and believe that what He says is the way it is! Walk in truth before Him.

The Modern Language Bible (ML)

The New Berkeley Version in Modern English

Amplified Bible (AMP)

Made in the USA
Columbia, SC
21 September 2019